Escape to Freedom

Chronicles of a Life on Two Continents

My Escape from Communist Romania

An Autobiography

Irie Glajar

Also by Irie Glajar,

WE ARE ALL ONE: The End of all Worries, Scientific and Spiritual Testimonies to the Unity of all Things,

TEACH FOR LIFE: Essays on Modern Education For Teachers, Students, and Parents.

To Terry Jayanty

Love

Imran Glajar

Escape to Freedom

Chronicles of a Life on Two Continents

All Rights Reserved
Published By
Positive Imaging, LLC
9016 Palace Parkway
Austin, TX 78748
http://positive-imaging.com
bill@positive-imaging.com

ISBN 978-0-9856876-1-8

Dedication

To my family, my relatives, my friends, and to all who are curious about at least some details regarding my life on two continents.

Many thanks to Flem de Graffenried for his continued support, positive suggestions, and editing. His meaningful contribution to this project is greatly appreciated.

To: Terry Jayanty : March 28, 2014

Our friend Irie risked his life in 1981, at age 26, escaping from (then) totalitarian Romania to have a chance to live in freedom in the U.S.A., and has been helping the human race since he arrived in Austin in 1982.

You too, Terry, are constantly helping the human race in your medical practice.

Thank you Terry,
Flem de Graffenried

Terry! Thanks so much for your many contributions to life. We admire you and VIK greatly. You both, and VIK' greatly, you both, like Irie, have caused the world to be in a better place. Thanks, with appreciation Jo

Table of Contents

Introduction

For several years I had the intention of writing an autobiography. The main reason for such a project sprung from frequent inquiries into my past, especially motivated by occasional discussions with friends, family, or even strangers. During such interactions I found that at least some of my life experiences were significant from different points of view while others were on the verge of slipping out of my active memory. As I thought it was also important for my family, especially for my son Sergio to have an account of the main events from my past, I vowed to myself that one of these days I would start putting things in writing.

That day came sooner than I was really expecting. After recounting my "escape from Romania" story several times at different occasions (including it also in my first book WE ARE ALL ONE), my friend Flem suggested that I should dedicate an entire project exclusively to that theme. I immediately mentioned my intention of writing an autobiography and we both agreed that such an approach could be a good idea. My perspective was that presenting my defection from Romania as a decisive chapter of my life, but not as a separate story, would offer a much more comprehensive picture of a life on two continents, hence the "Escape To Freedom" title.

Consequently, I set up an outline that would take me through all the significant periods of my life that are still vivid in my memory. Very rarely I went out to check some facts in order to prevent inaccuracies, and several members of my family were of great help in this respect. However, as one should expect, it is impossible to write a 100% complete biography, not even an autobiography, since it is impossible to recount one's daily experiences (significant or insignificant) in complete detail. The autobiography you have in front of you is no exception. In order to keep the volume manageable and the content engaging, I focused on what I considered most significant and on what also interests me most. Of course there is much more to add, even more significant facts and events, but at least at this point in my life I consider this volume a good and comprehensive enough true story for those interested in reading it. Perhaps some years from now I will go back and expand it to include more details and more experiences although that will not necessarily change the core of my life on two continents, from prison to freedom.

The table of contents presents this volume in its step-by-step progression, so I will not venture here to point out the book's makeup. However, I do want to respectfully ask all family members, relatives, and friends who are mentioned even if ever so briefly in these chronicles to offer their understanding considering the circumstances illustrated earlier, and I extend my humble request also to those whom I didn't mention at all. I mean absolutely no disrespect or lack of consideration relative to anyone's part in my life. The contrary is true. I am firmly convinced, as one can conclude from this and my previous volumes that we all interact with each other meaningfully, even though many times that seems not to be the case. In this respect I express my sincere appreciation to absolutely every human being with whom I have ever interacted. Sharing at least a few moments of my life with you had carved me into what I am today, and for that I am very grateful; I hope you can say the same.

Finally, I want to thank you for your interest in this story and I hope you will find enough food for thought for you to consider with respect to your own quests, as well as your own missions to help the human race, in order to make it worth reading. I welcome any questions, suggestions, or comments for which I want to take this opportunity to thank you, and … I wish you well!

Prologue

Among many anonymous wisdom stories circulating around the world, there is one that I find pertinent to any quest for freedom. Here it is.

"There once was this village that happened to be conquered by a brutal tribe. As soon as they took control, the conquerors put all the men of the village in prison and kept them in very poor living conditions: unsanitary water, bad food, and they suffered of cold at night. However, that village was also the home of three sages. In light of the situation they were witnessing, they felt they should do something to help their co-villagers. So the first sage came to the conquerors and asked them to allow him to donate all his wealth in order for the prisoners to receive clean water. The conquerors accepted, so now the prisoners had clean water. Soon after, the second sage came to the conquerors with a similar request. He offered all his wealth, such that the prisoners would receive better food. The conquerors accepted once again, and now the prisoners were given better food. At last, the third sage felt that he should also do something to help, so he went to the conquerors and offered all his wealth to provide each prisoner a blanket to keep them warm at night; they accepted. At this point the three sages felt they answered their personal responsibility call to help the co-villagers in time of crisis.

In the meantime, that village was also the home of a saint. As he was witnessing this entire scenario developing before him, the saint felt that he should also do something to help. Consequently, he went to the conquerors and politely asked to be allowed to visit the prison. They granted his wish and as he was walking around the prison, he noticed where the conquerors kept the keys of all the prison cells. At the end of his visit, he thanked the conquerors and left. However, under the cover of that night, he snuck in the prison compound, found the keys, and carefully released all the prisoners from their cells, offering them their freedom."

What I find as the moral of this story is profound. The three sages did their best to help their co-villagers 'suffer in comfort,' while the saint did the optimal thing: he released the prisoners, granting them the freedom to take charge of their lives. I find it most illustrative of what really happens around the world in societies where people are kept under dictatorships that offer their population a 'suffering in comfort.' This is what Communist regimes did or still do in the world. Under such political systems people don't live in true freedom since they are denied freedom of movement, freedom of speech, freedom of assembly, freedom of religion, freedom to protest, and many other liberties included on any list of human rights in the free world. Therefore, we should praise any effort to promote true freedom, of course, under reasonable laws, for human beings of all nations. At the same time we should protest false claims of providing freedom, offered by regimes that actually oppress their own population. We should know that, at best, their people are 'suffering in comfort.'

1

Childhood in Romania

The Kindergarten Years

The night was black and the only sound around was the monotonous screech of the baby stroller's wheels rolling on an unevenly paved road of 1961 Romania. My sister Ligia, who was only a few months old, was asleep under the wooden cover of the stroller and I, a six years old boy, was sitting on the cover as my mother was carefully pushing the stroller toward her place of work. This is the picture of many a night from my childhood in Communist Romania, and is still present in my memory. Its significance surpasses that of ordinary days for reasons of deep complexity, and I will forever remain grateful to my family for keeping such memories alive over the many decades since.

After they got married in 1954 my parents moved in with my grandparents on my father's side of the family in Ucea de Jos, a village of about 300 people in the district of Brasov. Immediately after her graduation from the Pedagogical Institute of Sibiu, my mother found a position as a kindergarten teacher in the near-by village of Ucea de Sus which was just about 3 miles south from my father's home-village, Ucea de Jos. This might not seem like a distant place, but the lack of regular public transportation between such villages made it difficult to commute.

Consequently, my mother rented a room from a family in Ucea de Sus and we moved in. Before my sister was born, only my mother and I would live there, while my father would start his career as a Christian Orthodox priest in Ucea de Jos. After my sister came along, there would be the three of us living together, and during my mother's working day we would have a nanny caring for my little sister. We would travel to spend some weekends with the rest of the family at my grandparents' house, hence the stroller 'rides,' and we would spend the rest of the time at my mother's place of work, Ucea de Sus.

My memories of Ucea de Sus are centered on childhood play with friends, attending kindergarten with my mother as my teacher, and waiting for the Saturdays when my father would come by bicycle to visit us. Those weekends carried more excitement than usual for me not only because he would come loaded with fresh food and reserves for the following week, but also because I would get to ride his bike on the unpaved streets of the village.

Moreover, another significant memory of that time is related closely to our host family. The gentleman of the house had been a teacher in the village prior to the Communist take-over and during the first part of the Second World War he took an active part in the military while Romania fought on the side of Germany. In 1944 Romania switched sides and joined the Allies till the end of the war, but he had already gained a negative political reputation in the eyes of the Romanian supporters of Communism. In rapid and swift retaliation, the newly formed government ordered his capture but this proved to be a difficult task since people in neighboring villages offered him secret shelter. He spent five years hidden away by families in Ucea de Sus and Ucea de Jos but in the end he was turned in and he did have to serve time in prison. As far as I remember, he was a nice and well-intended man, also with great affinity for classical music. In fact many evenings we would hear him practice his violin in his room even at the end of long days of hard work in the fields.

Of course, his story was well-known in the village, but it was never brought up in open discussion out of fear of repercussion. The Communist party made sure to come down hard on any idea of political dissension especially in the early years, in order to establish undeniable dominion of the country. The late 1940s and the 1950s offer clear examples of cruel retaliation in different parts of the country practiced against isolated anti-communist groups hiding in villages, in the woods, and in the Mountains of Romania. There were many who lost their lives and were buried in common graves, as it was discovered later.

Life in Ucea de Jos

Under such political pressure, although as a child I wasn't really aware of its implications, in 1962 I was ready to start my first grade. In order to be with the rest of the family, my mother had located a position as a kindergarten teacher in another village close to Ucea de Jos, and she took it. The name of the village was Arpasu de Jos and the advantage was that this time she would be able to commute since the new place was on a bus route.

In the meantime my parents had started a major remodeling project of the old family house, and to help me adjust to the change in environment, to my insistent requests, I received a little puppy as a present. However, it wasn't to be a long-term joy.

One day, as we were playing around the house, my six weeks old puppy died instantly. A heavy oak door-frame that was leaning against the wall of the newly built house collapsed unexpectedly as I sat on its edge. Without a sound of pain, the little puppy was crushed by its weight and I was devastated. One can imagine the horror such an event brought especially to a child who longed for a pet so fervently. My desperate crying alerted my parents and the few craftsmen who were working at the house, and they all rushed in to find me petting my dead little friend.

To help me cope with the unbearable pain, my parents took me in the house and under their comforting care, in a few minutes I fell asleep. The following days impregnated my memory with a deep feeling of love and compassion for such innocent creatures, a feeling that follows me to this day.

Some time later, my mother gave in to another of my requests: I wanted a couple of pigeons, a hobby that I started with a friend of mine who lived in my home village. My mother had located somebody at her place of work willing to give her a couple of young pigeons. That pair of ordinary birds captured me for a while, until I 'evolved' and I started raising the well-known homing pigeons that bring me joy even today.

I spent most of my childhood in Ucea de Jos, in the South of Transylvania, Romania, where we enjoyed an optimal geographical location. About 7 miles South one could admire the majestic Fagaras Mountains with the highest peak in the country which stands at 8,346 feet. To the North, less than a mile away, one of the largest rivers in Romania, Oltul, had dug its bed at the foot of the Transylvanian hills since time immemorial. Overseen by the mountain chain and the hills, more or less parallel to each other and passing through Ucea de Jos along the river Olt, a national paved road and a railroad connected the three largest cities in Southern Transylvania. From my native village almost in straight line, Sibiu was 35 miles to the West, Fagaras about 17 miles to the East, and Brasov, the district's capital, about 60 miles to the East.

This was the larger scenery of my childhood sheltered by a great family that followed the old Romanian traditional set-up. My parents, my sister, and I lived together in the same household (two buildings) with my grandparents from my father's side who were farmers (peasants) like their parents and grandparents their entire lives. As I was growing up, my grandfather would take me to most of his work places as long as I was not in his way. So, from an early age I grew up in a country-style environment rich with farm animals (mainly horses, pigs, sheep, and water buffalos), poultry, vegetable gardens, fruit trees, green fields and hay, and the woods. Those early years I was blessed with my grandfather's attention who, although exhausted after a long hard day in the fields, would take the time to give me one of the greatest satisfactions a child in that environment could get: riding horses. His unspoken message was that he loved what he was doing and, together with my grandmother, they were proud and happy to provide for the entire family.

Self-sufficient Villagers

The norm for the entire village population was a virtual independence from the national · market. Over many generations they inherited and perfected techniques of preserving food. Some of the few items they would buy in the store were sunflower or vegetable oil, sugar, salt, vinegar, and petrol. Since most Romanian villages were deprived of electricity in the late '50s and early '60s, petrol was the way to provide light at night. I vividly remember how during my first few grades I was doing homework sometimes at night in the dim and flickering light of a petrol-lamp.

My Grandfather's passport photo
for a trip to the U.S. prevented by WWII

As far as food was concerned, people had long figured out ways to manage the basic household necessities. Every village family would rely on sizable vegetable gardens and a number of animals and poultry to ensure the entire year's supply of food. Since there was no electricity there was no refrigeration as means of preserving food, so the solution was to make use of deep underground basements where the temperature would stay pretty constant and low all year around. That was an ideal place where potatoes, carrots, apples, cabbage, onions, and garlic would be stored for the winter along with large glass containers of pickled cucumbers and green tomatoes. One important and well-known source of vitamin C was the sour-cabbage used both as a winter salad/side-dish (sauerkraut) and (its leaves) for the traditional Romanian stuffed-cabbage. For this purpose whole cabbages would be set in huge wooden containers with salt and water and kept in the basement for the entire year. In respect to meat and eggs people relied most of the time on chickens, geese, and ducks. However, a major meat supply for the family would be pork. Almost every family would raise at least one pig starting in the late spring so that by December the animals would weigh close to 400 pounds each.

This was an interesting process of its own. The pigs were traditionally kept closed in with only occasional 'free time' in the backyard. Since they would devour all the grass around, I remember many a time when my grandparents would ask me to go out in the nearby field aside the river that was flowing about 20 yards from our fence, to fill up a few large bags of fresh grass for the pigs. At that early age it would take me a while to fill up the bags by hand, but as I grew older I 'optimized' my work by using a scythe. During the fall months my grandparents would feed the pigs mainly corn, potatoes, and leftovers from the kitchen, and they would make sure the pigs' movement range would be gradually restricted in order to fatten them up.

Late December, usually before Christmas, would be the time to sacrifice the pig. As sad as that day was especially for us kids because a pig would die, it was actually a celebration of life. Like in many parts of the world, the life of an animal was taken for a human family to live. The day was almost like a ceremonial day. Several relatives and/or neighbors versed in that process would come to our house to help, and instantly the proceedings would become a fascinating 'live show' for the kids. The 'festivities' would start very early in the morning and would last the whole day, culminating with the first meal prepared with fresh pork meat and offered as an almost mystical light dinner to all the participants. Remarkable is the fact that virtually no part of the animal would be thrown away. Even the intestines would be saved, cleaned, and prepared for sausage making, not to speak of the rest. As kids we didn't give it much thought, but in retrospective the entire procession seemed to be the crowning of a plentiful year and the insurance that the approaching holiday and the coming year were off to a good start. To close the day's hard work, the short dinner would be started by a few shots of 'rachiu' (the traditional home-made brandy) for all the adults in the party, and it would be joyfully ended with a glass of home-made wine.

The process of making brandy is another significant childhood memory for me since I was part of the unofficial 'team' at work. Throughout late summer and early fall I would help, of course to my limited ability, with the gathering of ripe fruit from the backyard and the two other gardens my grandparents owned, in order to prepare the composition that would eventually be set for months of slow fermentation in huge wooden barrels. The best brandy came out of plums, but since the supply of plums was not always to expectations, people would mix in every other kind of fruit they had. When time would come, I would often join my grandparents at the local distillery for the almost ceremonial 'making of rachiu.' The government would tolerate such enterprise in order to allow people to exploit their fruit production, but simultaneously they would heavily tax the final product: 30% of the brandy made by a family would become state property. However, the actual distilling process, although done in the most basic of ways, was not free to the customer. Large volume of firewood would be needed and many hours of careful physical labor would be required. Sometimes we would spend a day and an entire night to complete the process, but of course that depended on the quantity of raw material we would have available. Even though I was just a kid, this kind of involvement brought something new and different in my life and I liked it so much more because I always enjoyed the company of my grandparents.

The Nationalization

All this was taking place during the heavy efforts of the Communist Party to take over the entire economy of Romania. This process culminated in 1962 with the nationalization of virtually all the agricultural land in the country, including people's homes. Of course, my grandfather, who owned about 20 acres of fertile land, vehemently rejected the 'voluntary' donation of his land. Since it was his inheritance from several generations and since it was his only means to support his family, he opposed this takeover in every conceivable way. However, the Communist Party was not too sensitive to logic and was determined to follow through with their plan in spite of any opposition.

At that time my father had just become an ordained Christian Orthodox priest in his home-village. As I would find out only in 1975, this was his last option to higher education due to his earlier choice to join an anti-communist youth-group which membership condemned him to one year of prison at the end of high school. The irony of the entire situation was three-fold and profoundly affected his life. First, all through high school he was hooked to the study of sciences in which he excelled. However, soon after prison, the Communist regime prohibited him from entering university studies in that field, the only chance to higher education left being theology, which was for some reason tolerated since it was outside of the national Ministry of Education! As he was an avid learner, he accepted his fate, but he promised himself that upon graduation he will only accept a librarian job, away from preaching the gospel in a church. Second, as some invisible destiny had it, since nothing was available in that respect, and having to support his family, he had to give in and take a priest position as the last resort for employment. He searched for a place away from his native village, Ucea de Jos: "In your home-village you shouldn't even be the village's shepherd, let alone the priest," said his mother! And third, since the only other such opening in the region at that time had been given to a priest with an unusually large family, out of desperation, my father was forced to accept the position in his own village that just became available!

In the meantime, the Communist representatives in charge of that region took advantage of the situation and started the process of nationalization with the priest's family in order to set a clever example to everybody else in Ucea de Jos. Since they were coming to our house under the cover of darkness, I remember many evenings of heavy discussion meant to convince my grandfather to give in. My father was equally reluctant, but under the pressure and the threats set forth through the Communist propaganda, he slowly drifted and finally begun to convince my grandfather that opposing will only cause hardship to the entire family. One well-known strategy practiced by the Communist regime in power was to threaten the future of the young generation by interdicting access to higher education, much like my father experienced right after high school. Consequently, under dual pressure, my grandfather conceded and the land nationalization process in our village was off to a good start as far as the Communist Party was concerned. Later on, halfway jokingly, people in the village would accuse my grandfather for being the one who started the collectivization in the village. In retrospect, giving in was probably the right choice at the time since the one single family in the village who did not, and who happened to live across the street from us, had a tremendously hard time working their land alone and, as 'promised' by the party in power, their daughter was denied entrance to college education.

Starting with 1962 the people in the village would work the nationalized fields (compensated for the number of days they worked that year), would live in nationalized homes, and would use nationalized tools, machinery, farm animals, and all other resources. As a child, I lived through this period not realizing the obvious implication regarding the morale and the well-being of the people around me. My parents and grandparents would do all they could for the family, in spite of the shortages that soon started to manifest as a result of Communist politics and economic mismanagement all around the country. That year I started the first grade and during vacations and other free time I had great opportunities to take part in most activities that involved my grandparents. The small piece of land around the house was used mostly as a vegetable garden, and together with the two other isolated gardens in the village that were old family properties now nationalized but tolerated for personal use, provided for the entire family. I remember vividly many summers spent around the village helping with whatever work I was able to and most importantly taking part in the traditional celebrations, let them be religious or otherwise.

Summer Vacations in Seica Mica

My mother was born and raised as the daughter of the priest of Seica Mica, a village of about 500 people surrounded by Transylvanian hills in one of the best wine-producing regions of the country. It must have been the climate, the soil, and the two well-known rivers, Tarnava Mare and Tarnava Mica that created a close to perfect environment for quality wine producing. My mother's father was a Greco-Catholic priest before the Communist regime took over and now, along with all the other followers of his faith in the country, he was forced to convert to the wide-spread Christian-Orthodox creed. My mother had four siblings, and one of her sisters got married to another priest in the same situation as my grandfather. They met at my parent's wedding in Seica Mica, he being a good friend of my father from the Theology Seminary years in Sibiu. He was originally from another city of Transylvania, Medias, about 35 miles Northeast of Sibiu. They were now living and professing in Medias and they had two daughters, Monica, the younger, and Marinela, of my age.

Many summers, all of us four cousins were taken to Seica Mica to spend several weeks with our grandparents. We always had a great time and I really enjoyed the change from my home-village, to this place marked visibly by the hills that appeared to be raised on purpose to protect the community. On the North side the hills were full of grapevines and fruit trees, with their steep slopes falling almost dangerously in people's backyards. We always wondered when those households will be swallowed by giant mudslides, but as far as I know it never happened. My grandparents' house was just across the street from such a neighborhood and it was built basically on two floors due to the natural inclination of the land. About 60 yards further down there was a seasonal little creek almost dry during the hot summers, but occasionally threatening with flooding after heavy rains, since it was collecting huge volumes of water from the hills. Across the creek there was another neighborhood and immediately behind that the other chain of hills displayed their majesty but this time virtually bare: no trees or bushes found their home there, and the only vegetation consisted of some grass and wild flowers that were struggling to survive the summer heat. As kids, we loved those hills and we climbed them often seeking the beautiful views of the village they offered. We enjoyed this so much that we would scream our lungs out and wave to make ourselves noticed by our grandparents who we could watch down in the valley doing their household chores in the yard, delighted by our delight.

The village had one of the most interesting communities I have ever seen. More than half of the population was of German origin (Saxon) as the result of a 12th century colonization of parts of Transylvania. Consequently, the village developed itself over centuries as a union of two ethnicities: Sasi (Saxons) and Romanians. One of the most vivid memories I still have from those long-passed years is sitting with the entire family on the bench in front of the house in the evenings while numerous giant wagons of hay were slowly returning from the fields to make it home before dark. In spite of the different ethnicity and religious beliefs, there was deep respect to be admired between the two groups. There were virtually no disputes and one example was manifesting itself every evening when Sasi would stop their wagons for a few moments in front of the Orthodox priest's house (my grandfather's) just to shake hands and exchange a few cordial words.

My grandfather was leading a pretty tranquil life as a converted Greek-Orthodox priest of Seica Mica, but one story that was only circulating among family members proved that it had not always been that way. It was during the last year of the Second World War, after Romania had switched from fighting alongside the German coalition, to aligning itself with the Allies. At that time the Russians had conquered Romania in their allied effort to push the Nazis and their coalition back toward Italy, Austria, and Germany. Seica Mica had just been occupied by Russian troops and there was a known fact that they would confiscate anything of value from the innocent civil population. Consequently, people would hide their valuables in order to save what they could, and so did my grandfather, although, as father of 5 children, he didn't really have anything of great value to be worried about. In any case, as soon as the Russian troops entered his house, they took him to the basement and at gun-point they demanded whatever he possessed of value. He obviously did not have anything to offer, so an angry Russian officer brutally grabbed my grandfather's pocket-watch, broke the chain that was securing the watch to his pants, and left. They also took some nice clothes from the house and my grandfather claimed he saw a Russian soldier wearing a pair of his pants the next day. Such stories would surface almost every summer when my grandfather had a chance to spend some time with his two sons-in-law, and of course, we as very curious grandchildren enjoyed every minute of it.

Our summer vacations in Seica Mica would end usually on the first week of September since schools were starting always on the 15th. So our parents would all come for the "grand finale" of the summer vacation and spend a weekend at my grandparents' house. Those few days were without exception remarkable. My grandfather's church was immediately adjacent to the house which in fact was church property, so on the Sunday morning of the big family reunion we would all take the short sidewalk to the church and attend the Orthodox mass. That, however, was not an ordinary occasion since my grandfather would offer the entire service accompanied by his two sons-in-law, my uncle and my father. Consequently, larger than the usual numbers of parishioners would attend in anticipation of the unique mass.

Those Sundays would carve a special place in my memory for yet another reason. In the evening, knowing that we would be leaving the next morning, neighbors from across the creek, good friends of my grandfather's and dedicated supporters of the church, would invite us all for a special treat. Just about that time of the year they would already 'test' the wine from the new harvest. The fermentation process would by far not be complete, but in their wisdom, the wine producers would check it periodically. So we would all join them in and outside their basements while they would present to the adults in our group the variety of their produce. Of course they would offer samples of each to everybody, and the socializing would last for hours. Since it was so early in the production sequence, they were only tasting the fermenting grape juice which displayed already a great aroma and color. Not to leave us kids outside this flavorful experience, we would each receive a small glass of juice filled mostly with foam. That sweet taste and unmistakable aroma have stayed with me ever since. Even now when I taste a sweet champagne I have the image of those evenings flooding my mind, and they take me way back to Seica Mica surrounded by great hills and inhabited by nice people versed in the art of wine-making. Our playful summers of true childhood freedom would usually end, therefore, with informal but tasteful and unforgettable celebrations.

Elementary Education

Of course, once school and daily homework started, only evenings and short weekends were open to play. The regimen of the six-day work-week as well as the six-day school-week imposed by the Communist party in power kept the entire country occupied most of the time. Sundays were the only days of true leisure and we treasured them immensely. Of course Sunday mornings were 'religiously' dedicated to the Christian Orthodox mass which I couldn't miss since my father, as the village's priest, had to set a good attendance example starting with his own family. In addition I started to develop some athletic ability mainly through playing soccer in physical education classes at school and evenings and Sundays in the street. The national soccer league games were mainly scheduled on Sunday afternoons, so after 1967, when our family was able to afford its first TV set, I was watching the games regularly followed by a game of our own with friends in the street or on the nearby soccer field.

School days were so structured that, with a 20-minute snack-break, lunch time was non-existent, and the 10-minute regular break between classes was often not enough for an 8:00 a.m. to 2:00 p.m. elementary school schedule. So, one day, along with two of my classmates, I was about half a minute late from such a break, and as I was running back to the classroom, the blow came quickly and hard across the right side of my face. My homeroom teacher, Mr. Oprea, who was in charge of the 4-inch hand-held bell calling the break time that week, swung his arm so fast that I could not get out of the way: his angered stroke met my face leaving a bloody bell-circle that covered part of my right ear. Dizzy, confused, and in pain, I ran to my desk and only then I realized the magnitude of what had happened. With tears in my eyes I muscled the day but I did not master the courage to tell my parents. The pattern followed by most parents was to side with the teachers, presuming the child was guilty, so only some years later I related the story to them ......

Unfortunately, the pedagogy promoted by the Ministry of Education under the directive of the Communist government was not exactly encouraging respect for students, especially under the presumption of guilt. Consequently, similar incidents, although most of them less drastic than mine, were not uncommon. Discipline, at least up to the secondary school level, was imposed with an iron fist, little effort being spent on logical and common sense teaching of the moral and ethical place it occupied in the realm of education. This was a 'natural' reflection of the more general approach implemented by the ruling Communist Party in order to impose its dominion over the entire society. Fortunately, this strategy was exactly what many years later had to exhaust people's patience, leading eventually to the radical political change of 1989.

'Red Scarf' Pioneers

Ever since 1949 the Communist regime institutionalized the 'voluntary' organization of elementary school young pioneers. This was a clever intent to indoctrinate the youth as early as possible in the Communist creed. It was declared 'voluntary' but it was the same kind of voluntarism required of people to give up their private ownership of land and houses in the Nationalization process: if people would not 'volunteer' they would automatically be placed on the black list of anti-communist ideology and subjected to gradual but decisive discrimination. To mark the festive day of adherence to the Pioneers Organization, schools would run a formal program culminating with the oath of allegiance to the Communist manifesto and the distribution of the infamous red scarf to each one of us, students.

In spite of this reality, families were doing their best as the education of the new generation was concerned. My family decided, for example, that learning foreign languages was important, so beside French that we were learning in school since the 5th grade, my father wanted me to learn German. He, therefore, initiated what would become a long-term practice in Ucea de Jos. He contacted an old lady who spoke German fluently and I became her first student–it lasted on-and-off about two years during my elementary school. As a common trend, many Romanian families realized that one major way to overcome the oppression exercised by the Communist government was to secure a higher education diploma. However, that was only possible if the student had a complete and thorough elementary education. The four years of high school were not meant to fill in previous major educational gaps. That is why to enter secondary education (the Lyceum–the 4-year Baccalaureate program–which was and still is the requirement to higher education) one had to pass a very serious admission examination. Those who would not pass had to follow a 2-year trade school since the 10th grade education was mandatory. Consequently, my parents were pretty insistent regarding my academic preparation up to 6th or 7th grade. From there on I became sufficiently responsible to take care of my preparation for the high school entrance examination, and I was very successful at it. Ever since first grade, mathematics was what appealed more to me under my parents' guidance. I also liked literature and grammar, so the high school admission exam was not really a problem.

Apart from academics I became deeply interested in sports such as soccer and, during the last two years of elementary school, volleyball. Sundays were almost regularly "game days" in the village when the youth, mostly men, were gathering on a grass volleyball court for two or three games. It was pretty competitive and it captured my attention. I really liked it and I started playing alongside 'stealing' the craft from the older players. First year of high school was the decisive one in this respect since I started training and playing with a well-organized high school team in the near-by town, Victoria, about 6 miles from my native village, where I attended high school. Beside school, volleyball had become my main preoccupation and had followed me everywhere I went in my life. In fact my first coach, the high school coach, Soni, expressed it best during the introduction to the first training session in front of all 12 of us aspiring volleyball players: "You may not make a career out of volleyball, but volleyball will open many doors in your life." He spoke from experience and he was certainly right!

2

The High School and University Years

High School: 1970-1974

The first semester of high school was off to a mediocre start. Used to very good grades all through elementary school, during the first week of 9th grade classes I displayed my high level of confidence and I volunteered to be one of the first to be examined, in a class of 36 students. Part of the examination was done individually at the blackboard in front of the entire student body, when the teacher would ask questions and give an assignment to be completed on the board. The grade I took home after such an examination in chemistry was a 6, on a scale from 1 to 10 with a passing range from 5 to 10. A 6 was very low compared to my usual grades of 9 or 10 in elementary school so it worked like a great wake-up call to the new academic reality and my parents reinforced that message abundantly as soon as I arrived home that day. However, despite this poor start, in respect to mathematics, physics, and most other subjects there were no worries.

In parallel to academics, athletics became a priority in my life. The love for volleyball and the junior team I joined slowly convinced me that I should opt for a career as a Physical Education teacher. Consequently, Human Anatomy and Physiology captured me since it was an integral part of the college admission examination at the end of the 4-year Baccalaureate program (the standard secondary education in Romania). In many respects, therefore, along with Mathematics, this helped me gain a pretty broad scientific perspective on the human condition that would guide many future decisions in my life. Team physical training opened my taste for almost anything having to do with track-and-field, gymnastics, stretching, bicycle racing, and mountain hiking.

One day, as I was searching for math books among hundreds of books collected by my father, my eyes stumbled upon two books that would open new horizons in my life. The first was a Yoga book by two Bulgarian authors, husband and wife, who had spent 8 years in India studying and practicing it. The color pictures of a variety of "asanas" (body positions) at the end of the book really took me by surprise and ever since, Yoga stretching exercises, controlled breathing, and meditation became part of my routine. In fact, based on later knowledge, I credit my openness to spirituality and, most importantly, to the Eastern philosophy of unity, to the practice of Yoga exercises, since it is assumed that it helps activate related energy centers in the human body. The second book was a translation of *Chariots of the Gods* by Erick von Daniken, in which he advanced the idea that Earth has been visited by extraterrestrial beings from times immemorial. He traveled the world and discovered much evidence to support his theory. From the Egyptian pyramids and archaeological sites in Mexico, Central and South America, Middle East and Asia, to the Indian ancient literature and the Bible, he also appealed to mathematical and astrological evidence to support his hypothesis.

However, such books were very much the exception to the 'rule' and I have been silently grateful to my father for including them in his collection. Also, years later, I was surprised to realize how, in a destined moment, I found these two in an amalgam of books stored away by my father in a cellar ostensibly due to lack of space on the shelf. The 'rule' was that the cultural censorship imposed by the Romanian Communist Party vehemently prevented the translation and publication of work that could undermine its dominion in the country. So it appears that only once in a while, as long as the subject matter seemed to be neutral or inoffensive from a political standpoint, they would allow such works in order to prove their claim of openness and support of freedom of thought and democracy. My father took advantage of this and collected books on anything of value in accord with his life-long hunger for knowledge. In fact, most of his adult life he had some kind of an unwritten commitment of his own, namely not to leave a bookstore without buying at least one book. Over the years he ended up with thousands of books that he at least partially read, which many years later had to be stored in a remodeled horse-stable that he called "the stable-library."

Music, Film, and Education

The censorship strongly imposed all across the country also included music and film. The Communist propaganda was based on a pretended conviction that the Western Capitalist culture had a negative influence on the population and consequently they banned most of the artistic values of the West, including music and film. By music I mean the modern music: blues, jazz, progressive, and rock-and-roll. Classical music and inoffensive opera and ballet were encouraged in the idea of providing inspiration to young Romanian talents who could successfully compete with the West. As far as film was concerned, they censored any trace of freedom of expression, freedom of religion, and, of course, anti-socialist political themes. They tolerated Hollywood historical movies along with action pictures and modern serials that, in their view, were depicting the negative side of life in the West: the capitalist greed, the unemployment and drugs in run-down neighborhoods, and, of course, pornography. In this respect, the famous American series "Dallas" was at the top of the list. Behind closed doors though, the Communist higher-ups were enjoying all that they prevented the larger population from experiencing.

Music was something that touched a sensitive cord in me ever since I remember. As soon as my parents could afford the first radio, in 1964, any musical program I heard on the radio would grab me. The main long-wave national station broadcast from the capital, Bucharest, did have a pretty good variety extending from Romanian pop music to folklore that was geared to praise the party in power. In order to justify their presumed openness to world-wide culture, it also touched on international top hits (politically selected) mostly in English, Italian, and French.

However, in his anti-Communist wisdom, my father made sure to get a radio with short-wave capability. Ironically, the radio he bought was a SPIDOLA, a Russian-made little set that had several set-ups for short waves. His great intention was to gain access to the international news furnished by the famous "Free Europe Radio" broadcast from Munich, West Germany at the time, and sponsored by the United Nations in an effort to undermine the Communist regimes of Eastern Europe. In fact, Free Europe Radio had programs specifically directed toward the Eastern Bloc countries, in the respective languages, such as East Germany, U.S.S.R., Poland, Hungary, Romania, etc. Beside Free Europe Radio we were also able to listen to The Voice of America, from Washington D.C. Of course, the Communist Party declared them illegal radio stations in Romania and people caught listening, especially in groups, were severely punished. However, in spite of the dangers, many used them as underground sources of information and my father was one of them.

Before high school I would just overhear fragments of "real" rock-and-roll on short-wave between the news programs my father followed mostly at night on Free Europe Radio. Since the little specs of English and American rock-and-roll and progressive music captured me so deeply, starting with the first year of high school I became an avid daily listener. Cornel Chiriac, a multi-talented journalist escapee from Communist Romania, was the most inspiring and knowledgeable DJ working for Free Europe Radio for many years until his assassination, presumably by the Communists, on March 4, 1975. Out of love for music, I would do my daily math homework during his shows culminating with Sunday afternoons from 1 to 5 when, in a special show called "Metronom," he would respond to musical requests he was receiving almost miraculously from his listeners.

I say "miraculously" because it was virtually impossible to write a letter straight to Free Europe Radio not to be intercepted by the Securitate (the secret police of Romania, the equivalent of the KGB from U.S.S.R.). The Communists worked long and hard to keep away from us, the general population, the waves of freedom directed toward Romania by the Free Europe Radio. The music and all other programs were constantly flooded with static audio distortion to diminish the reception quality as much as possible. In spite of that, we persisted in listening, this being one of the very few sources of good music and news that one could count on. That was how for 4 years I received my rock-and-roll and progressive-rock "music education." Because of time constraints, only the best bands and albums were broadcast so we had access to the most successful and best quality music, the top of the charts so to speak. Bands like The Beatles, The Rolling Stones, Pink Floyd, Yes, Queen, Jethro Tull, Deep Purple, King Crimson, and many others were very popular, well-known, and highly appreciated especially by the youth of Romania in the 1970s. The fact that it was virtually certain that we will never find their albums in music stores, let alone see them live in concert, was one major reason for deep dissatisfaction and hate directed toward the Communist Party. However, no manifestation in the streets or in writing was possible without risking one's freedom–so tight was the regime's control and domination over the Romanian society. The Securitate employed a vast and very complex net of informants to keep the 20 million people under their watch– a severe case of 'Big Brother' reality if you wish. Any sign of organization and conspiracy against the Communist regime was, therefore, immediately crushed. In this respect, I don't remember any such attempts, except isolated cases of individual protests which were met with torture and many years of prison sentences. Two rare examples are those of a dissident Orthodox priest named Gheorghe Calciu-Dumitreasa and a professor of French Doina Cornea.

Under these circumstances my first year of high school had started great, as far as my love for music was concerned, obviously dependent on the Free Europe Radio. During the fall of 1970 I savored every one of Cornel Chiriac's radio shows and I became pretty well-informed regarding most of the big names in rock-and-roll. As the end of the year was approaching, Marinela, my cousin from Medias, invited me to spend the New Year's Eve traditional party with her and a few of her high school classmates. I joyfully accepted and I

37

took the trip to Medias a couple of days before the New Year. That party blew me away. We went to one of her friend's home and as soon as we entered the place I was swept away by what I saw: huge posters of some of the greatest rock stars were hanging on the walls of his room. Immediately I felt small and insignificant in my rock-and-roll experience since I did not have even a small picture of any of my favorite stars. The Beatles, Jimmy Hendrix, and Janis Joplin 'were' there, but the one that impressed me the most was a life-size poster of Mark Farner in concert (the voice and guitarist of the American trio Grand Funk Railroad). And there was more. Soon enough the music started. It was not coming from a small radio, which I was used to, but from a turntable with loud speakers. That was my first encounter with a nice collection of vinyl records and I instantly imagined what Free Europe Radio must have had in their arsenal. However, the moment that really brought tears to my eyes, was when they played one of my most favored pieces ever: "In-A-Gadda-Da-Vida" by Iron Butterfly. To listen to this 17-minute masterpiece loud and clear was, up to that point, only a dream for me. Then came "I'm Down" by The Beatles which shook the room as we were dancing like crazy. The entire night was laced with fantastic music, food, and of course discussion of the availability of such treasures in Communist Romania. The black market was the only way one could secure them, and apparently in larger cities this possibility was real as long as one could afford the high costs involved.

That reality served even more as a motivator toward education in Romania, especially higher education, since such a degree would secure a decent standard of living under the circumstances. Consequently, all through high school my focus was mainly on academics but I also continued with my hobbies. Volleyball and music took most of my free time while by the 11th grade I had made my decision to pursue a higher education degree in mathematics. The preparation for the university entrance examination was brutal. The high school Baccalaureate program of study in mathematics was set to very high academic standards (up to Calculus II level) so the entrance exam was a serious one. More importantly, we were competing for a limited number of positions since the entire system in the country was based on "planned" development: there will be no more entry seats than the anticipated number of people ready to retire the year of our anticipated graduation. For good or for bad, this was meant to ensure that all graduates will find jobs in their field of specialization eventually. In my case there were 72 places available and we were about 250 candidates. In other disciplines (medical studies, physical education, etc.) the competition was much higher. Therefore, one had to reach a high level of academic readiness in the chosen field to have even a chance to higher education.

After a long and steady preparation especially during the last two years of high school, in the summer of 1974 I passed the university entrance examination and I was enrolled at the University Babes-Bolyai of Cluj-Napoca, about 4 hours drive from my home town. However, I happened to be part of the second generation of high school graduates in Romania who, by governmental decree, had to complete their military mandatory service *before* entering university. So, for 9 months we had to follow rigorous military training as it pertained to any soldier preparing for war. The regular term was in fact 1 year and 4 months, but since we had to start university the following fall semester our term had been reduced to 9 months.

"The Union of Communist Youth"

The Communist regime's resolve to indoctrinate the youth of Romania beginning in elementary school with the so called Red Scarf pioneers would continue in the secondary school with the famous UTC (Uniunea Tineretului Comunist) or the Union of Communist Youth. Presuming a deeper level of maturity, the oath of allegiance was crafted on a deeper message as it underlined the 'voluntary' adherence to the Communist organization under the promise to live at its service. There were no real exceptions: all high school students would be inducted in UTC. This membership also implied an appropriate dress code and behavior that were systematically enforced by the schools through regular checkups and inspections in the classrooms. For example, most of the mornings during the school year would be marked by the principal of our high school, the Theoretical Lyceum of Victoria, waiting at the entrance to make sure all the male students were wearing the required neck-tie as part of the imposed school uniform. Non-compliance with this requirement would force the respective students to miss the school day, along with other disciplinary repercussions.

The 'voluntarism' did not stop with just membership in Communist youth organizations. Ever since the 5th grade, 1-2 weeks every fall, students, supervised by their teachers, would interrupt the academic program of study in order to participate in the agricultural harvesting campaign. So, early in the morning students and teachers would be taken by buses to the fields and would help the villagers harvest potatoes, corn, apples, grapes, etc. Most of the time we did the best we could to learn new things and have some outdoor fun in the process, but we would often also go through undesirable cold and rainy days. Over the rest of the academic year schools would do their best to recuperate the instruction missed during the so-called 'productive practice,' sometimes with more success than others.

The Transfagarasan

During my high school years, 1970-1974, Ceausescu's government had decided to build a 'strategic' paved road through the tallest and the most pristine mountains in the country: the Fagaras Mountains. I say 'strategic' because one of the justifications for this gigantic project was a military one: a fast connection between Transylvania and the Southern part of Romania in case of war. However, that was just an excuse. Not more than 35 miles West there was already an old and well established pass through the mountains at the low level of the river Olt. In the opposite direction, at about 55 miles and again at about 70 miles there were two more crossings. So, this new mountain-cross turned out to be just another grandiose project to establish Ceausescu's legacy. Coincidently, the project was also named "Nicolae

Ceausescu," to accompany the better known name of "The Transfagarasan."

The road was supposed to follow the beautiful valley of the mountain river which creates the famous Balea water-fall, originating from the 6,560 foot high lake Balea. This was about 20 miles away from Victoria, my high-school and my volleyball city. At the lake level the road was supposed to pass through an almost mile-long tunnel through the mountain to connect Transylvania with the Southern region of the country. That in itself was a monumental part of the project, along with all the many viaducts over the length of the road on both sides of the mountain.

This fact alone shows how fragile the 'strategic' purpose of the road was: one bomb over a bridge or the tunnel would make the entire road useless for a long period of time. This was made very clear to me since occasionally we had a high-level supervisor from the project join us at our volleyball practices. He was an ex-volleyball player and used our practices to relax and to get away from the stress of construction. That is how we were given significant details regarding the project. We learned that many soldiers and prisoners who were deployed to this project died, some in his own arms, due to the risky and poorly protected working environment; dynamite explosions were frequent and the weather didn't always cooperate.

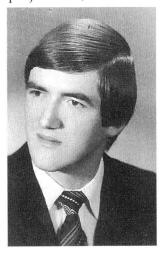

During the summer of 1974 I experienced the entire scenario for myself. After the high school graduation followed by my passing the difficult admission examination to college, I went on a 5-day bicycle trip which took me about 200 miles in the Southern part of the country. Knowing that the Transfagarasan was almost complete and planning to save some time, on my return trip I decided to try it. Although I

High school
Graduation photo

41

enjoyed every minute of it, my climb in the fresh and cool air up the Southern side of the mountain was heavy. I had to walk pushing my bike for many miles. As I was admiring the majesty of the mountains and a sheep herd in the distance, a number of sheep-dogs started running down toward me in an infernal barking concert. I stood motionless on the road, with the dogs running all around my bicycle until the shepherd came and rescued me.

Shortly after that I arrived at the tunnel. It was complete all the way through the mountain, but not finished. There was water dripping through the rocks of the ceiling and it wasn't yet paved. As I was ready to enter the tunnel in order to cross over, a number of agitated soldiers showed up running toward me. I became instantly worried not knowing their intention. However, one of them started screaming in exaltation: "Oh my God! I have not seen a bicycle in a long time. Can you please let me ride it just for a minute?" Of course I said yes, and that took all my fears away. We chatted for a few minutes while they told me how hard their life was and how heavy the working conditions were, and then I left continuing my adventure, this time down the mountain.

The view was magnificent. I passed Lake Balea with the cabin on its side, and soon enough I faced the snake-like serpentines down through the valley. Obviously the ride was almost effortless and in about 45 minutes I arrived home.

My mother greeted me with some anxiety, worried about my long trip, but all was soon well. Over a light mid-afternoon snack we talked about the trip and, among other things, we made some plans for the approaching new adventure of my life: the mandatory 9-month military term.

Military Service: 1974-1975

The military base to which we were sent was, fortunately enough, about 2 miles outside of Cluj-Napoca, our university city, and that helped us, student-soldiers, cope with the politics imbedded into such mandatory service. The first month was a heavy disciplinary period meant to indoctrinate us as deeply as possible into the military communist vision of the world. The West was always portrayed as the enemy and we were reminded almost daily of the threat of war. The Cold War tension, coupled with the centuries-old disagreements between close-by Turkey and Greece were used to keep that torch burning. Not knowing any better, we didn't realize that there we were, in 1974, training on old military equipment left over from the Second World War, while the West had made obvious technological progress on all fronts including, obviously, matters concerning the military. The Romanian progress in this respect was far behind even the Russians since they were the main protagonists in the Cold War. In the meantime, their efforts were also fueled by their intention to exercise control over the entire Eastern Europe.

However, one of the very few good decisions Nicolae Ceausescu made for the country, as the Secretary General of the Romanian Communist Party since 1965, was to keep Romania as far as possible from direct Russian influence. He more or less succeeded. The Russian invasion of Czechoslovakia in 1968 demanded immediate action since Romania could have been the next. So, almost instantly he flew to China and signed an agreement of mutual military assistance if either partner would be invaded by foreign military forces. Of course this spoke volumes to the Russians given the perennial problems they had on the huge length of the Russia-China border in Asia. At a personal level though, as Ceausescu returned from China, a major shift took place in his self-image as the leader of a Communist country. He fell in love with the attitude of total adulation the Chinese leaders enjoyed and their iron-fist approach on keeping the country under control. The new self image Ceausescu adopted would be one major cause of his eventual demise.

Under these circumstances we had to serve for 9 months as regular soldiers in training. However, there were a few officers who apparently understood our place in the service as future university graduates and consequently, they did whatever they could to make our life as comfortable as possible. Almost daily we had "office hours" following lunch, where we were supposed to read the papers and at times be given specific materials to study. As we were also fresh graduates from the Baccalaureate program many of us brought our own books, and some were using this time to enjoy them. One day a funny episode took place. One of my colleagues was reading a book by the classic Russian writer Nikolai Gogol. Suddenly, the colonel in charge, a Second World War veteran, entered the room by surprise and caught him reading the book. With anger in his voice he exclaimed: "So, soldier, are you reading literature from across the ocean?"–meaning American literature. Of course, we could not hold down our laughing at the colonel's literary ignorance (he thought we were laughing at our colleague who got caught); beside that, he was not one of those who were trying to make our 9 months easier. Of course, our colleague was punished with several days of arrest, but we took it lightly and joked about it for the rest of the 9 months.

To cope with the suppression of freedom, censorship, and with the draconic daily regimen, we were using whatever personal ability or talent to make our own life in the military go faster and smoother. In this respect my volleyball and my music helped. During the last years of high school I played drums in our improvised rock-and-roll band, so when the opportunity presented itself to play drums in the military band for the New Year's party I took it gladly. Not only did the rehearsals take me out of many hours of pointless military training but joining the band also promised me to spend the New Year night playing in the city of Cluj-Napoca at a nice restaurant where most of the officers from our military base would celebrate. It all came true and it rewarded me yet from a different and unexpected perspective.

During our rehearsal period for the New Year's party, in December 1974 my grandfather from my father's side of the family passed away unexpectedly at the end of about a week of illness. Born in 1902 and living most of his life in my native village, he was very close to me especially since we lived in the same household for practically all of my 19 years of life. He loved taking me with him everywhere when possible and also loved teaching me all I could learn. So, I was crushed when I received the news, and even worse, due to very rigid military rules, I was not allowed to go home for his funeral–

such permission was granted only for death of "relatives of the first degree" which meant parents or siblings. I wasn't a person to cry easily but with the official refusal on my mind I could not stop my nightly tears especially on and around the day of the funeral. I loved my grandfather dearly and I always will! In spite of a simple life of very hard work as a peasant, limited to his home-village, and in spite of losing all his property to the Communist nationalization in 1962, he had a mostly positive take on life. He, being a talented singer of folkloric songs learned by ear, enjoyed the role of the entertainer of the family and coworkers. Consequently, as related by my father, some of his last words on his deathbed were: "I will be missing this world very much!" Among my own life experiences, this statement has served me well as a sensitive and personal reminder of the truly valuable aspects of the human existence, and a helpful chosen world view.

Due to my good soldier status and my contribution to the New Year's party band, my superiors rewarded me with a rare long-weekend permission in January 1975 immediately after the New Year's party, to visit my family. It was a few weeks after the funeral but I welcomed it anyway and I took the first available train to Ucea. As soon as I arrived home I felt the obvious void left by the passing of my grandfather. The atmosphere around the house was dense and we all imparted the sadness of having him gone. A variety of pictures and a few songs I managed to have him record during the last few years of his life will aid our memory of him. Of course, my grandmother, his wife of 47 years, made sure to remind us of him almost every day until her passing in 1980.

Consequently, my return to the military base was not an easy one. However, the rest of the 9-month term went relatively uneventfully and in June 1975 I finished the military service when we all received the lowest officer rank. In four years, as university graduates, we would go back for two more weeks of training in order to be promoted to the rank of lieutenant.

1975: Caution!

As he was helping me settle in my first year of university life, my father found the opportunity to convey to me a very well-kept family secret. That calm September afternoon on a park bench in Cluj, he related to me for the first time in my life the story of his capture by the Securitate in 1948 when they came and arrested him from his home in Ucea. During the few minutes of that morning encounter, my father managed to slip a piece of paper into his grandmother's hand, who without hesitation, instinctively realizing the gravity of the moment, swallowed it instantly as the Securitate officers were preoccupied elsewhere. Since my father was the secretary of the anti-communist youth organization he had joined, he kept all the names of the members on that paper. Therefore, one can easily realize the gravity of the situation: if that paper had fallen into the hands of those officers, several other young members, not yet identified by the Securitate, would have been arrested and jailed immediately.

On that park bench in Cluj, my father continued to bring to my attention the significance of his words that day in September. He reminded me of something we all knew: there were informants everywhere. Over the years, the Securitate had made sure to infiltrate their informants in all area of public life in order to catch any sign of rebellion before becoming dangerous to the totalitarian Communist regime. Consequently, he cautioned me not to be tempted to fight the system since any such movement would be doomed to fail; the Securitate was much better organized by the 1970s compared to the late 1940, and the 1950s. He went on to warn me that even in the student body and the faculty of my university there will be numerous ears for the Securitate. I assured him that, although I was unhappy with the entire Communist propaganda and censorship, I wasn't really interested in any political activity and I asked him not to worry about me from that perspective. To close the discussion, he wanted me to know that he did actually know of informants among the clergy, even including the higher ranks of the church. That was news to me since I had never suspected such cooperation with the Securitate, but suddenly it made sense that some people would stoop so low just to gain favors from the regime including perhaps the security of their jobs.

My father left Cluj by train that day wishing me a good start of my first university semester. We embraced and promised to keep in touch by writing letters since that year he had accepted his new (additional) assignment as a lecturer at the Theology Seminary of Sibiu where he would spend most of every week. I waited until his train left the station and all the way to my dorm room I had plenty of time to reflect especially on our latest conversation.

University Years: 1975-1979

Although the 9-month military service, where we lived in a large one-room dorm that held 72 people, should have prepared us for the college years, my first semester was rough. A few weeks in, I felt some sort of a depression mainly caused by the busy 6-day a week school schedule and the living setting in a 4-bed dorm room with three of my classmates. The fact that we knew each other from the military service certainly helped, but I still felt the pressure of the new life style.

The salvation, once again, came from music and my 4-5 times a week volleyball training regimen, since I had been accepted on the university team in the first division of Romania. Notable is that there was no differentiation between university sports and the national league, Divizia A. There were 12 teams competing in the first division, a few from universities, and the others from different areas depending on the nature of the predominant industry in the respective cities. Of course, due to the recruiting power, the financial support, and the political interest to represent Romania internationally, the two strongest teams were the ones representing the police (Dinamo) and the military (Steaua). The Communist government never recognized professional sports (that was one of the stigmas placed on the West). However, to show the world how much better Communism was, these teams and the national team, were training according to Western professional standards and the players were paid solely for playing, with virtually no other obligations.

Since all industry in the country was nationalized, there was no issue of private sponsors and, therefore, private financial support for sports was virtually non-existent. As I was playing on the University of Cluj-Napoca team, I benefited only of what the university could afford according to the money they were allotted. However, it was good enough for me. For 4 years I received free room-and-board, which was more than I ever expected. This supplemented well the financial monthly support from my parents (students from lower-income families would be financially rewarded according to their academic performance, but due to my parents' income bracket I was not one of them). With the money I was able to save monthly over the 4-year university program, I accumulated about 60 reel-to-reel tapes full of western rock-and-roll and progressive-rock (my high school infatuation), a tape-recorder, and a turntable with about 50 world-class records. I must say that most of these records I bought at very high second hand prices from foreign students from Greece, Congo, Syria, and other countries who were studying in Romania.

In parallel, the specialized stores in the country were receiving maybe once a year a very limited number of selected albums (vinyl records) from the West to be sold as a 'testimony' to the 'true democracy and free market' the regime so vehemently claimed. At one point during my university years I learned of such a unique opportunity: a certain music store would make available a very limited number of copies of the most famous Pink Floyd album *"The Dark Side of the Moon"* and Paul McCartney's *"Band on the Run"* at a *regular* Romanian market price which was actually very low. That day I arranged for a colleague of mine to take notes for me as I was planning to miss school that morning in order to wait in line to buy the two precious albums. I waited 4 hours in a very unruly crowd which reminded me more of a mob than an orderly line in front of a store. At the opening moment, people stormed in the store, the doors flew out of their hinges and a couple of glass windows broke down to the ground. I couldn't believe it. I was squeezed in somewhere in the middle of the crowd and I was fervently hoping to get my hands on those records before the store would run out of copies. However, it was not meant to be. The last copies were sold to a person two people in front of me! I thought I would faint. I breathed deeply and I took my turn to the register. I was simply told: "We ran out of copies of those two albums, but we have some other foreign records available." Consequently, after my 4-hour wait, I ended up with one jazz record by a Polish band that I had never heard of. That day's great disappointment reconfirmed my deep unhappiness with the Communist propaganda and censorship and I recharged myself with the determination to save more money for albums I would find elsewhere.

Beside the money I was able to save to spend on the black market, one other great benefit from being on the volleyball team was the chance to travel all around the country. That offered me the opportunity to visit cities and historical monuments for free. As the Communists were vehemently against religion and therefore, to discourage church attendance, the games were always scheduled on Sunday mornings during the Christian Orthodox mass. Traveling by bus or train, usually we would arrive at remote locations on Saturday and return Sunday night. One such memorable trip was to Tulcea, a city close to the Russian border in the South-East part of Romania. With a few free hours on Saturday I felt I wanted to visit an old and modest looking church near-by our hotel. In the cold of the autumn evening I entered the church and I was shocked: the mass was in a Slavic language I couldn't understand. I stood up near the entrance for 30-40 minutes absorbed by the unfamiliar night ceremony and rituals. There were 15-20 people in attendance, but none of them very young. When I decided to leave I was once again taken by surprise. A very old lady followed me outside, took me by my right arm in the dimmed light of the late evening and with visible emotion in her voice said: "I am very happy to see that there are still some young people interested in our religion. Thank you for coming." I explained that I was just a visitor in town and that I was curious about different traditions and especially spiritual-religious rituals. That incident reminded me once more how fragile old customs were when the Communist Party perceived them as a threat. However, some benign practices were tolerated and more so if they prevented minorities from claiming any kind of discrimination, as it was the case with this church in Tulcea.

The Academics

The 4-year university program was, in the pre-1989 Romania, the first step in a 2-step higher education model: the Diploma de Licenta and the doctorate. It was, therefore, very academically intensive, with 6-8 course hours per day and 6-day weeks as the regular work-week. The courses and curriculum were mandatory and completely pre-set by the Ministry of Education for each specialization which, for me, was Mathematics and Computer Programming (Informatics – a relatively new discipline in the 1975 Romania; in fact ours was the second generation of students in that field). On top of the rigidity of the program of study was the fact that we had to pass each course during the respective Fall or Spring semester, or at least in the summer. If a student would not pass a course, that student would have to repeat the entire school year. Consequently, one can see how much academic pressure we were under (same rule applied at all levels of study, from first grade on). The first two years went well from an academic point of view. In addition to the specialization courses, I enjoyed a course in philosophy and one in higher-level physics meant to continue the undergraduate courses we completed as secondary education requirements of the Baccalaureate program.

However, students were taken aback by the mandatory course in Socialism, since most of us had a 'natural' repulsion toward anything having to do with the Communist party's agenda. In order to maintain a decent level of political sanity many of us developed a nice habit, I would say. As we studied mostly in the large university library, we would reserve desk-space and spend our first hour or so searching the library for books and periodicals in line with our other hobbies. My preferences were Eastern philosophy, Yoga, archaeology, spirituality, health, sports, and music. I must say that the entire four years of university life were very prolific in this respect since we had found a way to minimize dangerous anti-communist political debate.

Many of us had been forced to become members of the Communist Party but I was spared because of my 'unhealthy origin:' my father was a priest and my mother's father had also been a priest, now retired. Not only that, but as I mentioned before, my father took a lecturer teaching position at the Orthodox Seminary of Sibiu. He kept his position as a priest in his home village, so he was basically commuting 2-3 times per week mostly by train. Over his career he faced at least a couple of 'dates' with the Securitate Police who were trying to make him an informant. He vehemently refused and consequently, he was denied the opportunity to expand his religious studies in Viena (Austria) or Paris (France) for which he was definitely qualified.

With my father's 1975 cautionary remarks in mind and as I was deeply involved in my volleyball training and traveling, I was not really tempted to embark on any subversive activity against the party in power, not that there was any such visible movement around at the time. Even the Free Europe Radio anti-Communist broadcast was kept at a distance since we, students, were very aware that some of our classmates, roommates, including good friends, could be informants for the Securitate. In this respect, there was even a joke going around: "When two Romanians are talking to each other, one of them is an informant." So great was the suspicion and the fear infiltrated in our society. In such an environment I focused on doing as well as possible in my studies, while the communication with my family was mainly by mail and seldom by phone. My sister was in high school living at home, so my mother and father were busy on three fronts: two children to support, their occupations, and the household. On top of everything, my grandmother from my mother's side of the family had been hospitalized in February

1977. The month of March of that year remained one of the most memorable ones of my life.

The 1977 Earthquake

Beside school and volleyball I was able to join a few "cultural exchange" activities organized by my university in concert with other institutions of higher education from Romania. One of them was a trip to the University of Bucharest in early March of 1977. As I was visiting my cousin Marinela who was a student there, a 7.2 magnitude earthquake with the epicenter close to Bucharest took Romania by a shocking surprise.

We were in the lobby of her dorm around 9 p.m. on March 4th when the foundation of the building started to shake violently. The people present panicked and we all instinctively ran toward the door which was obviously way too small for all of us. In a totally disorganized manner we were trying to figure out what was going on, when a loud voice announced: "It's an earthquake, run outside!" The 10-12 concrete stairs that separated us from the ground were vibrating under our feet like the waves of the sea: it was hard to find your next step. In a few seconds we found ourselves on the ground in between two 4-floor dorm buildings. The earth was still shaking. Glass-windows were falling to the ground, and some students, even halfway dressed, were jumping off their windows desperate to survive. On top of the whole picture a super-loud siren alarm-like noise started, adding to the entire drama: it was coming from a near-by electric plant that released air pressure to prevent an explosion, as we found out later.

The actual extent of the disaster was difficult to estimate at the time since it all happened at night and almost instantly the entire city of Bucharest was in darkness. The streets were crowded with people since the public transportation system was all brought down. We went all possible ways in search of a place to stay overnight. The next day we faced the true magnitude of the earthquake: thousands of people died under thousands of buildings collapsed to the ground, and this included some well-known figures such as Toma Caragiu, a notorious name from the entertainment industry. The tragedy was multi-faceted since it touched all aspects of life in the large city. Notable is that most new buildings, raised according to a watered-down construction code during the Communist era, were among the ones that gave in, while older, sturdier constructions together with the monumental hotel Intercontinental, built under Western standards, survived.

On top of these intrinsic worries, a phone message had been received at my cousin's dorm a short time before the earthquake and it was conveyed to us the next day: "Your grandmother passed away in the hospital, and the funeral will be held tomorrow." That was totally unexpected and we had to make a quick decision on how to proceed. My cousin chose not to take the trip to Medias, her home-town where the funeral would take place, due to the virtual impossibility to travel out of Bucharest by public transportation that day. However, I chose to go, and the 15-hour trip to Medias via hitchhiking and two trains placed me at my aunt's door (my cousin's mother) at 2 a.m. the next day. My entire family was there also and they sadly informed me that the funeral took place the day before – apparently the note we received in Bucharest was already a day late. After a little rest, a visit to the cemetery and a sad family reunion the next day, I took a train back to Cluj to continue my spring semester.

The Graduation and Repartition

The last two years of university life were very challenging since during that time, in addition to a full schedule of standard courses, we had to complete the graduation thesis in our specialization. Combine all this with my continued passion for volleyball and music and one could see how I had chosen to lead a very busy life during those years. However, the defending of the thesis and the graduation went well. Almost immediately after that we had to go back to the military base to finish our training. It was two more weeks of instruction and, of course, we were treated slightly differently than four years earlier since we were now university graduates. We ended up with the rank of lieutenant and we were placed on reserve, ready to be mobilized in case of war.

In the meantime, we had to consider the selection of a place of employment. That process was called "the repartition" since there were supposed to be enough job openings around the country in their respective fields for all the graduates from all universities, following the long-term governmental plan. The repartition took place according to graduates' GPAs: graduates with higher GPAs would have the right to choose first their places of employment out of a nation-wide list of offerings. This process ran exactly opposite to the Western norm where *the employer* is the one selecting the best candidate out of a pool of applicants. Therefore, in Communist Romania most places of employment had no say-so in the process of selecting their employees, which might at least partially explain the gradual economical deterioration over time. In the end I managed to get a job in the small town where I went to high school, since I had always intended to return as close to home as possible. The position was as a Computer Analyst at the Computer Center of the Chemical Plant of Victoria in the district of Brasov.

3

Employment: 1979-1981

I started working in September 1979 and my life became gradually more complicated as time passed. During my last year at the university I started dating, mostly at a distance an old high school classmate, Lidia. Due to my mandatory 9-month military service, Lidia was one year ahead as she had already graduated from her university and was now working at the Chemical Plant of Victoria in the financial department. Over the summer of 1979 we got married and we were living at home in Ucea de Jos with my parents, my grandmother, and my sister, commuting to work mainly by bus.

Within this already crowded set-up my old hobbies surfaced once again making the whole situation even more interesting. Very soon that Fall I joined a rock-and-roll band as a drummer and vocalist and we played gigs 1-2 weekends a month; these were large all-night dancing parties and also weddings. The demand was high due to the shortage of such bands around our area so we were making good money. Along with that, my old high school love for homing pigeons resumed, and I built a spacious coup and I started raising them again.

In addition, I rejoined the local lower division volleyball team and now, with the financial support offered by the Chemical Plant, we were dreaming of promoting the team to the second division. Even with my 4-year experience in the first division, that was not to be an easy endeavor, and in the end was not successful; the competition was tough and the higher level interests (unfair push for certain teams) made it even worse. However, we trained and played in the district of Brasov division and we had lots of fun in the process.

The Work Regimen

All went well at work as I was learning about the place and about what a Computer Center could do to help optimize the production lines of the plant. We were charged to write computer programs in cooperation with engineers from different sections of the plant, and we were working on huge, closet-size French-made Felix computers, programming in FORTRAN and COBOL on punch-cards and enormous memory discs. Soon enough I realized once again one of the hidden problems of the entire Romanian employment system. Due to the determination of the Communist regime to keep unemployment virtually nonexistent (an international political obsession shared by all Communist countries) there were more than necessary people employed by one institution, which meant not enough work for everyone. In my case I would easily finish what I had to do in about 2-3 hours out of the 8-hour regular workday. This fact gave me enough time to do other things during work: solving math problems, offering math tutoring, reading books, writing, and socializing, but we had to be 'at work' daily, Monday through Saturday, from 7 a.m. to 3 p.m.

In this environment it became obvious that promotions, especially in my line of work, were almost impossible due to the low productivity and the nature of the department. On top of that, since I was not a member of the Communist Party, my chances for advancement were virtually nonexistent. Compared to other professions, my income level was decent but only meant for basic survival. However, I managed to supplement it substantially with my music, and living in my parents' house for free was also a big financial help. Under these circumstances I was doing my best to flow with the situation without getting my expectations too high.

The Market

As one could expect, most people in their mid-twenties, even in a Communist country, would like to have the opportunity to satisfy their personal desires, whether those be cultural, spiritual, or material. The strict censorship enforced by the regime in power was such that most Western values tolerated in the country were drastically limited. As a result, the black-market flourished and bribing for goods and services became routine. One could find Western products occasionally but at very steep prices. For example, the price of a pair of brand-name blue jeans, only available on the black market, was about an average monthly salary, and a rock album was close to a quarter of such salary– that was the cost during my university years. Prices for musical instruments were astronomically high also. The guitar player on my band bought a used Marshall 100-watt amplifier for 20 times the average monthly salary. In respect to cars which were really a luxury, the situation was similar: a new Romanian-made Dacia was sold for about 35 monthly salaries. We can see how, if one desired to keep up with the fashion of the day or wanted to satisfy some extravagant hobbies, it was all at a high price and often took the shape of heavy sacrifice.

This situation played very well financially in the hands of foreign tourists visiting Romania, foreign students studying in Romania, and Romanians who managed to leave the country and now were just coming for a visit. Especially in Transylvania, my native province, this phenomenon was wide-spread due to the beautiful Carpathian Mountains and the ethnic German population both of which attracted many tourists. In this respect, West Germany of that time crafted an agreement with Ceausescu's government: for a certain amount of money (paid to Ceausescu) some ethnic Germans could legally emigrate to West Germany. Many such 'repatriated' Germans would return to Romania once or twice a year to visit friends or relatives, which would give them the chance to bring in a variety of 'Western' goods. Using them as presents, to trade or even to sell, they helped fill at least part of the huge void created by the strict economic policy (censorship) enforced by the Communist regime.

On the other hand, the regime did allow a scarce number of small 'shops' (literally called "SHOP") where people could purchase such goods (cigarettes, brandy, soap, deodorants, and some electronics) but only if they were in possession of a foreign passport and foreign currency. In addition to special stores for the higher-ups in the party, in their hunger for foreign currency, the Communists furnished these 'shops' to satisfy mainly the needs of foreigners for decent merchandise during their stay in Romania. However, many foreigners will buy such goods for resell, for presents, or for trade. In spite of how much our income was and how much we could afford, Romanian citizens were not allowed to possess foreign currency; this was actually severely punishable under the law. My first-hand experience in this respect was helping a co-worker with English translations. She was taking care of her uncle who lived all his life in the United States and came back to retire (and eventually to die) in Romania. They were using her uncle's pension money to buy different things from these 'shops,' which was basically the only way to spend it, since it came in U.S. Dollars.

'Voluntarism'

As was the case with students beyond the 5th grade, including college, even office workers like me were mobilized 1-2 weeks during the fall harvest season to help the agricultural cooperatives in the fields. Apparently, the new agricultural approach helped produce more crops than the aging peasant population could handle during harvest. This is how the government found a way to engage, and I must say, exploit students, faculty, the military, and others not directly engaged in such work. Not only was this an interruption to the normal flow of a school year but it was also an impediment to the continuity of the production line of economic enterprises such as the chemical plant where I was employed.

One possible motivation for this strategy was that the government searched for the least expensive way to harvest. Of course, other than the peasants in the fields, no one else was paid for this kind of work. This played well with Ceausescu's plan to save as much as possible in order to sell on the international market for a maximum profit. In the process, though, people in Romania had started to taste real shortages in almost everything from toilette paper to food. Aware of this situation, the party in power, in fact Ceausescu personally, advised the population not to plant flowers in front of the city apartment buildings, as was customary, but vegetables. In some cases that was truly one solution at least during the warm seasons. Half-way comically was also the governmental recommendation for a vegetarian life-style. Of course, since most meat was exported, that was the sensible thing to do. One could see then, that people living in villages were a little bit better off, food-wise, since they did have means to more or less provide for themselves.

Scarcity

Not everyone owned a car in Romania but those who did had to do their share to help the national program of savings imposed by the government on all fronts, including gasoline usage. In this respect the 'weekend driving' law was that you could use your car only every other Sunday, according to your license plate number: odd or even. One can easily imagine the frustration and the problems resulting from such a law.

Over the second year of my employment at the chemical plant of Victoria, several other shortages surfaced. Not only were gas and electricity limited but also food gradually became scarce: "We don't have cheese today, but try again tomorrow or after tomorrow" became a typical kind of answer in the stores. Week after week it got worse and worse. People were aware of the governmental plan but that did not offer any comfort. Within its determination to pay the international debt the government was actually starving the country. One could find chicken feet in the store but not the rest of the chicken; could find pig feet but not the rest of the pig, etc. Milk, oil, bread, and sugar had been rationed and when they were available, long lines of people were forming. Even then, one was not assured of getting the items sought. In many cases people would join lines without knowing at first exactly what for. This shows the desperation and the fear people had to absorb in order to survive. One way to cope was making fun of the leaders and sometimes of the entire situation. Here is a popular joke circulating at that time: "People were waiting in this long line to receive passports to leave the country. Suddenly Ceausescu comes and joins the line without knowing what the line was for. When people saw that he wanted to leave the country, all left the line saying 'If he's leaving, I'm staying.'"

One can see, then, how a majority of people in Romania had lost hope for a better future as long as the regime stayed in power. With all the censorship and economical restrictions, there appeared to be no light at the end of the tunnel called the future. The Securitate officers and the informants were doing their job in concert to keep the rest of the country under control. However, in spite of the dictatorship, or perhaps exactly because of it, some people were contemplating extreme tactics to escape it. Many were seeking a better life for themselves and especially for their young ones. In a majority of cases the solution was not to be found inside Romania since people were not inclined to organize an anti-government movement, due to the overwhelming and omnipresent fear of immediate and swift retaliation; in fact, the 20-million population of the country lived in a virtual prison guarded by the all-powerful Securitate. Since only some Communist Party members were given passports to visit Western countries, it was impossible for regular citizens to receive such privilege. Consequently, as an obvious path to true freedom and the protection of human rights, the West provided help for those who would risk their lives in order to defect from the Eastern Bloc. The help came in the form of refugee camps funded by the United Nations in Western Europe, such as the ones in Austria and Italy. Although very risky, this became the preferred form of protest against Communism, and many people from Romania embraced it in search for a better life in true freedom.

4

My Defection Plan

Vacation Sites

The working regimen provided for 2-3 weeks of vacation a year, depending on the number of years of employment. After my first year at the Chemical Plant of Victoria, in the summer of 1980 I spent my vacation hiking in the mountains and taking a family trip to the old monasteries from the North side of another Romanian province, Moldova. Some people would choose to go to the Black Sea beach which was about an 8-hour drive each way, while some would just spend their free time around their homes. That summer there were, however, a few colleagues who chose to spend their vacation taking trips to other Communist countries from the Eastern Bloc such as U.S.S.R., Bulgaria, Hungary, East Germany, etc. Since the number of these opportunities was very limited, one had to qualify to secure a seat. That was why I didn't even try it the first time around but I had it in mind as a possibility for the second vacation, the one of 1981.

On vacation in Romania, 1980

As early as February 1981 the Youth Communist Union at the Chemical Plant of Victoria published a list of vacation sites in other countries for that year. These vacation programs were set up by creating groups of about 40 people such that the transportation within those countries was suitable to tourist buses. Usually the trips were organized over an entire district, so ours, the district of Brasov, had a few such programs lined up. Among several Eastern Bloc countries, the options for 1981 included also Yugoslavia, Romania's neighbor to the West. One of the restrictions the organizers imposed was not to accept entire families. This was meant to prevent possible complications during the trip resulting from special accommodations.

In this respect, the vacation trip to Yugoslavia was marked by even more drastic restrictions. The reason was clear but unspoken: it was well-known that Yugoslavia was the path most frequently chosen by defectors from Romania to the West, namely to Italy and Austria. This was because the Yugoslavian government, although still a Communist regime, adopted over the years a milder policy relative to the West. Virtually free from Russian influence, Yugoslavians were allowed to travel and work in Western European countries such as Italy, Austria, West Germany, France, etc. That was how Yugoslavia profited economically and it had the highest standard of living among the Eastern Bloc countries. Consequently, besides not permitting whole families on vacation trips to Yugoslavia, the Romanian organizers had decided to form the 40-person groups by picking two individuals from each of many industrial centers in the district. It was silently understood, therefore, that the intention was not to facilitate the formation of organized groups on the trip where people were friends or at least knew each other. Obviously this policy was meant to prevent defection.

The Plan

With all this in mind, in February 1981 I checked the list of available positions for trips to other countries and I noticed that out of the two designated to Victoria there was one left. The first one had been taken by the secretary of the Youth Communist Party, Olga, who was a friend of mine also involved in athletics: she herself was an excellent ex-team-handball player. As I was contemplating the list in front of her, she said: "Why don't you sign up for the trip to Yugoslavia; we can go together." After a little hesitation I answered with a probabilistic "I will think about it." At that moment a negative scenario ran through my head: I was firmly convinced that, for several reasons, there was no possible way I will get the visa for such a trip; the scrutiny of people allowed to visit Yugoslavia was very thorough.

First of all, as mentioned before, I was not a Communist Party member since I was coming from an 'unhealthy' family. Secondly, although I was well appreciated at work, I was not necessarily leading a politically correct life. I was part of a band playing mostly English rock-and-roll, and during the Fall months of 1980, I went through some marital problems (all of my own making, I must add) that got out of the realm of confidentiality since she even moved back with her parents in Victoria for a while. At the same time I was running evening musical auditions in town where I would also play mostly English rock and progressive-rock records collected during my university years. The youth of Victoria, most of them well-educated by the underground Free Europe Radio, were in love with recordings that were hard to find in Romania. Live albums, such as Emerson Lake and Palmer, Rainbow, and Deep Purple were at the top of the list and the audience grew weekly.

However, in spite of my lack of optimism, and after several tries, Olga convinced me at least to put my name down on that list and take that spot. She was right: I didn't have anything to lose. So I signed up adding my name next to hers and simultaneously, with a decisive inner conviction I said to myself in a grave silent voice: "If they let me go, I will not come back!" That was in February and the vacation trip was scheduled for the 4th of September.

The next six months were totally eventless in this respect, but my inner decision was present in my mind. Occasionally

I would talk to friends about the possible trip trying to collect whatever information was available. However, for periods of time I would forget about it since there was complete silence from the officials and even from my friend Olga.

Therefore, I stayed on the busy schedule I was entertaining at the time and I even went to the try-outs for the first division volleyball team in our district, Tractorul Brasov. This was a solid and very prestigious team, usually 4th or 5th in the country and they were recruiting players for the next season. I received the acceptance notice together with two good friends and teammates of mine from Victoria, Silviu and Vasile, and during the summer of 1981 all the preparations to be transferred to Brasov were finalized. We even went to several practice sessions and we enjoyed every minute of them. The challenge was enormous but all three of us were up to it.

On the music scene I also continued playing with my band with the understanding that in September I would move to Brasov. We still had many parties to play for and one of them in particular became especially significant. The 23rd of August was the Liberation Day of Romania from the German occupation in the Second World War. As part of the celebration we played at the all-night dancing party for several hundred people from all around Victoria and we had a blast. During one of the breaks I met an old classmate of mine from elementary school who together with his sister emigrated legally to the United States of America at the insistent request of a very old relative of theirs in need of care: she had been living for many years in the Chicago area. This had been a rare exception to the rule when, in order to appear that they honored international human rights agreements, Ceausescu's regime would allow it to happen at persistent requests via the American Embassy in Bucharest. After several years my classmate and his sister were able to return for a visit to Romania and it happened to be that summer. We talked for a few minutes, but mostly about life in the U.S., and that was when my possible vacation trip to Yugoslavia and my escape plan came back vividly in my mind. However, overly cautious, I didn't mention a word about it but I managed to get their phone number and address in the U.S. Aware of the censorship and the political oppression in Romania, they in turn didn't elaborate much about their life in the States, their dry comments being minimized to "It is nice. We can find anything we want in the stores so we are OK." We wished each other the best as they left, and that was the last dancing party I played for in the summer of 1981 in Romania.

The Visa

Several uneventful days passed; we entered the month of September and I gave up even the last trace of hope for my trip to Yugoslavia. For six months I had not received one piece of news from the authorities regarding the trip. I didn't know if I received the visa and to my best knowledge neither did Olga. The 4th of September was near and I started making plans to spend my vacation some other way. The mountains looked great and I couldn't wait for another hike.

The morning of September 4th came about and I went to work like on every other day. I had packed my lunch the day before since the store nearby my office had almost nothing to offer and I started my work-day as always at 7 a.m. I was about 45 minutes into whatever I was doing when I received a phone call. At the other end Olga was almost hysterical: "Irineu, we got the visas, yheeee! We need to be in Brasov at the train station by noon to catch the train to Bucharest. At 8 p.m. we will be on the fast train to Belgrade, Yugoslavia!"

That was the greatest and the most triumphant shock of my life so far. It all started to make sense. They had waited until the last minute on purpose. They did not want us to have any time to prepare, to make plans, to get money, to establish connections, all meant to prevent an organized defection. However, the main question in my mind was: "How did I get the visa?" I had no trouble understanding how Olga got it, but I was at a loss regarding mine.

Soon enough I was able to put all the pieces together in order to explain it away. The references from my supervisors were good, I was in a stable marriage at the time (with the old problems patched up) which counted as an incentive to return since I was going alone, and I assumed Olga herself put in a good word for me. Besides, I didn't really have any obvious anticommunist antecedents, so there was probably nothing on the Securitate file to prevent me from going, in spite of the 'unhealthy' family tree. Later I discovered another important fact that, no doubt, had contributed to the release of my visa. Just a few weeks before the departure date, the senior Securitate officer in charge of the Chemical Plant of Victoria, went on vacation. His replacement was a young officer who graduated one year before me from the same high school, so we knew each other fairly well. As the vacation trip applications arrived at his desk for approval exactly in that period, he was the one signing the local approval, which most likely allowed me to get the visa from the higher office in Bucharest.

After Olga's phone call, it took me a few moments to get back to reality and that morning, the morning of September 4th, turned into an exciting agitation. In less than four hours we had to be in Brasov, about 70 miles away, ready to depart. In the meantime we had to secure vacation approvals from our immediate supervisors, which was no problem but it took time. Then we had to figure out a way to make it to Brasov before noon. Since there were no trains and we were running out of time, we made the trip by car. On the way I had to stop by my parents' house to get ready and to get the money for the trip, including some pocket money. I did not prepare anything in this respect, so my mother gave me the amount I needed, borrowing it from the church money my father was overseeing. He was not at home, so in the rush of the moment I hugged my mother and said goodbye as she whispered in my ear: "Don't you even think of not coming back!" To this I answered with a half-assuring "Don't worry mother, it will be OK." It all sounded eerily familiar: in some of the last conversations we had, my wife of that time expressed vehement disinterest in following me if I decided to defect. With these thoughts in my mind, Olga and I took off to catch the train in Brasov.

5

The Road to Sarajevo

The main railroad station of Brasov was the meeting point for our 40-person group set to spend a 12-day vacation in Yugoslavia. When we arrived, the entire group was complete. During the introductions we realized the obvious: there were two persons from each one of many factories and industrial centers in the district of Brasov. At that time we also learned that we will be accompanied by a translator, a guide, and a Securitate officer who was in charge of the 'common passport' which was a simple list with all our names. Therefore, beside our personal ID cards, we didn't have individual traveling documents (passports), so once in Yugoslavia we were supposed to stay as a group at all times.

After we all took care of the financial obligations for the trip, we embarked on a train to Bucharest where that evening we were supposed to take a fast train over night to Belgrade, the Yugoslavian capital. That exact week my new volleyball team was in Bucharest for the mandatory pre-season national physical preparation tests. Knowing they were staying at a hotel near the Bucharest main railroad station, I paid them a visit before departing. My two close friends from Victoria, Silviu and Vasile, joined me back at the station and we chatted until the last minute. Among other things we made plans for me to complete the physical tests upon my return. Even during those last moments on Romanian soil I kept my inner promise not to tell a soul about my defection plan. So, within this atmosphere we embarked and we were on our way to Belgrade.

Fast Train to Belgrade

The train was called "Rapidul Decebal," named after the famous king of the "Daci" tribe who lived on the present territory of Romania conquered by the Roman emperor Traian in 101-102 AD. Once on the train, we took a few compartments and, of course, we tried to be with people we knew. So I, together with Olga, made almost instant friends with a couple of vacationers from Fagaras which was the closest city to Victoria.

We did the best we could to make the trip as pleasant as possible. We talked about a variety of things and we expressed our eagerness to step on the ground of another country, which was a definite first for me. An hour or two later we were paid a visit by the supervising 'team': the guide, the translator, and the Securitate officer. They had been visiting all the compartments in order to meet and know the vacationers a little better. At that point I took out of my bag the half-liter bottle of the home-made brandy I packed while I was rushing out of my parents' house. We welcomed their visit and proceeded to party (I did not drink at all, since I was following my well-established athletic alcohol-free lifestyle). We all had a blast by seeing how much they enjoyed the brandy and we continued socializing until we arrived at the Romanian-Yugoslavian border.

Entering Yugoslavia was less dramatic than I thought. As we were waiting for the border patrols to check our documents one by one on the train, the image of thousands of Romanians caught or killed on the border in their desperate attempt to escape from Romania came very strongly to my mind. The Romanian side of the border was heavily watched 24-7 by armed border patrols with the order to shoot anybody who didn't surrender. In the woods, on clear land, or across the Danube (one of the largest rivers in Europe that makes a good portion of this border), this was a territory that witnessed many traumatic events over the years. Of course, such stories were never headlines in Romania since the Communist regime censored any sign of dissent. However, within close circles everybody knew. With these thoughts going through my head we finally crossed the border into Yugoslavia and after a short night sleep and an uneventful day on the train we arrived to Belgrade.

Belgrade

From the main railroad station of Belgrade we boarded an excursion bus and went to the designated hotel. After we took our rooms and settled down for a while we visited some historical sites in the city. We were kept in a tight group, and between sites we had only minutes to glance at the stores we were passing by. Even so, we were all shocked. The abundance and the design we witnessed surpassed by far anything we knew in Romania. In this respect, we did expect a different economical picture but the reality on the ground was way over our expectations.

In the evening we went back to the hotel to have dinner and retire for the night. The day had been pretty tiring but some of us still had the energy to sit around a chat. With the image of the beautiful stores we saw during the day, among other subjects of discussion, we were investigating ways to exchange some Romanian money. There was no exchange office we were aware of, so some of us had other ideas. I had with me a Russian made photo camera and, since I had little pocket money, I decided to sell my camera. I asked our translator to find me a buyer and he made arrangements for the next morning.

I went to bed running my unspoken plan in my mind, and any extra dinars (the Yugoslavian currency) I could get would have been a plus. I was not, therefore, interested in spending my money on things, at least not just yet. At that moment I only had about 400 dinars (exchanged by our organizers), but this was very little since, for example, one vinyl record in the stores was a little over 100 dinars. This was in fact our quick revelation. Yes, there was an abundance of merchandise in stores but the prices were very steep, at least for our vacation budgets. In parallel we asked about the average income level of the Yugoslavian population, and it turned out to be much higher than that of Romanians, comparatively. Consequently, I was very excited about the prospect of selling my camera, knowing how much I will need that money later.

In the morning we had breakfast and right after that we were ready to board the bus for the second leg of our trip. As we were rushed to depart, I missed the meeting with the buyer of my camera. However, since I had not bought anything yet, I still had my 400 dinars, so that was my budget on the way to the next city, Sarajevo.

Sarajevo

Sarajevo was a beautiful city on our way to the Adriatic Sea, the very well-known West coast of Yugoslavia, which was our vacation destination. The road to Sarajevo took us through a nice countryside that we admired only from the bus, and we arrived in Sarajevo around noon. After lunch we took our rooms in a hotel at the outskirts of the city and then we visited several historical touristic sites.

The one site that impressed me the most was the spot where the assassination of Archduke Franz Ferdinand took place on June 28th 1914 which started the First World War. The supposed foot prints of the assassin, Gavrilo Princip (a Bosnian member of the Serbian terrorist group called The Black Hand) were carved in the concrete of the sidewalk and the story behind it was even more amazing. Apparently, the soon to be assassin was walking the streets during Franz Ferdinand's visit to Sarajevo and at one point the driver of the car from which the duke was waving to the people in the streets *took a wrong turn*. This simple mistake completed the picture. The archduke was riding now parallel to the sidewalk where the gunman was walking: he stopped, took aim at the archduke's car, fired, and the rest is history. That decisive historic event, through its serendipity, and my visiting that site in Sarajevo, would resurface in my memory on and off for a long time.

Soon after, we all went back to the hotel. It was around 5:30 p.m. and we received a very welcome message from our tour guide: "You have two and a half hours of free time. Be back in the lobby of the hotel for dinner at 8 p.m." At first this was very surprising: free time? What could we do with this free time? Then quickly and almost instinctively, without wasting any precious moments, we made little groups and vanished from the hotel in all directions, anxious to walk around and visit as many stores as possible. Naturally, I made a little team with Olga and the two new friends from Fagaras and headed on the first major street we could find.

6

The Choice: Two Trains to Freedom

We left the hotel behind and in a few minutes we found ourselves on a strait away mini-boulevard which promised a lot of shopping opportunities. As we were very excited about the free time we received, we were walking briskly and talking simultaneously with the intention of using to the fullest the two and a half free hours we had been granted.

The Taxi

Within a few minutes I spotted a music store on the left side of the sidewalk. My little group knew how drawn I was to anything musical so it did not come as a surprise when I said: "You go ahead. I will check this store out and I will catch up with you soon." Without hesitation they understood my calling and continued their walk further up on the sidewalk which stretched as far as you could see straight ahead.

I approached the store and suddenly I noticed four taxicabs lined up along side the building. That was the moment that instantly revitalized my plan: "If I get the visa, I am not coming back." That was the moment when I made my life changing choice. Almost subconsciously I went straight up to the first taxi driver in line and I tried to explain what I wanted to do. However, I did not speak Serbo-croatian; he didn't speak any of the languages I understood so I moved quickly to the next one. The story repeated two more times since I wasn't able to communicate with any of the first three men. But my destiny greeted me with the fourth taxi driver, apparently the youngest of the four, who could speak a little German. That was when the private lessons in German I took in elementary school came in very handy. I explained briefly what I wanted to do and, as naively as one could be, I asked him how much he would charge to take me all the way up North to the border with Italy. I soon realized that my 400 dinars could only cover about a quarter of the cost and I paused to think for a few moments. He, however, came to the rescue when he said: "Why don't you take a train? It's very cheap." At this idea I looked quickly up the boulevard and I couldn't see my little group anymore. Immediately I asked him how much will it cost to take me to the railroad station and he gave me a good deal having in mind the rest of my trip. We jumped in his cab and at my request he headed back to my hotel to grab my little bag.

In the heat of the moment I didn't realize the risk I was taking: I could have encountered somebody from our group at the hotel or even the Securitate officer charged to take us all back to Romania at the end of the vacation. Nevertheless, I took the key from the front-desk, I ran quickly to my room, I got my bag, I returned the key, and I ran outside: the cab was waiting with engine on, aside the building. I jumped in and we were on our way to the train station. It all became surreal: here I was leaving the group, I was in a cab rushing to catch a train heading North toward the Italian border, and I did not feel any fear.

Although at the hotel my improvised plan went smoothly, my 'great escape' was not over by any means. The risk was huge: what drove me to trust this man? He could have taken me straight to the police; there was, after all, a reward offered by the Yugoslavian government for every defector from the Eastern Bloc caught in Yugoslavia. But things went my way and we arrived at the station shortly thereafter. Aware of my inability to communicate in Serbo-croatian, the taxi driver joined me inside. The main hall was full of people: hundreds of passengers standing side-by-side waiting to depart in many directions. Sarajevo was, apparently, an important connection point on the way to different parts of the country.

The First Train

It was already after 7 p.m. and, glancing at my small map of Yugoslavia, I had to find a train ride to the Northern city of Ljubljana (in present day Slovenia) in order to eventually approach the Italian border. We checked the departures tableau and located a train that was leaving at 8:30 p.m. to reach Ljubljana at 10 a.m. the next morning. Since the taxi driver was aware of my financial situation he charged me only 200 dinars for his service, down from what he originally asked. Then he bought me a train ticket to Ljubljana, a sandwich, and a bottle of water, so I didn't have to talk to anybody else before boarding the train. According to his estimates, the rest of the money should have been sufficient to take me to the Italian border, since I was facing yet another train trip from Ljubljana to Sezana, a town about 2 miles from the Italian border. We shook hands, he wished me luck on my trip, and I could not have thanked him enough.

As he left the station I looked for a good place to await my departure. I found a small and less crowded spot near the kiosk from which he purchased the sandwich and the water. It was almost 8 p.m. and it stroked me hard: at 8 p.m. I was supposed to be back at the hotel to meet the rest of the group for dinner. That instantly became the moment of revelation for me: Alea iacta est (the die has been cast)! The decision had been made, I left the group, and I even had a train ticket to Ljubljana. So far, caught in the whole taxi adventure, I didn't really have the time to think about the immediate consequences. But now, as I was waiting for my departure, an entire scenario ran through my mind: not returning to the group on time will set me as a missing person and of course everybody will start looking for me. Maybe for a few minutes I will be considered 'late' but after that it will all escalate into an escaping attempt. Moreover, my missing bag from my hotel room will be a clear indication of the latter.

Soon I had to put all that scenario aside when I realized that the time was almost 8:30 p.m. and I had to embark. In preparation, I decided to scout out the crowded station hall. Suddenly in the distance, I saw the silhouette of a man who climbed up the pedestal of a light post to look over the entire crowd. He resembled closely our Securitate officer, which forced me to back up instantly and hide behind the kiosk. That was the only moment so far when my heart started racing since the possibility of being caught obviously surfaced in my mind. The departure time was drawing near, so I took a side route in the station hall toward my train to Ljubljana and I made sure I kept a low posture all the way. Soon I joined the crowd heading that direction and I took a seat in an empty compartment somewhere in the middle of the train.

The train left the station on time and it took me a while to be able to relax and to consider myself out of danger at least as far as my fear of Securitate was concerned. Not too much later I had to face another possible danger: the conductor. I had a train ticket but I was not able to speak the language. If caught without any valid tourist documentation, my future would have been very dim. Therefore, I adopted the obvious strategy: I curled up in a corner, I covered my head with my soft wind-breaker that I hanged next to my seat, and every time the conductor showed up I would just extend my arm with the ticket for perforation. It worked perfectly the entire trip to Ljubljana. At one time around midnight two young ladies came into my compartment and I had to entertain a short and harmless conversation, this time in English. Even though there were very few other people around I could not sleep at all the entire night. The thoughts of stepping on free Italian soil, away from the Eastern Communist Bloc, soon were swirling in my head and I let my imagination run through virtually all possible scenarios I might find myself in. In the meantime I crafted a tentative plan in my mind.

Ljubljana

At about 10 a.m. the next day the train entered Ljubljana with a loud whistle. The main railroad station was relatively empty and I quickly checked the departures to Sezana, the town very close to the Italian border. The first train to Sezana was scheduled for noon. According to my over-night plans I went straight to the ticket-office, I put my little map of

Yugoslavia on the counter and, as I was taking my money out of my pocket, I pointed to Sezana. It worked. The lady behind the counter gave me the ticket and some change and I quickly moved away to avoid any possible conversation. There were hardly any people around and after gathering my belongings I had to think of something to do until 12 o'clock. Since I hadn't slept a wink that night I did not want to crash on a bench in the waiting hall: I would have most likely fallen asleep soon and for too long.

Therefore, I took my bag and I walked out of the station toward town. In walking distance I saw what appeared to be part of the downtown, so I headed that way. The street was relatively large, clean, and the two-way traffic was not bad. I took the sidewalk and in about 15-20 minutes I arrived at a shopping center in a nice area guarded by tall historical buildings. Soon enough I found my preference: a music store. I spent most of the time I had in there, looking through the hundreds of vinyl records but, of course, not with the idea of buying anything. After a while I felt tired and I left the store, I looked around some more and I headed back to the station.

The Second Train

A few minutes before noon I located the train to Sezana and I took a seat somewhere in an empty compartment. Again, the train was almost empty and I followed my "working" strategy not to be forced to engage in conversation with anybody, especially with the conductor. The train ride to Sezana was supposed to take about three hours, so I had to make sure I would not fall asleep, which was not easy. I moved around a little bit in my compartment and in the hallway as I was admiring the beautiful countryside through which the train was rushing. Hills and mountains were dressed in autumn colors in tandem with the four distinct seasons that mark the climate of that part of Europe. The afternoon sky was turning from gray to dark gray with the anticipation of rain, which eventually turned out to be a positive development within my overall plan.

With a loud and prolonged squeak, a few minutes after 3 p.m., the train announced its arrival in the modest Sezana station. I grabbed my little bag and I descended to the side walk that took me to the main street behind the station. Based on my little map and my orientation on the ground, this was supposed to be the street heading through the small town toward the border with Italy. Finally being this close to the border, I stopped feeling tired, my heart was racing, so I had to calm myself down and think about the next step. I took a sip of water and I headed down the street in the direction of the Italian border.

7

Sezana and the Forest of Freedom

It was early September and the approaching rain had already brought cold air to the area. My windbreaker came in handy as I was walking on the right-hand sidewalk of the main street in Sezana, in the direction of the border. My mind was heavily preoccupied: I had to come up with a successful strategy to cross into Italy without being caught by the Yugoslavian border guards. I had absolutely no idea as to what to expect on my way to the border nor did I know what the border itself was: a wooden fence, an electric fence, a wall, etc. Therefore, I decided to ask somebody these exact questions, which in retrospective was yet another very risky move on my part.

The 'Advisor'

The street was virtually deserted; the wind had intensified considerably and I kept walking calmly on the sidewalk, when I spotted a man coming toward me on the same side of the street. He was about 100 yards away and was wearing a long coat with a protective hood over his head. As we came closer to each other I noticed he was about my age and his medium-long dark beard stood out. In a matter of seconds I built the courage to engage him in a conversation, and I did.

I approached him in my broken English and to my pleasant surprise he matched it pretty well. We were able to communicate that way, and of course I started by apologizing for stopping him cold in the street. He didn't seem bothered by it, but as soon as I mentioned my plan he took one small step back, turned and looked carefully all around, then said in a soft voice: "Let's meet in 5 minutes at the intersection of those two streets next to that fence and we will talk." He pointed out which intersection, I agreed and he continued his walk as if nothing had happened. Immediately the risk I was running came to my mind: "He could show up with the police, and there goes my entire plan." However, since I was convinced I needed the information, I didn't think I had a choice. Besides that, he did look like somebody from my 'league' so I said to myself: "Maybe I should just trust him." And I did.

I continued walking on my way for another block then I turned right and another right, and in about 3 minutes I arrived at the intersection he pointed out which was one block off the main street. He was on time, *alone,* and we walked a few more yards down the street to pause under the branches of some large trees extending over the sidewalk. He then explained his reason for being overly cautious: this was a border-town and local people seen in company of strangers could be eventually declared suspect. I told him that, coming from Romania, I understood perfectly the entire scenario and I thanked him for being willing to help me.

We talked for at least 30 minutes. In all this time I don't remember even one person to pass by. I asked all the questions that came to my mind, of course related to the border. Knowing the seriousness of the situation, he was very patient and grave–I don't remember if we even cracked a smile during the entire conversation. Since I didn't have any international documents (visa to enter Italy), we ruled out my walking aside the 1-2 mile long highway to the border check-point. Instead, he suggested that I could choose either side of the road, both heavily wooded hills, but to stay as far as possible from the checkpoint. I asked if the border patrols do actually watch the border yard-by-yard as they do in Romania. He said they don't, but they do walk around occasionally, especially during the day and in good weather. That was a promising piece of information since I was planning to wait until dark anyway and the rain was imminent. Then I asked the most stringent question: "How is the border actually marked?" He said that there was no fence of any kind and all I had to expect was a piece of land, a strip about 50 yards wide that was completely cleared of any trees or bushes. This was the so called "no-man's-land," the neutral strip that was neither Yugoslavian nor Italian. He said that once I step on it nobody can touch me anymore: any attempt, even by remote gun shots, was considered an affront against the other country and it was punishable under international laws. Then he insisted on warning me of one thing: "If you encounter border patrols in the woods you must give yourself up, otherwise they will shoot you, not knowing who they are dealing with." I explained that I understood, based on experience I had from my mandatory service in the Romanian military, and I promised to be very careful not to be caught. Then he mentioned that there were trails in the woods made by people of Sezana including shepherds, so I should follow the ones heading toward the border. However, he also cautioned me that especially at night, it was easy to cross the border back and forth on those trails. I took his advice, I thanked him immensely, he wished me luck, we shook hands, and we parted ways.

The Escape

It was around 4 p.m. by now and the September cloudy day started to lose some of the light to the early evening that was also preparing for rain. I went back to the main street sidewalk and in 10-15 minutes I left behind the last few sporadic homes of Sezana. These looked like country homes decorating both sides of the road on large fenced parcels of land full of fruit trees. The homes marked the last signs of civilization before the heavy wooded area covering the small hills that were presenting in the distance some majestic mountains. I was now walking on grass aside the two-way highway that in the distance was pointing like a straight arrow to the border checkpoint. The checkpoint consisted of a few small buildings enclosing both sides of the highway that turned into the actual crossing point into Italy. It was just about a mile away and I could even see the barriers rising and falling as they were letting few cars in and out of Yugoslavia.

The picture suddenly became surreal to me: immediately beyond those barriers was Italy, my destination!

Mostly out of instinct and basically ignoring common sense, I waved to a couple of Italian cars heading toward the border. My naïve hope was to hitchhike my way through, even without the proper documentation. One car stopped. However, as soon as the driver realized I wasn't Italian, he took off in a rush. That was another risky attempt on my part but, again, nothing negative came of it.

After a little while I decided to get some rest to gather my strength for what I envisioned to be another long night. I walked off the road and made camp under a fruit tree out in the open at the bottom of a small hill about 30 yards away from the pavement. A quick search through my bag revealed a last chance for a snack: a quarter of a sandwich and a couple of sips of water. After the 'meal' I plucked a few plums from the plum-tree above my head and I stretched for a few minutes on the grass, savoring the plums and watching the dark clouds drifting as they were gently guided by the invisible hands of the wind. There were hardly any cars on the road by now and in the quiet moments before dark I felt the first few drops of cold rain coming down. I scouted out the terrain in front of me on the same side of the road. For a few hundred yards there were no big trees and I already spotted a few trails that were heading away from the highway through some bushes toward the forest. I picked up my bag, I put the hood of my little windbreaker over my head, I took one of the trails, and I started a brisk walk to reach the cover of the deep forest.

While I was still walking on relatively open ground, I kept a wandering eye over the area but there was no trace of movement of any kind. It seemed that beside the deserted highway, all other forms of life had decided to take shelter for the rainy night ahead.

As I stepped into the woods, the dark night had fallen almost completely but I was still able to follow my trail hoping it would lead me to freedom. I welcomed the rain which was falling ever so softly, wishing it was hard enough to keep the border guards at the checkpoint. In spite of my conscious effort to stay as far as possible from the checkpoint I still felt it dangerously close. Consequently, I decided to take numerous breaks, kneel down to the ground and watch for but mostly listen for any sign of trouble. I was extremely careful not to step on dead branches that could give me away, so I was making small progress toward my goal. In the almost complete silence of this picture I was able to hear occasional distant voices coming from the direction of the checkpoint. Every time I heard human voices my heart was racing again at the possible danger; I remembered: "I must give myself up, otherwise they will shoot." However, I was not about to die this close to the realization of my dream. I slowly calmed myself down thinking that they were not close enough, but after a while I heard dogs barking. That familiar sound made me truly cringe! The picture of my dog, Hera, finding me in our hide-and-seek games over hundreds of yards in the woods around my home town, took my mind hostage. Therefore, I intensified my tempo a little and in a few minutes I arrived at what appeared to be some old, even ancient, brick-wall ruins. They were just about 3-4 feet off the ground and I used the site as a quick stop pretending I found better protection behind them. I caught my breath for a few minutes and when all voices and dog barks ceased, I continued hunched down on the trail straight ahead, yearning for Italian soil.

The night became even darker, but my eyes were already adapted to the September dim light of the Yugoslavian woods so I could distinguish my surroundings pretty clearly. It was around 9 p.m. by now, the rain took an unexpected break, and I carefully managed to cover 40 or 50 more yards in the dense forest on the trail that I was hoping to lead me to my goal: the border! Then I decided to take another quick break at the foot of a huge tree that provided me, after all, with a false sense of security: I could have been still within the radar of a guard dog or soldier who had been chasing me all along. With these thoughts running through my mind, I had sharpened my senses, ready to perceive any subtle threatening noise. Other than the soft murmur of leaves in the wind, there was nothing. The comfort of the virtual silence really helped me relax a little, and as I was breathing deeply the freshly oxygenated cold air, I scouted out the immediate surroundings one more time.

While I was leaning against the big tree, I eagerly let my eyesight to drift, focused over 180 degrees in the direction of what I was hoping to be the Italian border. At that point I couldn't even hear my own breath: the all-around silence made me feel one with the forest, so I felt even more secure. It seemed that all threatening noises, together with the rain were acting in concert, suspending their own being in order to pleasantly embrace and guide me to my immediate destination: the border.

My instincts did not betray me. As I carefully scrutinized the close proximity in front of me, my eyes sent an instant and long-awaited message to my mind: within 15 to 20 yards there was a distinct clearing in the forest! With all the unseen support around me I anxiously proceeded that way. It took me about 20 steps and, indeed, I located the strip. I stopped, I looked to my left, I looked to my right, and the clearing was obviously the border, confirming the description offered by my 'advisor' in Sezana. As far as I could see, tall and heavy trees on both sides were guarding it from above as to say "Don't touch! This does not belong to anybody!" My heart went crazy once more when I realized that the trail I was on was heading across the 'no-man's-land' strip, and that became overly significant. With my bag in my right hand, I squatted for a few seconds, I gathered my strength, and, although there was complete silence all around, I ran the 40-50 yards on the trail…to Italy!

As soon as I reached the other side I stopped. I set my bag on the ground, I turned around, I waved goodbye to the Yugoslavian side and implicitly to the entire Eastern Europe, and I murmured a heart-felt thank-you whisper to the Yugoslavian land and to all who facilitated my success so far. The emotions ran high. My heart was racing, but this time with the realization that I had just accomplished my life-changing goal. To the best of my knowledge I was now in Italy, finally free from the Communist Bloc! There was no turning back. My mind was processing all these thoughts almost simultaneously and that was the first time a trace of nostalgia entered the picture: "Who knows if or when I will ever see my family and my homeland again!" I said this to myself with my eyes resting back on the trail that brought me to freedom, while a warm and shy tear slowly lingered down my left cheek as if to say: "You can't experience joy without a little pain." How true has that turned out to be throughout my life!

8

A Great Night in Trieste

In the meantime the night became a little colder and the rain came back as a continuous sprinkle but gentle enough not to be a hindrance. I grabbed my little bag, I turned toward what was supposed to be Italy, and I continued my walk on the trail that took me to freedom. It was now late in the night and I had really no choice but moving along hoping to find some shelter. After a while my friendly trail headed straight into a railroad track. There I decided to take the railroad track as my next path toward Trieste, the largest Italian city close to the Yugoslavian border.

The area was still heavily wooded so the railroad track offered me a good clearance heading hopefully to a train station. As I was standing on the tracks, I had to choose: do I go right or left. As far as I could tell in the middle of the night and based on the direction I was coming from, I thought 'left' was heading back toward Yugoslavia while 'right' appeared to move away from it. So I chose 'right.''

The Train Station

Since visibility was drastically limited, I wasn't able to locate a trail parallel to the tracks. Therefore, I decided to step on and actually walk on the tracks, sometimes skipping one sometimes not. My steps were the only noticeable break in the late-night silence of the forest, blending rhythmically with the whisper of the soft autumn rain. The railroad tracks carried me for about 45 minutes when I spotted a small light in the distance. Encouraged by the prospect of finding a shelter for the night, I sped up my walk and soon I arrived at a small train station.

I stepped off the tracks and I went straight up to the front door. The sign above the door was reading something in Italian which confirmed that I was on Italian soil and put my mind at ease. Although it was a little after midnight, the door was still open so I entered what appeared to be a small snack bar. The room was deserted but off in a corner a middle-aged lady was cleaning up. She noticed my arrival and politely engaged me in Italian. Soon she realized that I wasn't speaking her language and we tried a couple more. However, French and English failed, but, surprisingly enough, German came to my rescue again. I briefly explained who I was and what I wanted to do and she was very hopeful to guide me in the right direction.

From the front of the station there was a two-way paved road heading out. She said I should walk up this road for about half a mile where I will find a bus station at the intersection with the main road heading to Trieste. I asked how I can get a bus ticket in the middle of the night and she said I should not worry about it because they rarely check and my situation was special anyway: I wanted to turn myself in to the police in order to get to the refugee camp. I thanked her very much for her help and I headed out.

In a few minutes I made it to the bus station. The surroundings were still part of a large wooded area but a few sporadic street lights illuminated the road so it was easy to find my way around. There were no buildings on either street and the bus station was in fact a metal post stating the obvious. Next to it there was a young couple waiting for the next bus. So, after meeting the lady in the train station, these people became my first unintended company in Italy. However, it was a silent one, since neither I nor they were willing to strike a conversation.

Trieste and the Carabinieri

Within 10 or 15 minutes the bus made its welcome arrival, breaking the deep silence of the night. We stepped away from the cold rain into the comfortable warmth of the bus and took our seats away from each other: we were the only passengers.

The following hour or so will turn out to be one of my most cherished memories of beauty and freedom.

Soon after departure, the highway took a winding course through the mountains, heading patiently down toward the city of Trieste. For awhile all I could see was what the headlights revealed, but later the spectacle turned into a magnificent show of lights. From our respectable altitude up in the mountains, through the very well pronounced serpentines, now I could see alternating to my left and to my right beautiful pictures of the port of Trieste. The port was hugging both sides of a small and narrow gulf of the Adriatic Sea, with shiny lights virtually everywhere. Several boats were showing their splendor as they were gently rocked by the calm sea waves, and short streets displayed a colorful panorama of a city at rest after a long September work day. The mountains were guarding both the port and the city with their protective majestic power, and gradually we left them behind as our driver found his way to the main bus station of Trieste.

By now it was almost 2 a.m. and there were hardly any people in the bus station. Since I hadn't slept for two days and I had no food left, I wanted desperately to turn myself in, so I inquired about the Police headquarters. Uttering the quasi universal word, Police, was quite sufficient, and the bus driver pointed me in the right direction.

A few blocks down the main street from the bus station I found the famous Carabinieri. It was a two-level building with a nice large front-yard enclosed by a metal fence. Without any hesitation, I approached the main gate and I rang the bell. Three or four times were not enough, so after the fifth, finally the door opened and an officer in a sleepy face showed up. He remained, however, in the door, wanting to know what my problem was. Not able to communicate in Italian, and being about 25 yards away from him, I shouted something relating to "Romania" and "refugees." He seemed to understand, but immediately he pointed to his wrist-watch and I was pretty sure I got his message: "It's way too late in the night. Come back at 8 a.m." As he went inside and locked the door I said to myself: "See? This is freedom. No sense of panic or urgency, even though I was a refugee with no documents, showing up at the police headquarters in the middle of the night. We will solve whatever problem in the comfort of day-light."

By then the rain had subsided so I was eager to find a place to lie down and rest, maybe even to catch a little sleep. Not far from the Carabinieri, on an adjacent street I found a very small Roman amphitheater, perhaps of about 100 seats all carved in stone that was standing tall as a testimony to the ancient past of Italy. It was not enclosed by any protective fence so I took a few steps up in the stands, I sat my hand-bag as a pillow and I stretched out my tired body on a large slab of stone. I slept for about an hour, but then I woke up freezing. My thin windbreaker, my Romanian-made jeans, and my light sneakers were no match for the cold slab, the cold September night, and the cool mountainous region. Therefore, I decided to get back to the bus station hoping it will stay open all night. Indeed it was open. I walked straight into the empty station hall and I lied down on a bench. It was much warmer than outside so I almost instantly fell asleep. However, it wasn't for long. At about 6 a.m. the cleaning crew came in and kicked me out since seemingly sleeping on benches in the station was prohibited. I grabbed my bag and, having all the time in the world, I slowly headed back toward the Carabinieri headquarters. It was still early in the morning and for the first time I was able to admire in the daylight the Italian architecture both modern and ancient. It was my first live encounter with such an impressive combination, and that was just an opening of what was awaiting me in the days to come.

I walked back and forth in front of the Carabinieri building for a while and at 8 a.m. sharp I rang the bell again. This time I was promptly invited in and I did my best to explain the situation. I am sure I was not the first. The two officers were very nice as they demonstrated their skills in such matters. They understood my intention and shocked me when they told me I needed to take a train to the refugee camp of Latina. The outdated information I received back in Romania pointed to a camp in Trieste, but apparently it had been moved to Latina, which was a smaller city about 40 miles West of Rome. At this news I explained to the carabinieri that

I was almost completely out of money, but they assured me that it wasn't a problem: my train ticket was covered by United Nations funds allocated especially for political refugees needs. Within a couple of hours I walked out of the Carabinieri headquarters with all the necessary paperwork (including a temporary personal identification card). Then I headed toward the Trieste train station.

9

Trains to Latina

The train station of Trieste received me with open arms as it did all the other hundreds of people that day. This time I wasn't afraid to be myself in the crowd and I felt free and comfortable to face a snack bar vendor where I spent my last money. All I had left was the equivalent of about five dollars so I bought myself a large sandwich and a bottle of juice for the trip.

The first leg of my trip was a 10-hour ride from Trieste to Rome and I had to embark at noon. At about midnight the next day I had to take another train from Rome to Latina, which was just about an hour and a half ride. I couldn't wait to get on the train. I was hoping I would find a seat and take a nice quiet nap at last. It wasn't to be. The train was super crowded and it got even more so as we headed on. Over almost the entire duration of the ride to Rome I stood up in the hallway of my train cart. This offered me the unprecedented opportunity to admire the Italian countryside and the multitude of villages, towns, and cities we were passing through. Most memorable was passing through Venice: from the train window I was able to see in the distance the sea water surrounding the city. Memories of pictures and movies I had seen of the water streets full of gondolas came to mind, but it will be only many years later when I will actually see them in person at close range.

The rest of the ride to Rome went on uneventfully. It was my first real ride in freedom and it felt wonderfully relaxing. I had enough time to review the events of the previous 2-3 days and the more I thought about them the more I felt a sense of guidance. As tired as I became over time I felt that all will be well; it was like a silent voice in the back of my head encouraging me on: "Go ahead, you're safe." I felt very little fear and even when I did it was more like helping me concentrate and not panic. So the long ride to Rome, outside of virtually any worry, was restful and refreshing in spite of the heavy lack of sleep.

Rome

Along with reliving the last few days, I had no choice but to also think about the immediate future. After all, I was about to arrive at the 'eternal city,' Rome. I didn't really know what to expect in the next few days. I was heading into the unknown, but this unknown was safe, or at least much safer than the very risky unknown I was facing leaving Romania and all the way through Yugoslavia.

After a long slowing down period the train stopped in the main train station of Rome, the Italian capital. It was around 10 p.m. and I knew I had a two-hour wait before the final leg of my trip to Latina. I was yearning to at least get a glimpse of the city so I went outside the station and I walked for a while back and forth in front of its grandiose building. It was good enough: I was in Rome! Even at night, or exactly because of it, it was very impressive. Although Trieste introduced me to what a true Western city should look like, Rome, or the little quarter I was admiring, already pushed me further. I was totally overwhelmed by the images in front of me. The liveliness, the lights, the ordered traffic, the multitude of travelers walking in and out of the station completed a picture of abundance that was horribly missing within the Communist Bloc. Even that late at night, people seemed happy, with a strong sense of purpose as they were following their bliss. There seemed to be absolutely no bliss in censorship, intellectual and ideological oppression, rationed food, and most importantly, there was definitely no bliss in living in a virtual prison since international travel was reserved only for a few. I instantly felt sorry for all the people left behind the 'Iron Curtain' since a majority of them will never experience anything like this. With such ideas running through my head I turned around and I went back in the station.

Before my departure for Latina I had to validate my train ticket. As I was searching for the proper teller I started deciphering the signs obviously written in Italian. To my amazement I understood enough to find my way around. After all, Italian and Romanian are both Latin languages, so there are plenty of similarities to help even a novice navigate from one to the other. This realization also put my mind at ease regarding my future proficiency in Italian, but for the time being I limited my efforts to the minimum necessary.

Latina

As soon as I embarked for Latina I ate the last piece of the sandwich and I had the last sip of juice. The train departed on time, at midnight; the ride was supposed to be short and I was wondering what I should expect upon my arrival.

The hour and a half ride went by fast and the train was relatively empty although Latina was just one station on the route to Napoli. I forced myself to stay awake not to miss the station in Latina and around 1:30 a.m. I descended at my final destination. There were very few passengers around and soon I understood why. There were about 6 miles from the train station to the city of Latina and the last bus to town left at 1 a.m. The bus system would resume its service at 7 a.m. so for the rest of the night there was no public transportation available. I could see the lights of the city in the distance but I didn't even consider walking in the middle of the night in the unknown. Under these circumstances I did the obvious: I found the station hall; I located a bench away from the door, and I lied down for a much needed sleep.

A 7 a.m. crowd inundated the station when busses brought in passengers from town. They were people commuting daily by train to their places of work in Rome, so that was an animated start of the day for me as I awoke and stood up from my 'comfortable' wooded bench. Immediately I searched for a bus to Latina. I located one, behind the train station, which was ready to depart, and I quickly jumped on. Once again with no ticket I was on my short trip to what was supposedly the main bus station in downtown Latina. The road took us through a brand new countryside for me. On both sides of the road an abundance of peach and olive trees, craftily aligned on well-maintained plantations, reminded me I was in Italy, moreover, in the warmer half of it. As we were moving away from the train station, I noticed in the distance, back on the other side of the railroad, some beautiful although pretty bare, tall hills, which I would find out later, were very old mountains, eroded over time. From their tops, a couple of small towns were shining their roofs in the early morning sun, and, intrigued, I had already made a commitment to myself: someday I will visit these places. Back on the road, the farm scenery gave way to more of an urban site, and soon enough, residential and commercial buildings announced the city.

From the outskirts of Latina to the station itself the city appeared to be different from what I remembered Trieste to be. Soon enough I found out why: Latina was a brand new city in Italy. It was built by Mussolini on virgin ground which was previously a swamp. Therefore, all the buildings were less than 40 years old at the time, most of them built in a modern architecture without a trace of Roman influence. With a population of about 100,000, Latina is located very nicely almost half way between the chain of very old and low mountains I saw in the distance, and the beach on the Western Italian coast.

I left the bus station and I immediately inquired about the refugee camp. I was instructed to follow the main street, take two turns and I will find it. Indeed, at the end of a 10-minute walk I was in front of the camp and the picture that awaited me was surprising but expected.

10

The Refugee Camp

It was a cloudy cool September morning in Latina and close to 8 a.m. I made it to the street where the refugee camp opened its walls to the city. I was surprised to see 50-60 people standing or sitting on the long sidewalk in front of the camp. Later on I found out that these were refugees waiting for black-market work offered very cheaply by citizens of Latina: political refugees did not have the right to work in Italy. From garden work to masonry, the range of black-market jobs was wide open. For 10-15 dollars a day refugees would accept such work in order to make some much needed pocket money.

As I was slowly and cautiously walking down the sidewalk toward the main entrance, I already heard people speaking Romanian. I waited patiently for an opportunity and, not wanting to sound too pushy, I approached two men who apparently were killing time waiting for some work. I explained my situation and, surprisingly, they became very receptive to my inquiry. They were nice enough to take me straight to the main office where I was supposed to start the official registration procedure, and to introduce me to the rest of the routine 'ritual' every newcomer would follow.

The Camp

The offices were located in an imposing two-story building very close to the main entrance which was guarded by tall white columns. As you passed that building there were sidewalks spreading into the compound and on either side of them you would find an ordered sequence of one-story dorm rooms with four beds each; occasionally there would be larger rooms holding more beds. At certain intervals there would be special enclosures hosting restrooms and showers, and somewhere in the back, somewhat symmetrical to the office building up front, there was another two-story building designed to host refugees with families with or without children. Aside that building there was the kitchen and the dining area. The entire camp was surrounded by a thick brick wall 7-8 feet tall, and later on I found out that in fact this compound was an 'inheritance' from Mussolini. During the Second World War these were actually military barracks used to shelter Italian soldiers. In 1981, as the statistics had it, it sheltered about 1,500 political refugees mainly from the Eastern Bloc.

I entered the main building and I was immediately guided to the registration office. After a short informal interview my file was put together. It included all the information I made available. However, in terms of official documentation it was all focused on my ID card from Romania, the only real identification I had, and the temporary card I received from the Carabinieri in Trieste. One of the crucial items in my file was supposed to be my choice for emigration (the communication in the offices was facilitated by a few Romanian refugees who somehow secured hourly work as translators). Not knowing all my options, I asked, and they presented them to me: the U.S.A., Canada, Australia, and ... Venezuela. The first three were obvious choices but Venezuela was not. So I asked: "Why Venezuela?" The answer came quickly and clearly. Apparently at that point in time the government of Venezuela was seeking skilled workers from the Communist Bloc such as electricians, welders, masons, etc. My choice came fast and easy, the dream of my life: the U.S.A.

In the next few minutes they gave me the tentative schedule for my stay in the camp. The first step was a relative formality, but important to some people. Within about two weeks I had to be officially interviewed by an Italian committee to determine if I qualified for political asylum in Italy, which meant I could stay in Italy for the rest of my life. If I will not be granted asylum in Italy I had to forward my application to a different office in order to emigrate to another country, which will imply an interview at the respective embassy, and so on. I was told that the entire process will take anywhere from 4 to 8 months, so I was bracing myself for a relatively long stay in the camp. The basic accommodation was room and board, so I was assigned a certain room in the compound and later I was supposed to receive a key and the immediate necessities such as towels and soap, toothpaste and toothbrush, and toilet paper.

As I left the office building I met one of the two Romanians I talked with previously. Apparently he did not find work that day so he was just hanging around. Since he knew the place very well he was happy to show me the room so we headed that way. We found it easily: it was empty and wide open. It seemed that I was the first one assigned to it, so I inquired where we could get the key. I hung my windbreaker on a coat hanger in a little iron closet; I grabbed my bag, I shot the door, and we left in search of the key. I didn't know it then, but I was in for my first shocker over my stay in the camp. It only took a few minutes, but when we returned with the key my windbreaker had already disappeared. That was a hard blow, the first wake up call. We searched for it and we asked the few neighbors who were around at that time, but my windbreaker was nowhere to be found. It wasn't a big loss except that in one of its pockets I had placed my little note book with addresses and phone numbers of friends and relatives. This included the address and phone number of my elementary school classmate (a U.S. resident now) whom I met in Victoria at the August 23 dance party.

The first lunch in the cafeteria couldn't be any more welcome: I was starving. My newly made friend introduced me to the entire ritual and I devoured everything I received. It was way over any of my expectations, and soon enough I grew accustomed to the Italian cuisine, at least with respect to the basics offered in a refugee camp. Later experiences would expand my culinary perception of the real Italian art of food preparation and its variety.

Later that day, my first day in the camp, I met again the other Romanian, Stefan, who did find work that morning. I told him the story of my lost windbreaker and almost immediately he offered me a place in his room. Apparently one of the four occupants, an older gentleman, a Romanian engineer from Bucharest, found steady work in Rome, so he was basically living there. I accepted the offer and I changed my 'residence' to the new room. My second friend took me to the warehouse where I received my bed sheets, towel, toilet paper, soap, toothbrush, and toothpaste. It seemed that, gradually, my friend and I found some personal affinities that helped us become closer over a short period of time. He had been a camp-resident for a few months already and he had already learned Italian well enough to communicate.

It took me a few days to get used to living in the refugee camp. The daily routine was pretty standard, the only set times we had to be in the camp being breakfast, lunch, and dinner unless we made other arrangements. There was no strict attendance policy and there were no other requirements. During the day one could attend free language lessons in English offered periodically in the camp, socialize, or take walks in the city. Those who had some money could go to the movies or other shows in town and one point of definite attraction was the weekend flea market. That was the preferred shopping place for most refugees due to limited financial potential as well as the bargaining option.

Phone Call to Romania

Two days before the scheduled date of return from our vacation trip to Yugoslavia I decided to contact my parents. I wanted them to hear it directly from me that I wasn't coming back and also that I was well. At that point I had absolutely no money left so Stefan offered to pay for a phone call to Romania; he had called before so he knew the procedure. That evening we went to the post office where they had pay phones for international calls, but since my parents did not have a phone at the time, I had to call a distant cousin of mine who lived in the near-by Victoria. His mother answered and as soon as I gave her the news she lost it: she started crying in disbelief and she gave the phone to my cousin who was a few years younger than me. In contrast to his mother, he was ecstatic and immediately responded with something like this: "Great! Well done. Take care of yourself and good luck!" I asked them to actually go to my parents to tell them in person, and of course, they soon did. As I found out later, my parents took it very hard. It was incomprehensible to them how and why I made that decision, and consumed by the despair of 'losing' their son, they suffered several days of deep sadness and depression.

Of course, after the phone call, not knowing its consequences, I felt good that I was able to send them the news instead of finding out at the vacationers group's return from Yugoslavia. Soon after, I also wrote them a letter and from then on we established a relatively steady correspondence. However, aware of the heavy censorship imposed by the Communist regime of Romania via the Securitate, we restricted the contents to mundane subjects of discussion hoping the letters would go through, and most of them did. In this respect, I vividly remember my father's first two letters (which were actually almost the same content sent twice just to make sure that at least one of them would make it): they were full of logical criticism toward my decision to defect. I am sure part of it came from his heart but I also wanted to believe that part was meant to please the Securitate so they will allow the letter to reach me. Some of the criticism sounded like this: "How did you decide to leave everything behind? You had a good job and now you have to start over from scratch, from the first knife and fork." I smiled as I read the letter but I felt their pain, regret, and, most likely, disappointment. However, mine was a one way decision since its reversal would have caused the same amount of damage to my life as if I were to be caught during my escape and sent back to Romania.

Finding Something to Do

There were around 400 Romanians in the refugee camp in the Fall of 1981 and many times people would strike a conversation with a stranger just for socializing and perhaps to commiserate about things. One such person approached me one day since I was the newcomer. As I was describing briefly how I crossed Yugoslavia, another Romanian overheard the discussion and invited himself in. His name was Gerry and we found out that he escaped from a similar group of vacationers coming from the Bucharest district to Yugoslavia about a month earlier and he arrived in the camp about 2 weeks before me. It turned out that he was about 2 years older than me and also in the computer science business, so, based on these similarities we became instant friends.

Such encounters happened all the time and soon enough we had a pretty good group of friends spending time with each other and especially joining together for meals in the cafeteria. Under these circumstances I spent the first two weeks mostly around the camp. After a few failed attempts to find some work I became restless and tired of sitting around so one evening I asked Stefan, my roommate friend, to accompany me as I wanted to go for a walk in town. That evening marked the beginning of a new and much happier part of my stay in Latina.

11

Life in Latina

Stefan and I left the camp at about 7 p.m. and were heading toward the popular streets where much of the youth of Latina were hanging out. Everything was in walking distance so it didn't take us long.

In search for something to do while waiting for my documents to go through the emigration process, I realized that maybe I could find a volleyball team that I could join to train and play as an outsider. That would at least occupy some of my time and also help me stay in decent physical shape. So I expressed my plan to my friend as we almost reached the center of town. One intersection in particular seemed to be favored by many boys and girls who were coming either on foot, on bicycles, or on small motorcycles, simply to socialize. It was a captivating happy picture of laughter accompanied by music played on portable stereos.

Soon enough I saw two young men about 15-16 years old bouncing a basketball on the sidewalk as they were entering an ice cream shop. That triggered my attention and, since I was not yet able to communicate in Italian, I asked my friend to approach them and see if they were aware of any volleyball activity in Latina. He did, but the two Italian young men did not have any direct information on volleyball. However, one of them said that he had a friend who might know, so he promised to talk to his friend and come back the following evening to tell us what he had found. So we made an informal appointment for 8 p.m. the next evening and left.

Obviously the next day passed very slowly for me. I was already imagining and planning the fun I will have playing volleyball and I couldn't wait for that evening. By now I had a routine during the day. I would go to breakfast, I would check with the refugee office for news (there was usually none), and after lunch I would go for a walk waiting for my friend to return from his black market work day. That day we met in the camp, had dinner, and took a long walk on the streets of Latina in anticipation of our appointment.

Volleyball in Latina

The Italian young man could not be more punctual: as my watch showed 8 p.m. he announced his presence by bouncing the basketball as he entered the ice cream bar. He looked tired and sweaty coming from his basketball practice and was ready for a juice and an ice cream. He came straight to us and delivered the good news: there was a lower division volleyball team in town and at that time they were getting ready for the upcoming volleyball season which was supposed to start toward the end of October. He also said that the team will have an informal get together and practice two days later on an outside court within a soccer stadium complex. My Romanian friend translated all this to me but I was happy to discover that I already understood some by myself. We thanked him for the information and went our way.

Two days later my friend was not able to join me to the volleyball practice so I went alone. I found the stadium and indeed I located two young teams playing against each other for fun. I was wearing street pants, a shirt, and the Romanian-made tennis shoes but I desperately wanted to at least touch the volleyball. So I took advantage of a break and I approached one of the players with my introduction question: "Excuse me, do you speak English?" That was enough to catch some attention. He said no, but he took me to another player who did. Apparently, Alberto was the only one in the group to be able to communicate in English and I was happy. I explained briefly that I was from Romania, living in the refugee camp, and I only wanted to play a little bit. Although I was in my street attire they didn't mind and I joined them for a few minutes. The team appeared to have fun having me around and, of course, it was a revelation for me: my first time playing a little volleyball in Italy! As a result they invited me to the next evening's practice, but that time their financial sponsor and coach will be there also, and they wanted me to meet him. I said yes, of course, and I expressed my deepest gratitude for their invitation.

Sergio Picone

Again, I couldn't wait for the next evening. It seemed a little bit unrealistic to find the possibility to play the sport I loved so much even as a resident of a political refugee camp. So that evening I showed up a little early, I waited for the rest of the team to get together, and I joined them for a brief warm up session. About half way through the practice the sponsor/coach showed up. He sat aside watching us for a while and only then did he make a few technical suggestions to a couple of players. At the end of practice we all joined him sitting on the first few rows in the stands of the stadium and Alberto made the introductions, acting very well as the translator.

His name was Sergio Picone; he owned a small business in telecommunications (telephones and operators) and he was an ex-top-division volleyball player in Italy. He stood at about 6 feet 4 inches, close to my height, and was very well built, especially for a non-active player. Via Alberto's translation I told my story of many years in volleyball and I was surprised to find a lot of appreciation for Romanian volleyball. I explained that I would be very happy if I could workout with the team, when Sergio shocked me with an offer. He wanted me to coach the team since he wasn't really able to do it, being pressed by time between his business, family, and volleyball. He took a note-pad and wrote down the monthly amount he will pay me. By shaking my head, I tried to explain that I wasn't as interested in the money as in having something to do. Not understanding exactly what I was saying, he increased the amount a couple of times and we finally settled. Later I found that kind of humorous and I related it as such many times.

My next question was, of course: "How do you think I can coach if I don't yet speak Italian?" With an open and happy little smile on his face, his solution came instantly from a very logical and practical perspective: "You do it and the team will follow your example!" I said to myself: "Wow! That is a very clever approach!" I thought it would work, at least while we will go through the 2-3 weeks of outdoor physical training, and I promised that by the time we move indoors I will be able to communicate in Italian. So I agreed, we shook hands, and everybody went their own way, except Sergio and I.

He invited me to his car and took me for a ride on the nightly illuminated streets of Latina. We went to a sports warehouse still open where he obviously knew the owners, and in a few minutes he purchased for me an entire set of volleyball attire starting with Adidas shoes, shorts, shirt, and a warm-up suit. He put them all in a brand new sports bag and handed it all to me. I was totally overwhelmed! I couldn't believe it! As we left the store, all alone, I gathered my drastically limited Italian vocabulary, together with a combination of English words, and with noticeable emotion in my voice I expressed my gratitude and thanks for his gesture. He smiled with what I thought was a compassionate feeling toward me and said kindly: "You're welcome!" Since his wife of that time was a high school English teacher in Latina, Sergio spoke and understood some English but apparently not enough to communicate fluently. Deeply moved by the entire evening, from there on I felt I should force myself to learn as much Italian as I could in the shortest time.

It was already pretty late at night, so after he gave me the short-term practice schedule, he took me straight to the refugee camp. Before I got out of the car I looked him straight in the eyes, and while we shook hands, I expressed my gratitude one more time: "Thank you very much Sergio. I will do my best!" As I grabbed my new sports bag, I followed with a formal "Good night!" and I promised myself that next time I will say it in Italian. His car's tail lights illuminated my face as I stood on the sidewalk for a few seconds watching him leave, then I headed on to my room. "I have a job" was the first thought going through my mind, but "not any job: it is volleyball" was the second. Almost instantly I remembered my first coach's words in September 1970: "You may not make a career out of volleyball, but volleyball will open many doors in your life." I walked through the dark corridor toward my room silently thanking Soni for such a timely and sensitive motivator phrase at my first organized volleyball practice back in 1970; not only that, but it came true at a wonderful moment of my life.

My camp roommates were very happy for me and they expressed it nicely the next day. They found it rather humorous that I will be a coach who will go through the physical training hand-in-hand with the team, at least for a while. However, I welcomed this approach being aware that I needed it and also wanted the training for myself. For this exact reason I couldn't wait for the first practice, which came two days later.

Physical Training

I was both proud and humble when I showed up for the first training session in my brand new volleyball attire; not only that it was new but it was a cut above everything I had been wearing in Romania, for obvious reasons. In the same time I sensed a little bit of anxiety from the group. They were mostly young athletes who didn't really know what to expect. I took Alberto aside and I briefly explained in my broken English what I had in mind for that evening. We were supposed to have a gymnasium reserved but only two weeks later, so for the time being we took advantage of the soccer stadium for two weeks of intensive physical training.

Then I pulled out basically my training routine I knew so well from my university years. We warmed up patiently with stretching exercises and light running around the soccer field, then we did a few laps of sprints on the track-and-field red clay, followed by rolls and dives on the grass. Since it was the first session I made sure we took plenty of breaks and I also included a short segment using the volleyballs. The stadium itself came in very handy: for two weeks, at every practice, we had heavy segments of running and jumping up and down the stairs in the stands. This is simple but very efficient not only endurance training, but also quickness and jumping training; good volleyball playing requires all three. The hour and a half practices also included many body-training exercises (push-ups, sit-ups, etc.) beside the volleyball-specific drills.

The training regimen went on for the entire two weeks more or less every evening so it didn't take long to have everybody tired and sore including me of course. Sergio would show up almost every day toward the end of the work out, and apparently liked what he saw and most importantly the feedback from the team. Alberto was very instrumental in translating but soon enough I started making a conscious effort to speak more and more Italian. Even making mistakes, it was the fastest way to improve. Slowly, I was able to make use of the Latinity of both Romanian and Italian to make use of many Romanian words and grammar rules that, to the best of my knowledge, were similar in both languages. It worked very well. I also encouraged Sergio and the team to correct me when needed and soon enough I was able to conduct our volleyball practices and basic conversation in Italian.

Those two weeks became very instrumental for the future success of the team and also brought me and Sergio closer. I was very happy when most of the players expressed their gratitude at the end of the two weeks: they felt very strong and comfortable as soon as we moved indoors. One of them said: "I feel I can fly." I knew the feeling. We were now training more volleyball specific so the physical readiness was quickly translating into better playing. Sergio, due to his extensive experience, knew it all along, so I was surrounded by a happy group. The volleyball season drew close so we had relatively little time to work on the actual game but enough to start with confidence.

Political Asylum

It was during that time that I was scheduled for my political asylum interview at the refugee camp. This was an important step in the emigration process since it could have opened or closed the door to remaining in Italy. In fact it was the decision of an Italian committee whether the respective individual refugee qualified or not to receive political asylum in Italy. Mainly the criteria were based on circumstances specific to each individual case. In accordance with international law the Italian government would offer political asylum to those refugees who had been heavily persecuted in their country. Persons who could prove that they had been put in prison, tortured, denied religious freedom, or that they had lost their jobs for political reasons in their native country, would be granted political asylum in Italy which meant they had the right to stay in Italy at their discretion.

However, as I was listing the reasons for my defection, the Italian committee concluded that my life in Romania did not involve hardly any of the circumstances invoked by its criteria so I was clearly denied a permanent stay in Italy. The next step was to apply for political asylum in another country, and of course, my first choice had always been the U.S. Within a couple of weeks I was scheduled for an interview at the American Embassy in Rome.

Periodically, there were groups of refugees from the camp, driven to Rome for such interviews in a most economical way: a small bus. In preparation for the interview I bought a cheap suit from the flea market of Latina in order to make myself a little more presentable, and I was on my way to Rome. At the American Embassy we had to plead our case for political asylum in the U.S. but we knew that it was more accessible than receiving political asylum in Italy. I took my turn and I was asked for the reasons I defected from Romania. Of course, by that time the embassy representatives were in possession of my file with all my declarations given at the camp since my arrival. I answered all the questions to the letter of the truth: I wasn't really persecuted in Romania but I was not a Communist Party member; I was against the Communist ideology; I had no prospects of advancement in my profession; I would have never had a chance to see the world, and my human rights and liberties were severely violated through the heavy cultural and intellectual censorship imposed over the entire country. I did my best to express myself in English, although we were provided a translator, which might have increased somewhat my acceptance chance. Indeed, I was granted political asylum in the U.S. and the next question was: "Do you have a sponsor in the U.S.?" A sponsor was supposed to officially offer room and board to the refugee for a number of months.

By that time my parents had sent me the phone number of a distant cousin of my father, a Romanian lady who had been living in Detroit for many years. So, to answer the question I was facing, I said yes but I did not have a confirmation from that person. Almost on the spot, the Embassy representative said: "Why don't you call and find out if they are willing to sponsor you?" And they took me to a phone in the embassy that I could use for free. It was about 3 a.m. in the U.S. but I had no other chance but call, and I did. After several rings she woke up and picked up the phone. I apologized for the inconvenience and I briefly explained the situation, making sure she understood that I only asked for the paperwork in order to be admitted into the U.S. but I wasn't counting on any financial or other kind of commitment from her. She reminded me that she was a single mother with her only son in college and she flatly refused to help me! I knew that her financial status could easily allow for the mostly formal sponsorship I was requesting, so I was really shaken by her refusal. I didn't know what to do next since at the time I didn't have any other sponsorship possibility in the U.S.

The Embassy representative came to the rescue. Learning that I didn't have a personal sponsorship they suggested to add my name to a list of political refugees, with the hope that a religious organization will find people in the U.S. willing to sponsor a political refugee like me. The organization was called The World Council of Churches (WCC) and, upon my return to the refugee camp, my name was included on their long list of prospective immigrants to the U.S. I didn't know much about the WCC but I was told that sometimes it might take many months for such a sponsorship to materialize.

Like almost everyone else, I wanted to shorten my stay in the camp as much as possible. I say 'almost everyone else' because there were a few refugees with unclear goals who spent up to a year and a half in the camp. Some of them would leave the camp for weeks, sometimes taking clandestine train rides even to Paris, France, only to come back to resume their emigration process. Therefore, not wanting to waste any time, I inquired if my parents could find other Romanian connections in the U.S., and they did. As a result of my father's suggestion, I contacted a family in New York, originally from Victoria, who had left Romania many years before 1981; to my delight, they were capable and willing to help. The family name was Mandrea, a pretty well-known name in and around Victoria. They had a very lucrative Taxi business in New York and they already envisioned me quickly getting my driver license and working for their small company. So without hesitation, through the Immigration and Naturalization New York office, they started the application process to become my sponsors. Since I had received political asylum in the U.S., my Green Card, the card for permanent residents with the right to work, was guaranteed, so there was no problem in being quickly hired as soon as I would arrive in the U.S.

From that day on I was basically waiting for all the international formalities to take place so I could finally fly to the U.S. However, my name was still on the WCC list and remained there for the entire time I was registered in the refugee camp of Latina. In light of all these events, the next few weeks would become very interesting from several other perspectives.

More Work: the Vineyard

We already had moved our volleyball practices indoors. Sergio Picone had rented a high school gymnasium and we scheduled our 2-hour practice time 3-4 times per week at 5 p.m. The team was very excited to get to play on a real volleyball court and also to go through the technical training for the upcoming season.

Over time, even during the outdoor training, Sergio and I became closer and closer friends. There would be many evenings when after the practice he would invite me to have dinner at his apartment, so I slowly became more or less a temporary part of the family. After long and persistent pursuit, I even gave up on my long commitment to be alcohol free, so mostly after dinner we would have a toast with a glass of wine. Stefano, his 4-year old son was a joy to watch and talk to and I already saw a good future volleyball player in him, which he became some years later. Sergio and I shared many ideas, and I was applauding his effort to take volleyball in Latina to the next level. In the meantime he had asked me to also coach a lower division women's team, so most of my evenings were joyfully spent in the gym.

However, my days were still open so, as I wanted to find something else to do during the day, Sergio came up with a great idea. A friend of his, also a volleyball player who would occasionally join our practices, was the owner of a large winery at the outskirts of Latina. October was the harvesting month of hundreds of acres of grapes, so they were hiring people. My name came up and I immediately got my second job: from 8 a.m. to 4 p.m. I and 3-4 other men were supposed to unload 50-60-pound baskets filled with grapes into waiting trucks. The pay was not significant but I was happy to find something else to do.

This second job lasted for about two weeks and it was a great adventure. The location was several miles from the refugee camp so Sergio offered to let me borrow his moped. That was an experience in itself since I had never ridden one before. Every morning I would have breakfast in the camp, then ride my moped to the fields, and come back in the evening most of the time barely making the volleyball practice. In this respect, my inexperience riding a moped and rushing to practice one evening set me for a potentially devastating crash. A soft autumn rain was falling as I entered a turn in downtown Latina, when, not counting for the wet road and my riding a little too fast, I caused my moped to slide and I fell on my right side, sliding behind my bike all across the intersection. There were no cars coming and my flea-market jacket protected me pretty well during the fall, so I collected myself quickly and, since the moped was still working, I made it to practice on time. However, the hard impact on the pavement left a mark: for a while I had to live with occasional sharp pain in my right elbow and my right knee.

That bike fall came as a good learning experience and I related it to Sergio as such. In the meantime I continued my volleyball practices and I kept my second place of employment where I was very impressed with the organization. Early in the morning there were several busses sent to villages around Latina to bring in mostly women who would pick grapes all day long. Fall mornings were usually foggy so we would start work at 8 a.m. Sometimes my moped rides were challenging but I grew to like the trip; my cheap flea market medium-thick jacket did an impressive job insulating me from the elements, wind or rain (in fact even now I use it around the house during cold winter days).

The busses were covering a countryside of a radius of approximately 30 miles so they were bringing many people from villages some of which were 50 to 60 miles apart. This was my first ever such experience and I enjoyed every minute of it: every day of those two weeks I found myself basically in the middle of a daily concert. We, the few men that were in the grape harvesting group, were the 'mobile force' since we were moving all the time carrying and unloading the big baskets full of grapes. The women, which were the large majority, would cut grapes and fill up the baskets, working orderly side-by-side on many parallel rows of the plantation as far as you could see with the naked eye. To help pass the day more enjoyably, the women would sing almost the entire time an impressive variety of Italian folklore. I was a little bit familiar with the famous Italian 'canzonetes' but being bathed in the gentle warmth of the autumn sun by such natural musical treasure was more than I could have ever imagined. It was virtually an outdoor women's choir singing in the most natural way songs they obviously loved, and although I didn't understand hardly any of the verses, I was deeply moved. The entire scenario reminded me so much of the 'shows' my grandfather would joyfully offer while working, which proved one more time how important music from the soul is for people anywhere in the world. In that actively meditative state, my mind went back to the origins of the blues on the American cotton plantations and I was wondering which part of the world harbored the oldest such sensible musical tradition.

Beside the beautiful music I was enjoying every day, there was one other fact that shocked me to the core. Apparently, some of the women were from villages far enough from each other that over the centuries they preserved almost completely different dialects. If they so wished they could express themselves such that the others couldn't understand, and they took advantage of it playing funny language games with the rest of the group. I had just started speaking some Italian, and I thought I could communicate fairly well, but this was beyond any expectation: I didn't understand a word of some of the dialects and neither did my co-workers from Latina. To find dialects that different within a distance of only 50-60 miles in a country like Italy blew my mind. They explained that over the centuries many villages especially in mountainous regions lived almost completely isolated so there was no need for the import of a universal language. In the same time, of course, the modern era brought in the necessity of connection and unification so the population of all these villages also became fluent in formal Italian.

As much as I enjoyed those two weeks, it could not have lasted too long. The harvesting season came to an end, I received my pay, and I continued my life in the refugee camp, every day looking forward to my volleyball practices.

Unrest in the Camp

Although I had met a couple of nice Romanian families in the refugee camp, I was mostly socializing with my two friends, Stefan and Gerry. Since now I was spending more time in the camp I was able to catch up on the latest regarding the status of my emigration paper-work, but nothing significant was taking place.

As October was giving way to November we started noticing some negative developments in the camp. One night I walked out of my room going to the common restrooms, when I realized that all the light bulbs in there disappeared.

I said to myself that I will figure it out in the dark, but it wasn't to be that simple. A nasty reality stroked me hard: I was only a few steps in the hallway when I almost lost my balance. My right foot stepped over something slippery and the terrible smell instantly sent me the message: it was human fecal matter. I was aware by then that many of the refugee camp international inhabitants were of dubious moral and ethical quality, but I didn't think it would go that far. Apparently, some were stealing the light bulbs for whatever reason, inflicting ugly consequences like my night drama, while others couldn't care less to report such acts to the camp administration. I did just that the next morning and I also found out that light bulbs had been missing for days.

And the ugly events were only escalating. Somewhat understandable was that in the internationally mixed population of the camp disagreements would manifest themselves. However, I couldn't believe that they might rise out of just about anything, but the facts convinced me that they could. This one scandal was started over a young lady, resident of the camp. A group of refugees from Albania which were notorious for their blunt ways to deal with conflict were determined to defend a friend who got into an argument with a Romanian man, both interested in this young lady. As night came, and after they all had way too much to drink, a wild fight started in the camp. Of course there was no shortage of friends to defend the Romanian man so the two 'armies' went at it in full force: knives were used, bricks were thrown, but as far as I know no firearms were available. By the time the Italian police stepped in to stop the fight they had to take several people to the hospital, a few critically wounded. Of course the event captured the headlines in Italy and even my father had heard the news on the Free Europe Radio, so he asked me in a letter: "Why did the Albanians beat up on the Romanians in the camp?"

That was the only major fight that took place while I lived in the camp and I was happy to be a distant observer. However, things were coming much closer to home. A few days after that fight I was brutally awakened in the middle of the night by a group of 4-5 Romanians, obviously drunk, who came to our locked room, kicked open the door, and with knives in their hands turned on the light and uncovered me and started yelling, questioning me. My friend Stefan, who was asleep in a bed on the other side of the room, jumped up and, as he recognized a couple of the intruders, he quickly explained that I wasn't the person they were looking for. I was totally scared at first, not knowing what to expect and being powerless in front of such an angry and drunk mob, but I calmed down once they left. Later I found out that they were searching for an older Romanian gentleman who had been seen in the vicinity of our room and whom they suspected to be a spy for the Romanian Securitate, sent by Ceausescu to report back from the refugee camp. In fact Stefan and I had met that person but, as far as we were able to tell, there was nothing to that rumor.

Of course the next day after the volleyball practice I related the entire story to Sergio over dinner at his apartment. He obviously also had full details about the fight between Albanians and Romanians, so without hesitation he proposed that I should move in their apartment; they had a small adjacent room I could sleep in. That really touched me. Over the last few weeks we had discussed the future of volleyball in Latina and I started to feel very comfortable in his company; we were becoming even better friends. I humbly accepted his invitation and I ran by the camp to pick up my immediate necessities for the night.

Coincidently, at that time Sergio and his family were in process of buying a larger apartment not too far from the old one, and they intended to have some major remodeling done to it. The day came when Sergio invited me to move in the new apartment, all by myself, while the remodeling was taking place. He also proposed that I could help with the work for some extra pay. The apartment was completely unfurnished so he brought in a foldable bed and a couple of chairs. Knowing about my love for music he borrowed an acoustic guitar from a friend and that's how I started teaching myself the basics of guitar playing. In fact, on that guitar I wrote one of my first songs that I have treasured ever since;

I titled it "Song for the Dead," a nostalgic, but not sad, tribute to departed souls who once were close to me.

Consequently, even though the hard living conditions in the refugee camp affected negatively a large number of people, the entire scenario helped me spend more time with Sergio and his immediate family. I was totally taken by their generosity and compassion, and I appreciated every little step Sergio took to make my stay in Latina as comfortable as possible. From the volleyball practices and Sunday official games, to going to the movies and having dinner together, we had plenty of opportunities to share ideas about life in general and volleyball in particular. They were often asking meaningful questions about the Communist regime of Romania, and I was striving to learn more about living in true freedom. Along the way Sergio and I had started building a common vision for volleyball in Latina, based largely on our honest mutual respect and friendship, and in the end that led to another surprising proposition Sergio offered.

12

First Fork in the Road: Italy or the U.S.A

Weeks passed by without any significant developments as far as my emigration documents were concerned. I really enjoyed that period for the parallels it presented: I was never bored. I would sleep in Sergio's new apartment, have breakfast in the refugee camp, I would go back to the apartment to provide a little unprofessional help with the remodeling, have lunch in the camp then back to the apartment, and in the evening there came the highlight of the day: the volleyball practices.

Both team practices were very rewarding. All players were very dedicated and anxious to improve and they enjoyed working as hard as I would ask of them. Occasionally Sergio and I would join the men's team for a practice game and it was fun to play aside my new friend: it cemented even more our commitment to the glory of volleyball in Latina. I was not by any means a perfect coach or player, but I strived every day to bring my best contribution to the realization of Sergio's grand plan and I felt he really appreciated my efforts.

The Proposal

Often, after the evening volleyball practices, some of the older players would join us for a snack and a drink before retiring for the day. I cannot forget the thin true Italian pizza I would enjoy almost every time: its unique flavor was the sign of authenticity and virtual perfection reached at the end of centuries of culinary evolution in the freedom of a proud nation as Italy. During many such evenings we would all be chatting, playing games, and crafting new plans for the future of the team.

One late November day, as we were relaxing with a drink, would become especially memorable for me. Sergio approached me in his warm but serious personal way, somewhat privately, and said: "Irineo, what do you think of staying in Italy instead of going to the U.S.?" Up to that point it never crossed my mind to change my final emigration destination, so hearing his proposal shocked me. I paused for a few moments as I was gathering my thoughts and I said: "You know, I really like it in Latina, I treasure your friendship, and I am happy coaching and playing volleyball here, but I was not granted political asylum in Italy so I cannot legally stay." And that was exactly how I was feeling at the time. Immediately he answered, as if he had already given the matter a lot of thought: "If you decide to stay, I am sure we can work together to change your political asylum status."

We debated the possibilities for a change in political asylum for a while and in parallel he presented an even larger picture. He was moving his business into a brand new three-story building which had a nice little apartment included: I would work for his company, I would stay in that apartment, and I would coach and eventually play volleyball. With a confident smile in his eyes he told me that his father had been the chief of police in Latina for many years and, since he knew everybody in the department, for sure he would be able to help with the change in political asylum.

Bumps in the Way

It took me a few days to weigh my options before making a decision. It wasn't easy. On one hand I really liked it in Latina, it was still closer to Romania than the U.S. would be, but on the other hand, I was wondering about the possibilities that might enfold if I would cross the ocean. To make my choices even more sensitive, I remembered what my father wrote to me in an earlier letter as I announced my decision to emigrate to the U.S.: "That is so far! If you stayed in Italy it would be like you were in our backyard!" So after long and arduous debates mostly with myself I decided to say yes, I will stay in Italy, and I embraced Sergio warmly thanking him for his thoughtful and caring offer.

The following day he asked his father to do his magic, but to no avail. His father contacted the local authorities who could shed some light on the issue of changing a refugee's political asylum and the answer was no. Apparently, their justification was that the Italian government enforced vehemently this policy: the decision of the Italian political asylum committee was irrevocable. However, he suggested that Sergio should contact an aunt of his in Rome who might be able to help.

Her name was Dr. Esmeralda Crucitti and she was a historian who researched and published material about the Christian persecutions during the Roman Empire era. Our hope was that, since she maintained a variety of connections with officials in the Italian government, she should be able to find out if there was any possibility for a change in my political asylum. One day, when Sergio had some business in Rome, we drove together and we met Dr. Crucitti at her residence. Not only did she express interest in my story of defecting from Romania, but she was also very receptive to our inquiries and promised to do anything in her power to help. And she did.

However, a few days later, at the end of her search, she offered us the same conclusion: there was no legal way to reverse the denial of my political asylum in Italy. I was very grateful for her efforts and I expressed my sincere thanks to Sergio and Sergio's father for trying so hard to help me stay in Italy. It seemed that there was really no possible way to resolve this problem so at least for the time being I gave up even thinking about it.

But Sergio had other plans. One evening after the volleyball practice he said to me: "Tomorrow I have some business to attend to at the Vatican. Why don't you come with me and maybe we can talk to somebody there." That was a sudden revitalization of our efforts so, of course, I said yes, and the next morning I was ready to go.

This unexpected journey offered several unmatched highlights. Sergio had some business with the 4th ranked

Vatican official after the Pope, the cardinal overseeing Vatican's telecommunications. That fact in itself raised my excitement level for the trip, let alone the possibility to find a solution to my problem. Moreover, the meeting was supposed to take place *inside* the Vatican. To me that was a major feat. Since Vatican City is in fact a country in a country, virtually all tourists going to the Vatican visit the public museums and St. Peter's Cathedral, but they don't get access *inside* the famous Gardens of the Vatican and the rest of the buildings.

The next day, after we made it through the heavy morning traffic of Rome, we arrived at the gates of the Vatican. The Swiss Guard, dressed in the well-known official attire, received us promptly, checked Sergio's documents, and looked inside the car. Sergio introduced me as his assistant, but curiously enough they did not ask me for any document – I didn't have any anyway other than my temporary card. So Sergio drove through the giant gates on a rock-paved road and soon we found a parking spot close to the building that held the offices of the cardinals. The gardens were all around us and they offered a breathtaking view. There were hardly any people in our proximity, so for a few seconds I paused in order to take in as much as I could of the unique picture. Yes, it looked like a photograph: a large variety of flowers were dancing with their colors through a maze of alleys marked by green bushes perfectly manicured by professional keepers with years of experience. Several enormous palm trees were showing their distinct majesty as if to say: "We are the guardians: respect the sanctity of this place." Indeed, regardless of the name, the beauty of the overall arrangement was out of this world.

At the end of my short reverie we stepped inside and after the proper protocol we were ushered into the office of the cardinal. Here we were: the cardinal over telecommunications at the Vatican behind his desk, Sergio Picone as the telecommunications consultant from Latina, and me, a Romanian refugee with a problem. We shook hands with the cardinal and, since my presence there obviously demanded explanations, Sergio decided to start with our inquiry. He explained the entire scenario and, in light of the close relationship between the Vatican and the Italian government, he appealed to the cardinal for a possible solution. At that point the cardinal displayed a warm smile, looked at me with obvious compassion and said: "I am sorry to say this, but a change in political asylum is not possible. However, I see a solution: if you marry an Italian you will be able to stay in Italy." We smiled as I expressed my gratitude for his time and consideration, and after they discussed Sergio's business issues, we shook hands and left the office.

The cardinal's suggestion had actually crossed our minds before and we flirted with this idea but mostly for fun; I have told Sergio that I would not like to get married just to be able to stay in Italy, even though my divorce in Romania was imminent. The drive back to Latina offered us plenty of time for analysis and reconsideration of the entire plan. It seemed more and more as an impossibility to stay in Italy so I proposed to make the best we could of the time I had left until my emigration papers were completed.

The Holidays

As the volleyball season was drawing to a close all players were making arrangements for holidays and they warmly invited me to join them. My friends in the refugee camp also had made plans for Christmas and the New Year's party (a very popular event in Romania), but after almost three months in Sergio's company I opted to accept his invitation to spend the holidays with his extended family.

I didn't really know what to expect so I was pleasantly surprised by the Italian celebration of Christmas. I took part in a feast that was as sophisticated as it was new to me: my first Christmas in freedom. The expanded table welcomed Sergio's entire family so throughout the evening from time to time I would get questions regarding Communism, the Romanian holidays customs, and of course, my escape. I did my best not to monopolize the conversation being deeply preoccupied to taste a little bit of every dish brought to the table, and there were many. Sergio also did his best to shelter me from the excessive curiosity of his relatives, so over all I felt almost like a natural member of his family. As soon as the copious Christmas dinner came to an end Sergio and I went for a walk and continued with our 1982 volleyball planning promenade somewhat in private.

His time and energy were heavily dedicated to his business so, in terms of volleyball, he counted on me to fill in as much as possible while I stayed in Latina. I repeatedly assured him that I loved what I was doing and I will keep working with the teams to the best of my ability, and we both started to feel the inevitable sadness of my eventual departure. Almost every day I would check with the office at the refugee camp for news regarding my emigration status but, especially over the holidays, I wasn't expecting any significant developments. Ever since I contacted the Romanian family in New York who offered to be my sponsors, I had that avenue in the back of my mind as the expected road to the U.S. Of course I had told Sergio all about it but there was no way to estimate the departure time. However, according to the average stay per refugee in the camp, which was 4 to 5 months, my time was drawing near. At the end of December 1981 I had spent already more than three and a half months in the camp so I was hoping for an early 1982 flight to the States. In the meantime Sergio insisted that we should welcome the New Year in style so he and some of the older players on the men's team organized the New Year's party.

It was supposed to take place at Mauro's residence and I couldn't wait. We all arrived late in the evening of December 31st and I was very impressed with the whole setting. Mauro had just finished building his house on a nice piece of land and that year he accomplished a lot. He showed us the spacious backyard full of young fruit trees, flowers, and ornamental bushes that did well in the relatively warm winter climate of Latina, while the house itself was the highlight of the party. His young daughter, Sara, had just started playing volleyball so that definitely marked the décor. Soon enough he took us to the basement which was already prepared for a night of eating, drinking, and dancing. While Mauro presented the spacious room, I was very pleasantly surprised to find a nice set of drums somewhere in a corner: what a familiar picture! Apparently Mauro had another hobby, just like I did. Almost immediately I asked if I could play a little bit and of course they encouraged me to do so. Even more, they played a vinyl record of one of my favored bands, Deep Purple, and asked me to play with the music. I did fairly well, in my opinion, but my audience was astonished: "You not only play volleyball, but you are also a drummer?" What followed was a short synopsis of my university years in Romania, familiar story to Sergio but mostly new to the others. The rest of the night went on just as expected. They had also invited a few of the ladies from the women's team and we had a great time all together.

At 12 o'clock some good Italian champagne helped us cheer for the New Year and we expressed our optimism and hope for an even better volleyball season in Latina. Everybody showed their gratitude to Sergio for his support and at the same time their regret that sooner or later I will have to leave for the U.S. Of course I promised that I will keep in touch especially via Sergio and I insisted that one day I will return at least for a visit. Since they all meant so much to me and especially because of my friendship with Sergio, all of that became reality in the following years.

The Departure

The first week of 1982 passed uneventfully, we resumed the volleyball practices, and Sergio made significant progress remodeling his new apartment. At the same time I offered a little help with the finishing touches at the new business location and I made sure to take a few short trips to the beach at the Tyrrhenian Sea.

Latina was just about 3-4 miles from the beach, so during the warm months it was the main vacation spot for most people. The sand was very finely and randomly designed in a variety of small dunes by an unseen artistic hand, with very little vegetation around. A long street that ran parallel to the beach was lining up all the hotels, stores, and restaurants, and it was virtually deserted in the winter. Once in a while you could see lonesome individuals or couples taking walks on the beach while the winter wind was showing off by making miniature tornadoes of sand. The sea was relatively calm and its favored unspoken invitation was to peacefully and calmly meditate. I would just sit on a bench, watch the waves and the seagulls exhibit the eternal changing of nature, and I would try to escape into my stillness. More and more thoughts about America were invading my mind and it wasn't long until I had to wake up and taste reality.

One day, upon my return to the camp from such a 'vacation' at the beach, I received the news: apparently, my emigration papers were in order for my departure. As soon as I read the note I went straight to the office in the refugee camp for confirmation. Indeed, the flight to the U.S. was scheduled for the 25th of January, 1982. In the euphoria of such news I didn't even asked for details. All I knew was that there will be a large number of refugees departing from Rome that day and I was one of them. Immediately I gave Sergio the news and, as expected, he was happy for me but still reluctant to accept that I would be gone.

There were just about two weeks left before the 25th of January so once again we wanted to make the best of it. The volleyball practices intensified and the time I spent with Sergio and his family was some of the best I had had in Latina. In the last weekend remaining he organized the so called "Farewell volleyball game for Irineo." It was out of this world. We formed two well-balanced teams and we played a real game with Sergio and I on the same team. The women's team and other spectators took a lively part in the exhibition game cheering for both teams. At the end of about two hours of play we all got together on one side of the court and took many pictures. They opened several bottles of champagne and sprayed some all around before offering small glasses to everyone in the gym. Then the climax came and I couldn't believe my eyes: Sergio took me in front of the group and handed me an envelope full of money; it was the sign of appreciation from the two teams I coached for four months. Apparently, the team members offered to contribute with as much as they could to my new start in the U.S. That gesture moved me so much that I was speechless; all I did, while tears were running down my face, was to embrace each one of them with my deepest gratitude. Then I gathered myself and I said a few words of appreciation for their devotion and patience over all that time. It was truly a wonderful group and that was the last evening together. At the end of four months we were all happy for a proper finale: a good game of volleyball and a short party, with many of us sharing tears of joy and promises for future reunions.

I used the last 2-3 days to prepare for departure and, of course, I spent as much time as I was able to with Sergio. At the end of my stay in Latina I was able to fill up a couple of large pieces of luggage of stuff, but my most precious possessions were a few rock-and-roll tapes, a small radio with tapeplayer, a couple of winter windbreakers, and the two-piece suit I bought for the interview at the American embassy. One of the windbreakers was unique: on the inside it displayed the entire map of the world; Romania was somewhere inside the left sleeve, while most of the U.S. was in the other. Jokingly, I used to say: "With this coat on me I can never get lost in the world." I still have both coats and I treasure the memories they helped me keep over all of these years.

January the 25th, the day of the flight, came, seemingly a little too fast. I wanted to have more time to say goodbye to friends both in Latina and in the camp. None of my closest refugee friends were scheduled for the same flight. Stefan would eventually emigrate to Canada and Gerry to the U.S. So I spent the last night in the camp and early that morning Sergio and a couple of volleyball friends came to say goodbye. I was supposed to embark on a bus in front of the refugee camp, coincidently in the same exact place where I arrived four and a half months earlier, also in the morning. Sergio parked his car next to the bus and helped me load up my luggage. All of the sudden those few minutes became hard to take. I was leaving behind, possibly forever, very good friends, and that nostalgically reminded me of September the 4th 1981 when I left Romania.

First I said goodbye to my Romanian friends from the camp as we embraced and promised to keep in touch. Then I turned to my small Italian team that was waiting aside. Realizing how moved I was in those moments, they wished me good luck in all my future endeavors, assuring me that everything will be fine. Of course I promised to send back news from America and I expressed my sincere hope that one day we would see each other again. Then came the hardest goodbye. Over those 4 months Sergio and I became almost like brothers, not only through volleyball but also blending our personalities, as we shared many ideals. Of course we were now beyond the level of compassion for a simple refugee in need of help and I was overly convinced of that. His proposing that I should remain in Italy was the greatest sign of devotion and friendship I could get and I truly appreciated every one of its implications. So to say goodbye to Sergio felt almost the same as expressing my unspoken goodbye to my family in Romania. However, this time I wasn't afraid to say it out loud as we embraced: "Sergio, thank you for all you did for me, and thank you for your friendship; I will treasure it forever, I will miss you, and I will definitely keep in touch!"

I waved to all of them from the window of the bus and with a short horn blow the driver announced that we were on our way to the international airport in Rome. The hour and a half drive to Rome gave me enough time for a complete retrospective of my stay in Latina: the loss of my light windbreaker the first day, the unrest in the camp, the many volleyball workouts and the dinners with Sergio's family, the visits to Rome and the Vatican, all culminated with the wonderful celebration of the holidays and finally with the departure day. I almost did not have the time to think of what was coming up: my first flight ever, in an airplane.

We arrived at the airport on time for all the necessary preparations for boarding. Many, if not all of us refugees, were facing our first flight so we needed as much information as possible. The route was nonstop Rome to New York and we were supposed to land at the LaGuardia airport that evening – counting the 7 hours time change.

We boarded the plane with no incidents and we took off almost on time. One can imagine the uniqueness of flying for the first time, and not just any flight, but a trans-Atlantic one!

Of course I could not sleep at all during the flight as I was admiring what I could see outside through the small oval windows, and also as I was making myself part of the large group of refugees since we were basically sitting together on our way to the United States of America!

This was the trip of a lifetime for everyone in our group. At the other end of it we would be arriving to our destination that will completely change our lives. The 8-9 hours flight passed relatively fast especially due to the inherent excitement, and during the last hour we were asked to complete some paperwork required to enter the U.S. The entire flight went on smoothly, as far as I could tell, but the landing became something very special. When we touched the ground and we heard the loud squeal of the tires, almost all passengers reacted instinctively with a joyful rampant applause together with some celebratory whistles. As for us, the large group of refugees, we were all thrilled we made it to the land of our dreams, away from Communism with all its infringements on human rights and brainwashing in isolation. We were finally free to create our own destinies according to each person's desire, persistence, and ability.

13

Second Fork in the Road:
New York or Texas

At the end of the long flight from Rome to New York and a well-acclaimed landing, our entire group of refugees was carefully guided by airport personnel to a specific spot in the terminal. It was about 6 p.m. on January the 25th, 1982, and, with our luggage near us, we were waiting for information about the next step of our journey.

The Surprise

Based on my correspondence from the camp with Mr. Mandrea in New York who agreed to be my sponsor, I was firmly convinced that New York City would be my residence in the U.S. At times I was fantasizing about my life in New York City and I couldn't wait to experience it first-hand. Now I was in the LaGuardia airport and I was waiting for him or somebody from his family to pick me up from the airport.

But it wasn't to be. I anxiously waited for my turn to receive information on my next step, and when I was called up it came with a big surprise. A young African American airport employee approached me as he read my name from a list, and with no hesitation pressed a sticky note on my winter jacket somewhere in the direction of my heart. He said briefly: "You are going there!" Of course, immediately I read the two words on the note: it said "Austin, Texas." I quickly responded with something to this effect: "No! There is a mistake. I am supposed to stay in New York!" Then he checked my name on the list one more time and he explained that Austin was in fact my final destination and my flight will be leaving the next morning at 8 a.m. Next, he instructed me to join a small group of us, refugees, to be taken to a near-by hotel for the night.

I was perplexed. How come I am not staying in New York? What happened with my sponsorship? Why am I sent to Texas? With these questions running through my head I had no choice for the moment but to follow the group and be taken to the hotel. We boarded a small bus and in a few minutes we entered the hotel lobby where we waited for our rooms. Soon I received my key and I went straight up to my room. It impressed me tremendously: I was all by myself in this wonderful one-bed room with a television set, a telephone, and a bathroom. The young gentleman who escorted me to my room reminded me to be in the lobby, ready to go, at 7 a.m. the next morning, and he left. By then I felt a little tired and, tempted by the nice bed in front of me, I lied down for a few minutes and gathered my thoughts.

The Investigation

As I really wanted to clarify the situation, I decided to call Mr. Mandrea to find out what had happened and why I was not staying in New York. However, the international traveling novice in me had to make it harder than necessary. I had no idea how to use the phone in my room, I didn't think of searching for a pay-phone in the hotel, so I decided to go back in the airport and use a pay-phone I had seen in the terminal upon our arrival.

That became my first real encounter with America. I didn't know and I couldn't see anybody around to ask how I could get back to the airport, so I decided to walk. It was pretty late by then and very cold outside. The hotel was close enough to the airport that I could see it and that gave me some courage. Thinking mathematically, 'the shortest distance between two points is the straight line,' I proceeded to walk accordingly. However, the daylight was fading and, in the cold of the evening, I had to speed it up. Moreover, a light snowfall reminded me that I was not in Latina anymore and I became instantly grateful for my 'map-of-the-world' winter jacket.

The first 'leg' of my walk back to the airport placed me under an overpass frequented mostly by taxicabs. I stood there for a few seconds watching in fascination many huge cars speeding on the already icy road. That brought back memories of rare collections of photos of American car shows I had seen in Romania. This time though some of them were right before my eyes and they were magnificent: they seemed to create a sentiment of power, energy, and durability that I had never felt before.

As I left the overpass behind, I walked through a large outdoor parking area, then I climbed up some stairs and I entered back into the terminal. It took me a few more minutes to find a pay-phone but first I had to change some Italian currency into dollars to pay for the call. I finally found an exchange office open and with a few dollars in my pocket I went back to the telephone. After a few attempts, the phone finally rang. Mrs. Mandrea answered and I briefly expressed what had happened. She told me that Mr. Mandrea is working (driving his cab) and she will let him know where I was so he could come to pick me up.

I left the airport terminal on the same route as I followed from the hotel, so the return walk to my room was easier and a little faster. Within an hour or so Mr. Mandrea made it to the hotel and we met in the lobby to discuss the situation. He was a well-built middle-aged man and strongly reminded me of home. Of course we conversed in Romanian and I explained in details the sponsorship procedure I went through in the refugee camp, and we both came to the most probable explanation. We concluded that, since my name remained on the WCC (World Council of Churches) list, that search for a sponsor went on in parallel to the application Mr. Mandrea filed from New York. Because the WCC nation-wide process had started earlier, most likely they had been able to locate another willing sponsor sooner. At that point I realized that my confusion resulted in fact from two sources. The first was that the refugee camp representatives never told me exactly where I would be going once I arrived in the U.S., and the second, was that, assuming I would go to New York, I never asked for that information and I did not read very carefully whatever paperwork they gave me.

The Choice

As soon as we cleared that up Mr. Mandrea made a surprising proposition. He said: "If you want you can stay with us. You don't have to go to Texas. Tomorrow morning we will go to the Immigration and Naturalization Service here in New York and we will change your sponsorship and your destination. You can sleep on the couch in the living room, in a few days you will get your driver license, and you can start working driving a taxicab." That offer really made me think. Apparently, in a few days I will be already working, hopefully making a decent living to be able to rent an apartment and start my life in New York City. He explained that they were members of a large Romanian community and that should help me make a smooth transition to living in America.

Mr. Mandrea's proposition was very tempting but while I was conversing with him, another thought came to my mind. Since I really appreciated his offer, I did not want to sound ungrateful so I had to think hard of how I could express my latest thought which was really just an idea. Therefore, I thanked him very kindly for his suggestion, I expressed my gratitude for his generosity, and then I said: "In the meantime I was thinking that since the other sponsorship went through, perhaps the people who offered to sponsor me are able to help me find a job in my field, computer science. What do you think if I first go to Texas, see what possibilities there are, and if that fails I will come back to New York. I have a little money that I made in Italy so I think I can fly back with no problem." He immediately agreed and asked me to call him by his first name, George; we shook hands, and he was ready to leave.

I escorted him out of the hotel lobby and to his cab that was parked aside the building, but when he tried to start it we found out that the battery was dead. He explained that he needed a new one and asked a fellow cab driver on the site to give him a jump. At the end of a ten-dollar transaction they started his car and he took off in the New York City night.

·

With this entire scenario in my mind, I returned to my room hoping that I made the right decision. After all, it was an important choice, but having in mind the possibility to return to New York in case of need, it was comforting enough so I wasn't really worried. After I had the last few bites from the little food pack I received as I was taken to my hotel room, I couldn't wait to go to sleep, tired at the end of a long and exciting day. I was ready to spend my first night in the U.S. getting some rest, to be able to face another day of traveling, this time from New York City to Austin, Texas.

14

Welcome to Austin, Texas

The next morning I was awakened at 7 a.m. by some very powerful knocks at the door; the same young gentleman from the airport personnel wanted to be sure I wouldn't miss my flight. I responded quickly and I promised to be in the lobby in 15 minutes. I didn't have much to do since I had not unpacked hardly any of my stuff the night before.

In a few minutes I was already walking side by side with him and a few others from our 'refugee group' as he escorted us to catch a shuttle to the airport. I almost wanted to tell him about my walk to the terminal the night before but I caught myself on time: I didn't want to appear ridiculous, although it could have been a nice story for him to eventually tell his grandkids. We made it to the gate on time, he gave me the boarding pass, wished me good luck, and then he disappeared in the crowd. I followed him with my eyes as long as I could, thanking him again but silently this time. He was a nice young man and he appeared to like what he was doing.

Welcome to Austin

I landed at the Robert Muller airport in Austin in the afternoon and, as I was walking from the airplane to the gate I caught myself thinking: "Here is another dilemma. What am I to face this time? Which facet of the unknown will I encounter?" However, I felt absolutely no fear, no regret, and no anxiety: just legitimate questions springing from my curiosity about the future. There was now a completely different scenario than the Yugoslavian adventure when any wrong turn could have led to disaster. From Sarajevo to the Italian border every minute encompassed the potential of reversing the path of my entire life: if I would have been caught I would have been most likely sent back to a life in misery, regrets, and despair in Romania.

Soon enough I had to leave all those thoughts gently aside since I had almost arrived in the waiting area where people were expecting to meet their loved ones, or, as in my case, to welcome strangers. I looked over the small expecting crowd and suddenly I saw a sign with my name printed in large letters. It was held by a middle-aged lady, kind of petite, and I naturally walked straight to her. I introduced myself and she said: "Hi! I'm Emilia Martin. Welcome to Austin!" Immediately I made an almost instinctive and a little bit out-of-place statement: "I thought I had to stay in New York!" That became the phrase that she would jokingly remind me of for years to come. Of course I explained myself the best I could within my limited proficiency in English, but it remained a humorous statement under the circumstances.

Dr. and Mrs. Martin

After I picked up my luggage I followed her to the parking lot, we loaded everything in her car and she slowly drove out of the airport. Over the next few days I learned fascinating details about the Martin family, my sponsors in the U.S. On the way to their home I did my best to converse and basically to answer questions regarding the refugee camp and the trip. I didn't even know what to ask about my future in Austin but I did express my gratitude for their willingness to help me come to America. Mrs. Martin explained that she and Dr. Martin were members of the Unitarian Church in Austin and their church received the list of political refugees from Italy via the World Council of Churches. She went on and said that in 1979 the Martin family took a summer trip to Romania especially to visit Transylvania, the birth place of the Unitarian Church (later I learned that the initial congregations were formed under the first and only Unitarian king, John Sigismund, starting in 1568). The Martins were impressed by the countryside, the people, and the history but they also had the first-hand chance to taste the poor quality of life and lack of freedom in Communist Romania. Mrs. Martin actually compared it to life during and right after the Second World War in Holland, her native country. Distressed by the whole political situation and out of pure human compassion, this deep feeling became one of the reasons they had decided to help Romanian refugees.

Eventually I would find out that Dr. Norman Martin was a World War II veteran gravely wounded during the allies' offensive against the Germans for the liberation of France. He was about 21 years old at that time and as soon as the war was over he continued his studies in mathematics/logics in the U.S. In 1949, as he was completing his Master degree, he was awarded a Fulbright scholarship at the University of Amsterdam, Holland. Over the last year before his trip back to Europe, he taught himself Dutch, and while in Holland, he met Emilia, a bright and beautiful young lady from Amsterdam. She was studying mathematics at the same university and within 2-3 weeks of dating they fell in love with each other. In the summer of 1950, they got married in Amsterdam and soon after that Norman received an offer for a teaching position at the University of Illinois. He accepted the offer, they came to the U.S., and they built a nice family together. In the meantime they had moved to Austin, Texas and by 1982 Dr. Martin had gained the stature of a long-time respected professor at the University of Texas at Austin, while Mrs. Martin had been pursuing her passion in the field of accounting. They made their home in the West side of town and that was my first contact with a real American family living in a nice house in the capital of Texas.

It was a relatively short ride from the airport to the house but long enough for me to get a quick glimpse of the northwest part of Austin. The streets appeared orderly, open, and well-maintained and, as we arrived in the vicinity of the house, everything changed to a wooded neighborhood where the residences where seemingly hiding behind giant oak trees. The Martins' home was built on a slope that allowed for a natural setup on two floors: the street floor with the garage, and the lower floor that opened up to a green belt down the hill.

Almost as quickly as we arrived home Mrs. Martin took me to a room on the lower floor of the house and said: "This is your room and you can bring your luggage in here." In fact all bedrooms were on that floor, so Dr. and Mrs. Martin had their master bedroom down the hallway to the left side of my room. To the right side of my room, at the end of the hallway past the bathroom, there was a larger guestroom which at that time was mostly a storage space.

Later that day I met Dr. Martin and immediately I realized how much they had in common: both were nice and gentle people, quiet in their ways, inspiring a sense of calm, self-confidence, and wellbeing. He came home from the university, and over a nice dinner we found out about each other as much as we could without any pressure. As I was trying to present different details about Romania, my escape, and life in the refugee camp, I realized once again my true limitations in expressing myself in English. However, both were very positive and encouraging, promising that we will speak a lot to each other so that I could learn faster. In fact, many evenings after dinner we would stay at the table and occasionally play cards just to give me more conversation time. One evening in particular remained memorable to me. At the end of the game I was left with one card in my hand and Mrs. Martin asked me: "What card do you have, Irie?" I responded without hesitation: "I have an ass." With a slight smile on her face, understanding my mispronunciation, she said: "I'm sure you do, but in your hand you have an *ace* not an ass." That was a quick and powerful language lesson and I was happy about it, although I did feel a little bit embarrassed. However, I was determined to improve so I was even more receptive when Dr. and Mrs. Martin suggested that I should watch television in my room while at home, that being another good way to improve my language skills; ever since then I had been an avid fan of sitcoms and, of course, sports channels.

Evidently, my first few days in the Martins' residence were nice, relaxing, and they felt like a welcome mini vacation after my first ever flight over the Atlantic. There wasn't much to do around the house and in the beginning I didn't really know what I could do and if I could help with anything. At times I was all by myself at home watching TV, reading a book, or listening to my radio or tapes. I also wrote letters to my parents and my sister to let them know where I was and how things were developing. In the following days, things would change. I learned how to use a lawn mower, for example, and found my way around the neighborhood a little better.

Soon enough though, at the dinner table, Mrs. Martin and I made plans to start searching the newspapers for possible employment. Of course, we looked mostly for openings in computer programming, informatics, etc. In fact, knowing my educational background at the time they decided to sponsor me became important criteria with which to select me out of the long list of refugees. Austin did offer a pretty good market in this respect. After several tries, calling phone numbers from the newspapers, we did go to a couple of interviews but to no avail.

Then Mrs. Martin suggested that I should get my driver license, so she started giving me driving lessons. Assuming I had absolutely no idea about driving, Mrs. Martin was really cautious until I first drove a little bit on their street: I did well, based on a few tries back in Romania without a license but only on country roads. When she realized that I was comfortable enough, she had me drive around the neighborhood and, in parallel, I started studying the driving booklet from the Department of Public Safety for the computerized test. A few days later I did pass it but I failed the driving test: "Sorry young man. You did OK, but you were winding too much in your lane; you need more practice with this car" said the police officer. Indeed, the power steering made every touch of the wheel very sensitive, so I did need more practice time with that car.

Unexpected Reunion

About two weeks after my arrival, Mrs. Martin made a surprising announcement: "Tomorrow we will go to the airport to pick up another Romanian immigrant who will fly in from Italy." I asked for details and it turned out that the Martins had sponsored me and this other person simultaneously. When I asked for his name I was very pleasantly surprised: his name was Gerry! Apparently we were on the same list of refugees sent out by the WCC and the Martins had been inspired to help us mostly due to our common background in Computer Science, a field with which Dr. Martin was very familiar.

So the next day, great was Gerry's surprise when he saw me waiting for him in the airport. We hadn't had time to communicate since my departure from Latina; that made our reunion in Austin even more special. Since Gerry was also able to speak a little bit of English, the three of us had a nice conversation on the way home.

Once we arrived at the house, Gerry was guided to the guestroom at the end of the hallway of the lower floor and I couldn't wait to hear all the latest from the camp in Latina. Later on that day he also met Dr. Martin and, over dinner, we were very impressed by Dr. Martin's familiarity with Europe and more importantly with the history of Romania. After dinner I rushed to Gerry's room to be updated on the news from Latina and I forgot that I had left my radio on, at a pretty high volume, in my room. Within a few minutes Mrs. Martin, obviously annoyed by the music, came in and asked me to turn it down. It was already after 9 p.m. and I felt terrible realizing my negligence: bothering our wonderful host was the last thing I wanted to do! I apologized profusely and I promised myself that it would never happen again. Gerry and I quickly learned from this experience and he continued with the news. I was pleased to find out that in the meantime, Stefan, my roommate from the camp Gerry also knew emigrated to Canada and we had a phone number to reach him there. He had no news from Sergio or the volleyball crowd in Latina and it seemed that the only way to find out was for me to call and write which I did eventually.

My First Job

Time was passing by without any significant developments, so one day I asked Mrs. Martin if she knew of a place where I could workout, or even better, a place to play volleyball. That day she took me to a public recreation center relatively close to the house and very soon I attended an open-play session in volleyball. That day I met several guys about my age from a team that was training for some upcoming tournaments. The level of play was pretty good, I fitted right in and I had much fun playing for the first time in the U.S.

However, they didn't really need an extra player so they recommended me to another team from Austin that could use another player. The captain/coach of this team was John Fulton and I had a chance to practice with them a couple of times. John was an ex-tennis-pro about 14 years older than me and also an avid volleyball player. He was the manager of a city-run tennis center so as soon as he found out that I had no job he offered me part-time work at the center: I was supposed to answer the phone, make reservations, replenish the water containers on the courts, and keep the reception area clean. The pay for the time being was the minimum wage, $3.25 an hour, and I was happy to finally start working (Soni's words from 1970 resonated again in my head: "You may not make a career out of volleyball, but volleyball will open many doors in your life"). I made my share of mistakes in the beginning until I learned to use the cash register, but John was very kind and patient, understanding that I had never done this before. On the side, occasionally I would hit some tennis balls against the wall and sometimes I would also play with pros who were giving private lessons. That is how I started playing tennis and I have been in love with it ever since.

Volleyball Again

It was February already and around the middle of the month there was an annual volleyball tournament scheduled at Texas A&M University in College Station. That was the traditional Valentine's Day tournament for teams from all over Texas. John entered his team in the tournament and he needed to register me quickly so I could play. He picked me up from the Martins' house early on a Saturday morning and off we went on the 2-hour drive to College Station.

Such tournaments would run the entire day, depending on the number of teams in the competition, and, at the Valentine's tournament there were plenty of teams. We played well but late in the evening we lost a tight game in the semifinals against a team from Houston. However, after the game, the Houston team's coach introduced himself to me and we talked for a few minutes while they were waiting to play the final game.

His name was David Olbright and he held the University of Houston women's team coaching position. He was about three years older than me; he had been a great college player in the past and then he played on the U.S. national team. So out of his love for volleyball, aside from coaching, he was also the captain/coach of the strongest men team in Texas, "Texas Stars." In fact, he had recruited some of the best players around and, other than playing tournaments, they were occasionally training using the University of Houston's facilities.

As soon as he understood my circumstances he immediately proposed that I should move to Houston, a much larger city than Austin, that promised a better chance to find a job in my field, informatics. He suggested that I could stay at no charge in the house the University was renting for him and the assistant coach of the women's team, until I got established. I told him I will think about it; we exchanged phone numbers, and soon after that I joined John on the road back to Austin.

Move to Houston

I presented the entire scenario to John and Dr. and Mrs. Martin and after a few days we made the decision that it wasn't a bad idea. I called David to give him the news; I bought myself a Greyhound bus ticket to Houston, and soon I was on my way to the city that potentially offered more professional opportunities for me. The early morning bus ride took about five hours and in the afternoon David was waiting for me at the Houston bus station.

Although it was a late February day, it was warm enough that David came in shorts and sandals to welcome me to Houston. I put my bag in his car and we left the bus station. He then explained that he had already called a few places that advertised computer programming positions, so from the bus station we went straight to a job interview. The location was very close to downtown Houston so I had the first chance to admire the majesty of the Houston skyline. Especially since that was my first visit, I felt so small and insignificant at the feet of those skyscrapers, mostly office buildings that ran their glass windows in perfect and seemingly endless alignment toward the open sky. The interview lasted only about ten minutes and we left empty handed. It was, therefore, not the best start to my stay in Houston, but I was grateful to David for trying to help me.

From the downtown area we made it to his house in about 25 minutes. Once at the house, David showed me my room which was separated from the kitchen by a sliding door. It was great for what I needed and I already felt at home. The three-bedroom one-level house was in a residential area in the southwest side of Houston and it was a 45 minute drive from the University of Houston's gym where the volleyball workouts and games were taking place. Later that evening I was introduced to David's fiancé and to the assistant coach, Michael, all living in the same house. They were all very nice in welcoming me to their home and offered to help with whatever I needed, including my English. In this respect I remember a nice lesson I received soon after my arrival. As I was getting ready to take a shower one time, I announced it loudly: "I need to make a shower before we go," which is the word-for-word translation from Romanian. The response came quickly from David: "I don't know if you can; you need a lot of wood, bricks, mortar, and other things. Maybe you want to ... *take* a shower!" Of course I took it as a nice and friendly joke meant to help me learn the proper phrase, and it worked perfectly.

The days went by pretty fast. In the mornings David would have some office hours, while I would check the newspapers for jobs. In the evenings we would all go to the gym and I would act as an additional assistant coach for the women's team. Occasionally, I would join David's "Texas Stars" team training, but due to the number of players, he had me actually play on Michael's team which was yet another competitive team in Houston. Soon I would find another common interest with Michael: he also loved rock-and-roll. In fact he was a long-time devoted Rolling Stones fan and from then on he helped me start my music collection of vinyl LPs and tapes.

David also loved music but apparently he wasn't as fanatic about it as Michael and I were. However, knowing my love for the most famous rock bands in the world, one day he shocked me with a great surprise: he handed me two tickets to a concert with Black Sabbath in Houston. It was 1982 and this was the 'new' band after Ronnie James Dio replaced Ozzy Osborne. I knew all about their history and I couldn't wait to see the show. That was my first such concert in the U.S. and, indeed, it was the greatest spectacle I had witnessed to date.

Environmental Awareness and My Driver License

Around the same time, my stay in Houston presented me with another life-changing experience. One late night I was on the passenger seat in a car, riding home from the downtown area. I had just finished a can of coca-cola when the old 'Romanian' primitive instinct took the better of me: I squeezed the can, and as I opened the window I threw it on the side of the road in the grass. That was when I received one of the best lessons in environmental awareness. Almost instantly, with hardly any words, the driver, a newly made friend of mine, turned the car around and pulled over on the shoulder of the road close to the spot where I threw the aluminum can. In that pretty tensed and embarrassing situation for me, we both searched for the can in the pretty tall grass in the middle of the night. After a few unsuccessful minutes we gave up and headed back on the road. The rest of the ride was a quiet one and it gave me plenty of time to reflect: apparently, all those years of witnessing such careless practices in Romania did not bring a deep enough personal conviction that they should be unacceptable. However, this incident in Houston did it; with that experience behind me I became one of the most fervent advocates for environmental awareness, finally realizing the meaninglessness of polluting the very environment that allows us to live.

In the meantime David insisted that I should attempt one more time to get my driver license, so whenever possible I would practice driving his car. One event though, became 'legendary.' As I felt more and more comfortable driving, he let me also drive on the highway. So I was driving him to the university one day on Loop 610 when suddenly he said in a sharp and short statement: "You just missed the exit!" Instantly, I checked in the review mirror, there was no car coming, and I stopped the car abruptly, I backed up about 20-30 yards, and I made it to the exit I was supposed to take in the first place. While I was backing up David did desperately say "What are you doing?" but it was too late: it was done. In spite of my re-assurance: "There was nobody behind us," his next comment was obviously "You don't do that. You don't back up on the highway. You take the next exit and turn around!" He was right, and I have never done it since.

After a lot more driving practice over the next few days, he decided that I was ready and he took me to the closest police station to take the test. Remembering my Austin experience in this respect I was a little bit nervous but as soon as I turned the car on, with the officer on the passenger seat, I relaxed and I said to myself: "It's OK, I am much better now." As soon as we exited the parking lot the officer said: "Turn right!" I did, and at the end of the block he said again: "Turn right!" Within about 2 minutes he said "Turn right" two more times and we arrived back where we started. He gave his verdict immediately: "Congratulations, you passed!" I thanked him and, while we were waiting for my temporary driver permit, I said to David: "Wow! This was easy; much easier than in Austin!" That was a Friday, and the next day, very early in the morning, we had planned to drive to Dallas to a volleyball tournament.

By then they had changed my registration from Austin to Michael's team and we made it to playoffs that day, of course,

Texas Stars being the winners. The tournament ended late into the night; we went to dinner, and, as if the day had not been long enough, the Dallas hosts invited us to a party. Since David's women team had to be back in Houston by Noon on Sunday, we all got only 2-3 hours of sleep after the late-night party and we had to safely handle the 5-hour drive back. We were loading our volleyball equipment into the van when David handed me the keys and said: "Here! You drive!" I was surprised and proud in the same time: I had a two-day old driver permit and he trusted me to drive a van full of sleepy volleyball players all the way to Houston. Then I said to David: "Good! This is my *real* driving test!" and he agreed. However, although the rest of the players slept the entire time, David sat behind the driver's seat mostly awake in case I needed any help. Although I was very tired, it all went well and I really appreciated the challenge: that was truly my optimal driving test.

Temporary Work

In the meantime, David and I kept searching for work in my profession and we spent more and more time together. He had a degree in History so we often talked about the history of Europe and especially about Communism in Romania. While he was on the U.S. national team he did have encounters with Romanian volleyball players, but he had never been to Romania. Some evenings we would have long talks while preparing dinner. Several times we would burn the food as we would be absorbed in our discussion, hence the term we came up with for the overly grilled meat: 'carbon chicken.' Day after day we became better friends and beside volleyball, our collaboration on searching for jobs finally turned positive: we secured another interview and I was offered a computer programming position with a small company located in a suburb of Houston. The pay was about $12,000 a year and it seemed acceptable for a start. In the meantime Michael offered to give me his old car for free (a rusted 1972 Ford that was in need of repair), but according to an old Romanian tradition I had to offer even a modest amount for it which in the end he accepted. We fixed it, we changed the title to my name and I drove the car to work every day.

However, due to obvious factors such as my proficiency level in English, my programming experience, and the new personal-computing hardware/software superior to the archaic system I used back in Romania, the company terminated my employment at the end of the first month. So, one Monday morning the owner came to me with a smile on his face and asked for my set of keys to the building. He justified his decision by their inability to extend my training, he wrote me a check for that month, and wished me luck in the future. I thanked him for the opportunity he gave me, I expressed my understanding of the situation, and I left. On my way out I was running the entire scenario through my head and I identified some positives that came out of it. Among those, the preeminent one was that during that month I had learned a new programming language, BASIC, beside FORTRAN and COBOL I had learned in Romania. As I was heading home, I wondered how David would take the news, but he understood and asked me not to worry too much about it.

Return to Austin

In the early May of 1982 we played in the South Texas regional final tournament, and, at the end of a very exciting day and a great game in the finals, we won. Michael's team, my team by now, did very well to win the AA championship while David's 'Texas Stars' played in a different region. With this accomplishment we were qualified to play in the nationals scheduled for the end of the month, but that was financially out of reach for me due to high travel expenses. Around that time David had hired a new assistant coach for the university women's team due to Michael's departure. His name was Brian; he was a good volleyball player and coach, and he moved in with us. Over the short time we had together as teammates and roommates, we became good friends.

During my entire stay in Houston I did my best to keep in touch with Mrs. Martin and Gerry in Austin by phone and

I even placed a few calls to Italy as I was trying to maintain a connection with Sergio and the Latina volleyball crowd. Since I was paying more or less my share of the household expenses for food and telephone charges, and since my financial status was not one of the best, some of my expenditures, including calls to Italy, seemed a little extreme to David. Moreover, one time I came home with a 15-dollar book by Carl Sagan (*Cosmos*) and I was gently criticized for spending my money on an expensive unnecessary book under the circumstances, and he was right. In spite of everything though, I had always preserved my interest in life in the universe, ancient history, Eastern philosophies, and the human condition.

In respect to long distance calls, keeping in touch with friends was important to me and soon enough I was very glad I did. In the early part of June, Gerry called to let me know of an employment possibility at the University of Texas at Austin. It was a training position for a computer analyst with a solid background in mathematics. Gerry was mostly interested in programming so he thought that I was better suited for that job. Immediately I called the person in charge of the interview and I scheduled it such that I could have time to return from Houston.

The day before the interview I packed up my car with everything I owned, including 30-40 vinyl albums, I thanked everybody in David's house for their honorable intention to help me get started and I took my 160-mile ride to Austin. Although old and rusty, the car did well and later in the afternoon I found myself in front of Mrs. Martin's home. I unpacked with Gerry's help and I took back my old room on the lower level of the house. After dinner I briefly told everybody the 'Houston story,' then I looked over all the available information regarding the position for which I was interviewing the next day, and I retired to my room for the night.

For whatever reasons though, I couldn't fall asleep until very late, so I got only about four hours of sleep before the interview. At 9 a.m. I showed up for my appointment and the interviewer, a nice middle-aged gentleman, explained to me that in fact I had to take two different tests. The first was mostly about mathematical applications and the second dealt with text and logical interpretations. He gave me the first test and left me alone in a room to finish up. After about 90 minutes he came back and collected the test with my answers. He graded it and a few minutes later he came back with my score: an A. Then he said: "You did well. In order to offer you the training position you need to also score an A on the second test. If you want you can take it now, or you can come back later this week to take it. What would you like to do?" So I had to make an important decision on the spot. I thought about it for a few seconds and, in spite of feeling a little tired, I decided to go ahead and immediately take the second test. I did my best, but after he graded it, he returned with the news: "Sorry, but you only scored a B on this one." I asked if I can retake it later on, and he said that this is an annual offer so I had to wait an entire year for a retake. I thanked him for his consideration and cooperation and I went back home. On my way back, alone in my car, I finally came to my senses and concluded: "Yes, I am tired. I should have waited a few more days to take the second test." But the decision had been made and there was no turning back at least for one year.

That evening I shared my experience with Dr. Martin, Mrs. Martin, and Gerry, and they were all very supportive assuring me that there will be other opportunities soon. Being very persistent, Gerry had found full time employment with a fast-food restaurant, so he had already proven that there was hope for work.

In the meantime I had been corresponding with my parents in Romania and they had found a remote way to send me a copy of my higher education diploma, and it was again via the Mandrea family from New York. So I was anxiously waiting, until one day when the U.S. post master delivered an envelope from Mr. Mandrea to Mrs. Martin's house. I went to pick it up from the street mailbox and I was shocked by the cruel truth: the envelope was there but it was open and empty! Immediately I went inside and I consulted with everybody. We came up with a variety of explanations but none had the potential to change reality: there were no documents in the envelope. That evening I called Mr. Mandrea and he was as surprised as we were and assured me that he did send the copies as he agreed with my parents.

Back to the Tennis Center

At the end of these few setbacks I had no choice but to continue searching for work, hoping that something in my field will turn up. In the meantime I paid a quick visit to John at the tennis center and he welcomed me back to Austin. We talked volleyball and tennis but for the moment he offered me a resumption of my part-time job at the center. I was happy to have something to do and I was very grateful for the offer.

It was now the middle of the summer 1982, and I had been working for several weeks. When time permitted, John and I were exploring new avenues for me to find work. Of course I had been checking the newspapers but so far nothing looked promising. I had a nice place to stay and great company but I couldn't live there forever. Dr. and Mrs. Martin were so preoccupied with my situation that they exhausted all resources known to them, searching for an employment opportunity for me. At one point I came close to calling Mr. Mandrea in New York to make the trip back. I had saved a little more money on top of the approximately $450 I came with from Italy, so I could afford an airplane ticket to New York. However, it seemed that I kept waiting to make that decision as if something else was waiting in the wings, and indeed it did.

15

Full-time Employment

The summer of 1982 was in full swing and the tennis center kept me busy for the hours I was scheduled to work. In the meantime I had also connected again with some of the other Austin volleyball friends I met in February. One of them in particular, Reza, became my doubles partner and we played several doubles and eventually triples volleyball tournaments around Austin mostly for fun (some did have small cash prizes). Reza was a graduate student at the University of Texas at Austin in mathematics and computer science and he was a very skilled player; we complemented each other well, hence our success. In the meantime I was still searching for full-time work and I was happy to receive suggestions from anybody who cared to help.

The Opening

The tennis center gave me ample opportunity to spend time with John beyond tennis; he was obviously receptive with respect to my struggle to find work in my profession. As a tennis pro, he was giving tennis lessons to a group of students from a small private high school, Perry School, located not far from the tennis center. He was, therefore, closely in touch with the administration of the school since tennis was also part of the physical education requirements. In fact, that summer the director of Perry School, Dr. Cooper – a French teacher - was running an international exchange program with students from France, and tennis was among the scheduled activities. So John would bring the students to the center and once in a while I would even assist him with the tennis lessons.

While this program was going on, one day John came to me with a light smile on his face and pulled me aside as if he had something important to tell me. He first reminded me about Perry School and his involvement there, and then he continued: "You know, I just found out that the mathematics teacher at Perry is leaving this summer. You know a lot of mathematics. Would you like to apply for that position?" In that moment a number of thoughts ran through my head and the most persistent one was that while at the university I took 6 optional educational courses in mathematics. Not only that but I loved every opportunity I had to teach even if it was just giving private lessons in Romania. So naturally I said: "Wow! Of course! That is a great idea. How do we go about it?" He immediately said: "Tomorrow I will schedule an appointment for you to see Dr. Cooper and we will go from there." I was thrilled; I thanked him for thinking of me in such an opportune moment and I started making mental plans for the interview.

In the meantime, I remembered that I did not have any documentation regarding my degree from Romania and I couldn't envision going to the interview totally empty handed in that respect. Of course, as soon as I got home I told Dr. and Mrs. Martin about the new developments and the solution to my problem emerged almost on the spot. Based on his vast experience and prestige, Dr. Martin offered to print and sign an affidavit for me stating that indeed I completed the four years of university studies in Romania and that I was eligible to teach undergraduate mathematics. That became my temporary document attesting my education and readiness to teach and I was hoping it would be sufficient to get me started.

The day of the interview came and I met Dr. Cooper at Perry School on a warm morning in August. The interview was short. We talked about mathematics and her experience with the European school system which she knew well, then she made a copy of my improvised document and she offered me the job on the spot. I didn't expect such a quick decision; apparently private schools were blessed with the freedom to hire outside of the constraints of public school bureaucracy. Instantly I felt a flux of positive emotions running through my body and I couldn't thank Dr. Cooper enough for giving me that opportunity. As I was talking with her I realized that she was a person of strong character, very professional in her approach to education, and obviously concerned with the well-being of the small private school she was leading. Over all, there were fewer than 100 students enrolled and the school was not religiously affiliated. The entire educational program was supported solely by the student tuition so teachers were modestly paid. However, the financial reality was less important to me than the opening I was given. In fact I felt a sense of relief by not pursuing the field of computer programming since I really loved pure mathematics more.

After the interview she introduced me to the secretary where I received all the pertinent information regarding the starting of the school year. I left the school with a great feeling of confidence that the future will be as bright as I had imagined it to be while I was in the refugee camp in Italy. On my way back to Mrs. Martin's house I remembered that I had never really entertained pessimistic thoughts in my life so I was counting on the new development to be on the right track. And it was.

From day one, teaching felt good. Although it took me a while to adjust to the new education system, being in the classroom brought back comfortable memories of success in mathematics. Not only that, but also the satisfaction of explaining mathematics such that it made sense to students became the trademark of my teaching. Even if it took more effort and skill, I always believed that clear explanations made teaching and learning more rewarding not only to students but also to teachers. I felt that not understanding the "Why?" of a mathematical procedure defeated the purpose of learning it; it is generically easier to teach *how* a procedure works and *what* to do to get the answer, but that is merely mechanical teaching. Gradually, students would grow to appreciate this approach to learning and that would translate into better long-term academic success. Throughout my education in Romania I appreciated professors who took the extra step to explain in a clear and concise manner the down to Earth applicability of a math concept, and that became my focus in teaching.

Extra Work

As soon as I received my first paycheck, Gerry and I moved into a two-bedroom apartment in walking distance of Perry School. In the meantime, the divorce initiated in Romania in my obvious absence had been finalized by the courts, so here I was, a single man sharing an apartment with Gerry who was waiting for his wife from Bucharest to join him in Texas. After a few months in the apartment, his wife made it to Austin and that was when we started contemplating a separation. Soon enough I located a one-bedroom apartment near-by and at the end of our first-year contract I moved to my own place. During the summer of 1983 my rusty old car broke down and I replaced it with another used one. The opportunity arose as a lady from a neighboring apartment complex was selling a 1974 VW Beatle at a convenient price.

By then I was already in my second year of teaching and I loved every minute of it. However, the financial burden increased so I had to look for some extra work. My volleyball playing also picked up as I joined David Olbright's 'Texas Stars' in Houston which added to my travel expenses, although my newly acquired economical VW did very well to take me all over Texas to tournaments in Dallas, San Antonio, Houston, and College Station. So in my pursuit for extra income I learned about the Austin Community College (ACC) and the possibility of teaching mathematics as a part-time instructor.

Ever since I related to my parents that I did not receive the first set of copies of my educational transcripts from Romania, they had never rested in their efforts to send me another set. At last, they had found a connection via Greece and they managed to safely send me photo copies of my documents, notarized by my father who made use of his own Orthodox priest seal. With these in hand I applied for a part-time teaching position with the ACC. Apparently, the ACC need for mathematics instructors was imperious at that time so a few weeks after I filed my application I received a phone-call for an interview. Based on my Perry School short experience and my transcript copies, I was offered part-time employment at ACC: I was supposed to teach 1-2 night courses and I started in 1984.

My new teaching schedule really kept me busy. I was teaching all the high school math courses at Perry School from 8 a.m. to 3 p.m. and college courses after 5:30 p.m. It was a very good learning period for me since it had opened up new horizons in my teaching career. I loved my small classes at the high school and I enjoyed my night courses at the college. There were virtually no discipline problems at either school due to the motivation intrinsically imbedded in the respective educational programs. That allowed me to really focus on teaching. However, simultaneously, some old hobbies surfaced ever so gently and I gradually started to divide the little free time I had among them. In this respect, I had even bought a used set of drums and I was spending many Sundays rehearsing. However, despite our efforts and a couple of live shows at prominent Austin locations, I did not register much success with either of the two bands with which I played over 2-3 years, and in retrospect I am glad; as much as I liked it, a life exclusively lived in the field of music would not have been for me.

Vacation Trip to Mexico

The abundance of books and television documentaries on subjects I loved, and to which I had access since my arrival in the U.S., was really a great motivator. Due to my limited budget, the Half-Price Books stores became my favorites. I connected again with subjects such as Yoga and ancient history. At every opportunity I enjoyed talking about these with friends and students both at the high school and at ACC.

Such discussions were taking me quickly to like thinkers. In this respect, I was fortunate to have in one of my first high school graduating classes a very bright student from Mexico, Ricardo. After many interesting exchanges of ideas we had both on the history of Romania and Mexico, he offered to be my host in his home country. I was totally taken by the idea and I was very grateful to him. We sat down and made plans for a vacation trip to Mexico and we tentatively had set it up for the winter break.

There was a problem however. At that time I did not have a travel document that would allow me to return to the U.S. after a trip abroad. I searched for and found a solution. I had to secure a so-called "Permit to Reenter" via the U.S. Immigration and Naturalization office.

Once I received my permit we set the days for the trip and we connected at the Mexico City airport. His family received me with open arms and Ricardo became gradually more of a friend than just a student. They took me on short visits around the impressive Mexican capital and, of course, I was very close to making one of my 'unrealizable' old dreams from Romania come true.

Throughout my high school and university years I had the pictures of ancient Mayan and Aztec historical sites in mind; back then I was convinced that I would never be able to set foot even close to them. My curiosity as to how they were made and, more importantly, as to what some of them really meant, had sent me on a search course that was limited to the availability of information drastically censored by the

Communist regime of Romania. Sites such as the pyramids of Teotihuacan and Chichen Itza, the gigantic Olmec heads, and the Toltec statues had intrigued me for a long time. But one of the most fascinating artifacts of which I was aware was the tombstone from Palenque which, in many researchers' opinion, depicts an ancient astronaut (great pictures of all these sites are available on Google). As I was aware of their geographical location, I did not expect to visit many of them, so we focused on sites within driving reach from Mexico City.

Tombstone at Palenque
Internet Photo

Full-time Employment

Our arrival in Teotihuacan brought tears to my eyes: me climbing the pyramid of the Sun all the way to the top? Wow: I was standing on the spot from which Erich von Daniken (the author of *Chariots of the Gods*, the book that fascinated me so much back in high school) elaborated his hypothesis! I stood there completely taken by the view of the entire city and I was wondering if Ricardo and his parents understood what that experience meant to me; they did. They were fully aware of my passion, so they showed their own appreciation for ancient history by going out of their way to make my vacation trip one of the most extraordinary I have ever had.

Teotihuacan - Internet Photo

One early morning we embarked on a 10-hour drive South of Mexico City, to the state of Oaxaca. My friends owned a large ranch there and we were supposed to spend a couple of days with their close relatives. Once again, I was welcomed within a warm family atmosphere that in many respects reminded me of large Romanian gatherings with similar customs. Several times I said to myself "It is still a small world" as I also remembered ancient artifacts we saw in a Mexico City museum that resembled in details similar ones from Romania or even India. However, there were new things to ponder. The evening we arrived, our host family planned something special for the next day. They built a large bonfire, then they filled up a deep hole in the ground almost to the top with hot coal, and then they placed a huge pot that contained all the proper ingredients for a special soup. They covered the entire setup completely burying it under ground and we uncovered it the next morning. I must admit: that was the best soup I had ever tasted up to that date. The aromas were so delicately preserved in the flavor, that even the heavy spices traditionally used in its composition were just right; it was a real feast for our taste and a wonderful new culinary experience in my case.

That beautiful sunny morning we all indulged in a copious late breakfast only to get ready for another shocking revelation for me. We took a short and pleasant drive on the dirt roads of the ranch and at almost every turn I was introduced to a series of ancient pyramids about which little is known; the only signs of human exploration or intervention were a few digs testifying that some 'tomb-robbers' had hoped to get rich overnight. The pyramids were of relatively small to medium sizes but very clear and obvious in their appearance. Although they were all covered with grass, bushes, and some even with trees, their steps and their square-based shape were evident. I was silently wondering about the abundance of historical information that might be uncovered through their exploration. I voiced my concern to my hosts this way: "Why isn't the Mexican government interested in such ancient treasures?" The answer came quickly and to the point: "Money! There is not enough money to continue excavation of larger and more prominent sites, let alone these." However understandable that reality is even today, I cannot help thinking about all the historical data still hidden underground at sites such as these throughout the Americas and beyond. I was and I am still pondering this issue: if the human race could only shift focus from amassing such debt and spending such incredible fortunes on armament to fight each other, we could invest in archaeological and anthropological research to render a more profound understanding of who we really are and of our place in the universe. Chances are that this realization alone would make fighting obsolete and would really advance the human race.

My marvelous vacation in Mexico ended with another long day of driving back to Mexico City, a trip that headlined another striking reality. In several towns and cities through which we were passing, I noticed that many Catholic churches had been raised on ancient foundations built long before the conquistadores' arrival; the demarcation lines between the old and the new construction were clearly visible on their walls. Apparently the new builders had torn down the ancient 'pagan' temples, but they had been smart enough to preserve the very well-built and meant-to-last foundations. One could not help but think how much the modern world lost by the destruction of all those temples, let alone the burning of countless volumes of Mayan and Aztec ancient writings. Over the many prolonged periods of silent driving I entertained an inner retrospective of books I had read on these issues. Now I finally saw it for myself: through their cultural and religious ignorance, the conquistadores deprived us of very valuable information. In spite of all the 'historical' testimonies and explanations provided by 'professional' guides at many of those sites, it seemed obvious that there was much more to the story. However, I understood that they did the best they could considering the education they received as tour guides, and I kept in mind a well-known saying: "you cannot ask somebody to give you what they don't have." In the end I had to remember yet another truth: "history is written by the victors."

The next morning, as we were approaching the Mexico City airport, I expressed my gratitude to my hosts one more time. They were glad that we spent a few days together and in spite of a little bit of a language barrier, they understood my interest in the ancient history of Mexico. With my precious souvenir in my luggage, a nice poncho from Teotihuacan, I flew back to Austin with a revitalized motivation to study ancient history. I couldn't wait to reconnect with Ricardo that spring, and we remain good friends.

Change in Employment: Kirby Hall School

Toward the end of my third year at Perry School I received a phone call from Mrs. Martin. We had been keeping in touch periodically but this time her message was out of the ordinary. She told me that there was a mathematics teaching position available for the following year at a private school she knew well, and she was of the opinion that I should apply.

The new school was Kirby Hall and Mrs. Martin confirmed what I had sporadically gathered from my Perry School students and parents: Kirby Hall served more students; it was located in the proximity of the University; it was a kindergarten through 12th grade school, and consequently appeared to be a little more financially secure. I was obviously very interested in Mrs. Martin's proposition and I expressed my agreement that, yes, I should apply. She promised to set up an appointment for me to meet with the Kirby Hall director and a few days later we were on our way to a meeting that had the potential to change my life.

That day Mrs. Martin and I drove together to meet the director of Kirby Hall at her house. Her name was Mrs. Rase and from the first moments of our interview I envisioned a possible long-term cooperation. Her house felt exceptionally warm and welcoming, and it displayed family memorabilia all around, which resembled somewhat homes in Romania. From her description of the mission of Kirby Hall in the Austin community I detected plenty of common ground with my newly developed philosophy of teaching undergraduate mathematics at both high school and college levels. I expressed the best I could my vision of modern secondary education with its foundation set on student and parent responsibility, and at the end of a short hour, we shook hands as she offered me the job.

Mrs. Martin and I left the house with a renewed sense of confidence in my teaching career and we made plans on how I should approach Dr. Cooper to announce my departure from Perry School. That was smoother than I thought. In fact I had almost completed three successful years at Perry School, and, although I was extremely grateful for the opportunity, I felt that I owed it to myself to move on as the opportunity arose. Therefore, I wrote a nice letter of resignation to Dr. Cooper expressing my deepest gratitude for all she had done for me, giving her plenty of time to fill the position I was vacating for the next school year.

Interestingly enough, or as one might say, 'as fate had it,' one year later Perry School went out of business. The closing of Perry, which would have left me without a full-time job had I not moved on, strengthened even more my old conviction in a positive destiny. As I received the news, I experienced a quick flashback to images from my escape trip through Yugoslavia when, even marked by sleep deprivation, I felt a sense of inner guidance: "Don't worry. Go on. You are OK." This time I felt it again and that was just one more stone in the foundation of what was to become my new look on life.

Being a member of the Kirby Hall School faculty opened my horizons in many respects. Not only was I teaching all the mathematics high school courses up to calculus, but I also had to assure a smooth academic transition from the elementary level. This was highly facilitated by great elementary school teachers and I was very grateful to them. On top of it, a high school academic credit in computer science had been introduced as a requirement for graduation, and my computer programming background came in very handy. We had some of the first generations of students at Kirby Hall to learn programming in BASIC on the new Apple personal computers and I was glad I could help the school fulfill that requirement. That was really during the infancy of technology in education and there was a lot of uncharted territory. Mrs. Rase, together with her husband, Dr. Rase, an esteemed University of Texas at Austin professor, were very supportive on all fronts, both professional and personal. For that, I will be forever grateful to them.

The Kirby Hall School

Visit to Italy

Meanwhile, I was contemplating a summer trip to Italy to visit my friend Sergio and the group of volleyball players I met during my stay in the refugee camp. Latina was a great place to spend a summer vacation but my plan provided also for a selective tour of Europe. So, by then I managed to save enough money, and with my U.S. "Permit to Reenter" I was certain I would be able to accomplish such a goal.

Sergio enthusiastically picked me up at the international airport in Rome and we spent a few days together while including a couple of volleyball practices with many of our friends from Latina. It was refreshing. Soon I started to feel relatively comfortable speaking Italian again and I was happy my ability to communicate in this beautiful language had not deserted me.

After I expressed my intent to travel through Europe, we made arrangements and I left on my new adventure. First I stopped for a couple of days in Paris where I was in for a big surprise. Suddenly, I saw a number of Romanian-made cars (Dacia) parked in the street, and there it was: the Romanian embassy in France! The fact was that the hotel I chose was one block away from the embassy which looked like a well-protected building on a relatively quiet street of Paris. A cold chill went through my body and the old fear of persecution came all over me one more time. How did I manage to select, out of all the hotels in Paris, the one that was so close to the very Embassy of the Socialist Republic of Romania (RSR)? While I was bewildered by the entire situation, a piece of disturbing news came back into my mind, and that made the entire situation even worse. One recent morning, a Romanian visitor had been pushed to his death off a window from an upper floor of this very Romanian Embassy building. Apparently, the person got in a violent argument with employees of the embassy and, to prevent further political complications, they staged a 'fall from the window' death as they justified it later in front of the French police and news crews. With all this running through my head I immediately turned around and went my way.

Those two days in Paris represented a great accomplishment for me and they were to be followed by more excitement than I was expecting. After I visited for the first time the Eiffel Tower, the Louvre museum, and the Notre Dame cathedral, I took a train to Versailles. It was all impressive and breathtaking. More of my dreams from behind the Iron Curtain became reality. And that was not all. One morning I took a train to Barcelona, Spain. Gaudi's Sagrada Familia is the most vivid memory I have from that leg of the trip. To step inside such a unique and out of the ordinary architectural monument became a true emotional moment for me. With that picture in mind I also visited a small resort town, Sitges, that distinguished itself by its touristic profile. The traditional Spanish afternoon 'siesta' left the streets virtually deserted, but as soon as the cool of the evening embraced the beach, this lively tourist town showed its natural side as a party place.

My trip back to Latina followed the Spanish, French, and the Italian Riviera, as the railroad carved its way through the amazing scenery offered by the Mediterranean Sea shore. Famous landmarks like Cannes and Nice came and went, and soon enough my voyage took me to the heart of Italy. With some time on my hands, while I was approaching Rome, I could not help but place side by side in my mind the Romanian Embassy from Paris story with my escape and my train ride from Trieste to Rome of September of 1981. What a difference a few years in the free world made for me!

I shared my trip impressions with Sergio as soon as I made it back to his house and we spent a few more joyful days together while making other plans. We spent some time at the beautiful beach of Latina, we played volleyball, and he helped me set up yet another trip, this time by boat to Greece. After visiting the Acropolis in Athens I ventured to some of the Greek islands in the Aegean Sea. Crete and Santorini pointed out the fascinating history, archeology, and geology of the Greek world. To step on the same slabs of stone that, presumably, famous Greek philosophers and mathematicians walked on many centuries ago, was another of my old dreams that came true. On that trip I even had the chance to visit

Trip to Greece and Turkey

Ephesus and Kusadasi on the Turkish coast. It was out of this world; I was overwhelmed and completely taken by the richness of ancient history that seemed to be still living through all the archeological treasures preserved over many centuries.

The return to Latina offered me a few more days of rest before the long flight home to Austin, Texas. Spending more time with Sergio cemented even more our friendship and we promised each other to keep in touch and to do our best to make such reunions more the norm than the exception. In this respect, I invited him to visit Texas. However, his many engagements would not make it an easy accomplishment. It became clear to me that especially his working regimen, with short summer vacations, and a heavy and necessary commitment to his business throughout the year would make a trip to Austin improbable at least for a while. In the end, as we embraced at the airport in Rome, although I was certain that in our hearts we will never be apart, I realized that I will still be the one most likely to initiate visits in person with Sergio, and I felt it would happen, nevertheless.

My Mom's Visit to Austin

For some time after my 1981 escape I was happy that my parents were not persecuted by Ceausescu's Communist regime. They had been interrogated but since they had absolutely no knowledge of my plan to defect, they had not been incriminated. My sister was able to continue and eventually finish her university studies in mathematics, and my mother was even granted a visa for a vacation trip to the U.S.S.R. That came as an encouragement to me and it seemed logical since other than defecting I wasn't really a public thorn in the side of the party in power. Although I was vehemently opposed to the Communist politics, propaganda, and heavy censorship, for some reason I wasn't determined to go public (newspapers, radio, TV) once I arrived to Texas. After all, from the beginning of my adventure of escaping from Romania, it was more of a personal endeavor, more of a quest for true freedom so that I can see the world and I could maximize my chances to reach my highest potential.

However, despite the good signs regarding my parents' well-being, one negative repercussion did take place against my mother. She had been a kindergarten teacher for all her life. Due to special circumstances, she had to commute by bus to a near-by school for many years and only late in her career was she able to find a teaching position in our home village. Due to her longer experience, as soon as she moved in, she was granted the senior supervisor position over her only other colleague and that was their school setup when I left in 1981. Immediately after my escape, the Ministry of Education decided that since her son was now a defector she could not remain the person in charge, so they ordered the switch: her colleague was put in charge and my mother kept the second teaching position. Soon enough, though, the number of children in the village decreased substantially and the second position had to be eliminated: my mother had just lost her job. Since she was only 3 years short of retirement, and after long and persistent pleas, she was allowed to teach first to fourth grade classes as such a teaching position became available in the near-by town of Victoria, my high school town. This way she was back on a daily commute and at the end of the three challenging but required years she was able to retire.

Encouraged by her successful trip to the U.S.S.R., I proposed that she should consider a visit to the U.S. to see me. At first the idea seemed crazy, but upon further reflection, we decided to give it a try. So after several tries and all the pain and tribulation embedded in each respective bureaucracy, she secured an okay from the Romanian government and a tourist visa to the U.S. from the American embassy in Bucharest. By then I had bought a house in Austin and that was a big plus on the affidavit I had to send to her, which was needed for the U.S. entry visa. After my living in the U.S. for four years, her receiving the entry visa was not a big surprise to me, but the permission to leave Romania granted by the Communist regime, was a shocker.

Her one month stay with me in Austin in the winter of 1985-1986 was a true joy for both of us. I did my best to show her as many places as possible and she even attended a volleyball tournament I played in Houston. With that occasion she met my best friend David Olbright; I introduced her to our team; we visited NASA which impressed her immensely, and we also took a short walk on the deserted but pristine Galveston beach. It was a great sense of awe for her to feel the cold winter water of the Gulf of Mexico on her hands. I could see the deep impression that simple touch of water left on her. Of course, this entire scenario was played from the perspective of the well-known negative propaganda against the West practiced behind the Iron-Curtain; the image entertained by the Communists was one of pollution and degradation of the natural habitat caused by capitalist greed. My mother knew better and now she had the chance to experience it for herself. Still, there was more to come.

With my mother at NASA

One early sunny morning we left for Dallas. I knew I had a little problem with my VW Bug's starter but I had no choice and took the trip anyway. As we were getting close I was inspired to take the West IH 35 to Fort Worth first, planning to visit Dallas second. I say 'inspired' because we arrived in downtown Fort Worth at the exact time of a major parade. It was all so impressive, even I couldn't believe it: the multitude of flowers, the people dressed in festive colorful attire, the dressed-up horses pulling gigantic decorated chariots, all moving to the music of a joyful marching-band. My mother immediately said to me: "Wow! What a surprise you had for me!" I answered quickly: "Not really; we are just fortunate. I had no idea there would be a parade." We bathed our eyes in the scenery for a while and we left for Dallas with the satisfaction of an already great accomplishment for that day. Of course, I had to push-start my Bug but it didn't bother me at all: the day was off to a great start already.

We arrived in downtown Dallas before noon and we went straight to the Kennedy memorial. My mother insisted on reminding me how in 1963 my father took me by bicycle to a near-by village in Romania where they had a TV set, to watch Kennedy's funeral; somehow the Communist regime found it necessary to broadcast it. Most likely their intent was to display yet another negative aspect of life in the West, namely the assassination of a beloved U.S. president.

With such memories in mind we left Dallas for a long-awaited destination: Southfork Ranch, the site of the well-known series "Dallas." This was part of our excursion plan that day since my mother was an avid fan of the series. Actually "Dallas" was on almost everybody's list of preferences in Romania at that time and it was a mystery how after its debut in the U.S. in 1978 the Romanian television elected to show it in the 1980s. Even I was taken by the series' family intrigue, up to September 1981, the time of my defection. It seemed that the Ceausescu regime allowed this to happen for the same old reason: to show the Romanian people some of the atrocities that could take place behind the greed of Texan oil magnates. However, I think, their politically motivated intentions back-fired since the series also portrayed very well the freedom in a land of abundance which was definitely in short supply especially in the 1980s Romania.

Once again this was a dream come true for my mom. I don't think she had ever hoped to actually walk on the stage of one of the best American TV series seen in Romania, but there we were visiting the ranch house, the swimming pool, and most importantly taking pictures of everything. Even though we were aware that most of the actual scenes in the movie were taped in studios, it was still a unique experience especially since I was able to share it with my mother.

Late in the afternoon I push started my VW again and we were on our way back to Austin. Of course, most of the 4-hour drive from Southfork Ranch was decorated with superlatives on everything we had seen that day; we couldn't stop talking. On top of it all, we had yet another great objective for the day. Knowing how much my mother loved music, and in that respect a variety of styles, I had bought a couple of tickets to a concert with Rush, the well-known progressive-rock trio from Canada. The show was scheduled for 8 p.m. in Austin and we made it just in time.

It was my first time also to see Rush live and it was a fantastic rendition of all the famous songs I had enjoyed so far on tapes and vinyl albums. The tastefully orchestrated light show and the music left my mother speechless in spite of listening to them for the first time. That show became one of the most treasured highlights of her trip to the U.S. and once again I was so happy to be part of the experience.

My mother's return trip to Romania was a cold one in the middle of winter but it all went well. Beside some souvenirs, she took back a good collection of pictures and, of course, a great volume of inner memories that she couldn't wait to share with my father and my sister. The few months that followed were marked by our correspondence which was abundant in positive sentiments based on the month we spent together in Austin.

16

Personal Development Continues

U.S. Citizenship

After my mother's wonderful visit to Austin I dedicated my free time to one of the most important goals I had set for myself: to become an American citizen. The Immigration and Naturalization (I & N) law asserted that after five years of permanent residence in the U.S. one could apply for American citizenship, and I did. January 25, 1987 was the fifth anniversary of my arrival in Texas and by then I had completed and already sent in the application required by law.

Soon enough I was called for an official interview at the I & N office in San Antonio and at that time I didn't know what to expect. However, it all went smoothly. The interview consisted of a few general questions to test my knowledge of U.S. history, a short conversation with the I & N officer that included a brief written statement I had to provide as proof that I had basic writing skills, and I had to sign an official form that stated my renunciation to any previous citizenship. The latter document made me think for a little bit, so I asked the officer for details. I was told that in order to be protected as an American citizen all around the world one could not hold yet another citizenship. Moreover, I was told that since my country of origin was under a Communist regime this became even more important although the U.S. could not guarantee protection in the native country. I signed the document while I was thinking that if I would ever decide to visit Romania my safety could become a serious issue.

Several months after my interview I received the confirmation that indeed my application had been approved and I had been called again to the I & N office in San Antonio to receive my naturalization certificate that would be presented in an official ceremony. It was a memorable gathering of a few hundred immigrants from many countries and I was really impressed by its organization. With our certificates in hand we recited simultaneously the official United States Oath of Allegiance that encompassed the so called "five principles:" allegiance to the U.S. constitution, renunciation of allegiance to any foreign country, defense of the constitution against enemies both foreign and domestic, promise to serve in the army if needed, and promise to perform civilian duties of national importance when required by law. It was a grandiose moment in our lives and I could read that feeling on all the faces around me. In a certain sense it was the moment that brought my entire life to a climax. The pictures of American cars I admired in my pre-college years in Romania, my love for American blues and rock-and-roll music, my inner hunger for scientific and historical knowledge censored by the Romanian Communist Party, all the other affronts to human rights practiced by the Ceausescu regime, affronts which seemed nonexistent in the U.S., and my escape from Romania, all came in concert in my mind to help me savor the grand finale: the earning of complete freedom by becoming an American citizen. That was a day I will treasure forever since it was *the day* that made my dreams realized.

A Call to Metaphysics

Over my first five years in the U.S., a persistent side of my life continued to be my passion for all things related to ancient history and spirituality especially in the light of the two books discovered in my father's collection during high school: *Chariots of the Gods* by Erich von Daniken and *Yoga* by the two Bulgarian authors. Of course my interest in such themes sprung from my adolescent disenchantment with the dogmatic view on spirituality propagated by the rigid orthodox practice of Christianity. From a young age I was hard-pressed to attest to its functionality and as I grew older I enjoyed entertaining a multitude of varied existential questions. Ever since high school, I had the inner conviction that what was generally accepted as the core philosophy of human existence was by far not complete. It seemed that something radically important was missing. What exactly that was I couldn't figure out even through my college years, but I was driven to find out. Consequently, by 1987, the year of becoming an American citizen, I had collected a large number of books on: the Egyptian pyramids, the Incas of South America, the Mayans, the ancient philosophies of the Far East such as Hinduism, Buddhism, and Taoism, all topped off by the most recent research on life after death, reincarnation, and near-death experience. After my arrival in the U.S. in January 1982, I obviously searched for more books by Daniken and I wasn't disappointed. Indeed, there were several new books translated into English and I found them via "The Ancient Astronaut Society." However, soon enough I was shocked to learn that the most recent of Daniken's books had been banned in the U.S. Apparently, their content undermined the established Christian theology by proposing that in fact in time immemorial our planet was visited by extraterrestrial beings who were actually mistaken for Gods by the unaware earthlings, hence the Indian Vedas, the Biblical stories, the Mayan writings, etc. That fact steered up my curiosity even more, so I became overly receptive to anything of value as far as those themes were concerned.

One late Monday evening I was watching TV when the telephone rang. It was a friend with a sudden announcement that would open a new universe in my search for answers to my existential questions. I was instructed to turn to a certain television channel where they were running something about Machu-Picchu and the Incas of South America. Indeed, as soon as I switched channels I was completely taken by the majestic views of the Andes of Peru and soon enough I realized that in fact it was a movie featuring Shirley MacLaine, the famous Hollywood actress. I watched the rest of the picture and then it all became clear. The movie was a mini-series played on the respective channel in two parts, the first on Sunday and the second on Monday, called *Out on a Limb*, and it was her autobiographical story. Per her recount, after she turned 40 she started noticing frequent unexplained synchronicities in her life, and this fact led her to meet certain spiritually gifted individuals who eventually became guides on her journey of personal growth. Over a number of years she devoured all the books she could find on spiritual matters combined with significant ancient history. The result was her book *Out on a Limb* followed by the four-hour mini-series which she produced, financed, and played in, obviously playing herself.

As I watched most of the second episode of the series which was shot mainly in Peru, I was struck by how 'normal,' logical, and common-sense-like the messages propelled by the movie felt to me. Perhaps it was the large volume of information on such issues I, myself, assimilated over the years, but I also think that we are usually exposed to the exact teaching that appeals to us, or in other words, "when the student is ready the teacher appears." Consequently, the very next day I started my search for Shirley's book and, once with the new treasure in my hands, it wasn't long until I finished reading it. All I had to say was "Wow! It all makes sense to me," paraphrasing Shirley's expression of her own awe relative to unorthodox explanations she received over time to mysteries of human life. As I silently suspected ever since high school, there seemed to be much more to the reality of life, a different dimension if you will, capable of explaining aspects of our existence left in the dark by modern science, traditional religion, and established philosophy. Finally it appeared logical to think that, indeed, in a world where cause and effect is a universal law, events in our lives happen for a reason, there are no accidents, and yes, even extraterrestrial life might not be just a utopian dream. Moreover, if God, or the Universal Intelligence is omnipresent, as it is proposed by the established religions of the world, then God is 'everywhere' including the human beings, which makes us drops of God, as drops of ocean-water are to the ocean. Also the possibility of universal unity being a factual reality gained significant ground in my inner debate over the nature of the universe, possibility proven in fact by the quantum physics of the 20th century. With these thoughts in mind I started visualizing huge benefits to the human race. Understanding life from this perspective would prevent most of the pain inflicted by humans onto humans, and the ideas suggested in *Out on a Limb* seemed to support a promising higher standard of moral and ethical living on Earth.

However, how good is a philosophy that's rarely applied? From that time on I set myself on a search for other people with similar views on life and I was hard-pressed to find any. My surroundings were marked by mostly nice people who were too busy to entertain new thoughts. Rarely was I able to find an individual who shared my interests and that was a discouraging factor on my personal path of inquiry, but I never gave up. Most of the literature on these themes underlined one common idea: if the human race will ever produce a critical number of positive thinkers about its future, that future will be attainable. This idea came very close to the scientifically researched fact known as "the hundredth monkey" phenomenon which states that if a sufficiently large number of individuals from the same species gain some new knowledge the entire species will adopt it much faster than the first few did. Consequently, I felt a sense of optimism about my endeavor and I continued my personal growth with new energy.

Contacts Renewed

While this entire scenario was developing, my professional life kept me deeply involved as I was teaching full-time high school mathematics at Kirby Hall and evening college classes at ACC. In addition, most weekends were taken by my persistent love for volleyball and the tournaments took me all over Texas and beyond. One of the few international tournaments we played was a two-day invitational in Miami, Florida. There were high caliber teams from the U.S., Canada, Mexico, and the Caribbean Islands, so most games were very challenging. We did well on Saturday and were preparing to play the final on Sunday morning against a club team from Mexico. Three or four members of our "Texas Stars" team, including David and I took good care to rest to be ready the next morning, despite the general trend to enjoy the weekend at all costs. We played well in the final and I was happy with my performance but we lost the game in two close sets.

Apparently the rest of our team was not completely up to the task and although we didn't win, that tournament remained one of my dearest volleyball memories.

Within the very engaged life I was leading especially after I took on the part-time teaching position with ACC, there were more exciting events taking place. At one time I received notice that a first cousin of my mother also defected from Romania and now he was in Yugoslavia. Soon he made it to the U.S. and eventually to Austin. I introduced him to the small Austin community of Romanians of which I was part and we enjoyed relatively often get-togethers, sharing the hosting responsibilities evenly within our group of four households. They were all hard-working people and, beside entertainment, we helped each other the best we could.

Another piece of good news came in 1987 also from Yugoslavia. Silviu, one of my best friends and teammates from Victoria and at the last moment from Brasov, defected from Romania across the border into Yugoslavia. He was one of the two teammates who escorted me to the train station in Bucharest for my departure on the 4th of September 1981. Now he was in a Yugoslavian jail awaiting their decision: should he be sent back to Romania or let go to a destination of his choice. As I learned later, the Yugoslavian police would conduct a search on each detainee via their connections in Romania, and if there were no significant reasons to be sent back, the person would be set free. In fact another friend of ours from Victoria was with him at that time but due to family complications in Romania he was sent back.

Silviu made it to Austin at the end of a pretty rough time spent in a Yugoslavian jail. He bribed some of the personnel in order to speed up his release. Once in Austin he lived with me for a while as we searched for work, and we registered great success in a few volleyball tournaments.

In general I wasn't inclined to be the captain or coach of the teams I played on and I was always happy to have somebody else in that position. However, that season was an exception since all the players on my new team from Austin declined to assume that responsibility. Especially with Silviu on my side, I offered to take charge but only for that season. I did not regret it. We had a great group of talented players and I remember one weekend in particular: against all odds, we won a tournament in San Antonio that was usually for the home team to win. Silviu and I played side by side as in the old days in Romania and we re-enacted our magic one more time. It's easy to imagine the excitement we all felt that Saturday evening. Moreover, the home team which organized the event had prepared for the winners the largest trophy I had ever seen on a volleyball court: it was about four feet tall and very tastefully constructed. In all modesty, I thought I played and I led my team well that day but I didn't think a great deal of it until during the trophy presentation when I was awarded the plaque for "The Most Valuable Player of the Tournament." Indeed, that was an impressive crowning of my volleyball career up to date and I was very grateful to the organizers, whom I knew fairly well, for honoring me with the MVP award. In memory of that unique victory I saved the

With volleyball trophy

distinguished trophy all these years, and today it is one of the highlights of my volleyball memorabilia.

A Life Changer

Within all these engagements on top of my teaching jobs, I couldn't say that the romantic side of my life was going that well. In fact, over all the post-Romania years it appeared challenging to craft solid and lasting relationships the way I envisioned them to be. Perhaps I became overly concerned with my emotional state of mind and I instinctively pushed away superficial attachments as I was firmly convinced that there will come a time for the right development in that direction. My newly established philosophy of life also supported my decisions in this respect and it had helped me end a relationship in Austin that had already ran its course. Under the new circumstances, and hungry for a meaningful and also spiritual connection, I wrote a letter to Soni, my first volleyball coach from Victoria, Romania. In that envelope I included another short letter and I asked him to give it to Valentina, an old friend of mine from Victoria with whom I kept in touch on-and-off over the years. She had been a student of German and English at the University of Cluj while my sister was getting her degree in mathematics there and they became good friends spending significant time together as students. By 1987 she had already graduated and she was now teaching German in Victoria.

As a good friend, Soni did forward the letter, and that was how Valentina and I actually reconnected after a long break in our correspondence. It only took a few letter exchanges to realize how astonishing the evolution we each went through had been. I was completely taken by Valentina's views on life as we were debating existential themes, and she was quick to point out some Romanian philosophers who had published extensively in and outside of Romania. Two names come to mind in Mircea Eliade and Constantin Noica, but there were several other remarkable ones. We found, therefore, very much of a common ground in terms of understanding the meaning of human existence, and I kept sending her several samples of my sources of information in this respect. Of course *Out on a Limb* was one of them and from then on we continued exchanging a variety of thought triggering pearls of wisdom and philosophically we moved gradually much closer together.

But the closeness was so far still at a distance, the huge physical distance between Texas and Romania. However, sentiments and emotions were running high with every sign of life from each other, and that kept us markedly close. There was, therefore, just one way forward: to eventually *be* together. Since her leaving Romania was a virtual impossibility due to the ever-more degrading political and economical reality brought forth by the Communist regime, it was I who could have taken the next step, and I did.

Not long after I became an American citizen I sent in the application for my American passport and I received it shortly. It was another significant day in my life and Silviu made it even more special: when I arrived home the envelope with the passport was hanging on a thread from the ceiling fan in the dining room as if it fell from the sky. We celebrated my new formal identity, and almost instantly the idea of my visiting Romania took over the conversation.

There was a problem, however, and the problem was one of security. Was I feeling secure enough to throw myself back in the hands of the Romanian Securitate who might invoke whatever pretexts to detain me? This newly developed worry came on top of many nightmares I had had for a number of years ever since the time I spent in the refugee camp. In those dreams I was finding myself back in Romania and in spite of my desire to leave again I was not able to. As soon as the feeling of being restrained was overtaking me, I would wake up from my dream testing my immediate surroundings and realizing that in fact it was just a dream. The feeling of safety that would comfort me in those moments could not be described; it was like I had had a sour taste of being in a prison and suddenly I would realize that in fact I was free.

Although during the interview at the I & N office in San Antonio I had signed a form renouncing any other citizenship, I had not done so officially as far as the Romanian government was concerned. Consequently, as I was contemplating a visit to Romania, I decided to renounce my Romanian citizenship via the Romanian embassy in Washington D.C., and I did. I envisioned my trip to Romania to be much safer as an American stripped of any former nationality. At the same time I saw my giving up the Romanian citizenship as a formal protest against Communism, the only reason I would have ever taken that step. Simultaneously, I really hoped this would enhance even more my American status especially in case of an emergency need for help from the American embassy in Bucharest during my stay in Romania.

Shocking Surprise

While all this planning was taking place in Austin, in the summer of 1988 I received a surprise phone call from Valentina. In a well-crafted code she let me know that she was on the verge of defecting from Romania. I was shocked. I didn't know the details and there was no way I could find out over the phone or in writing. The only certainty was that she would try to escape via Hungary from which it was slightly easier to enter into Austria where political refugee camps were still available. At the receiving end of the surprising news I didn't have that much to say so I wished her good luck and I braced myself as I was waiting for any new developments.

Not too long later, the news came. Unfortunately there was no good news. She and the group trying to escape from Romania into Hungary got caught as they were trying to cross the border and were immediately arrested and taken to jail for further investigation. Subsequently she was taken home and because she was the only one from the group who did not possess foreign currency, she did not have to serve time in prison, but she lost her teaching position in Victoria and she received as punishment one year of house confinement. In the meantime she was supposed to work for no pay in a field that required completely new training but she was still in her home town of Victoria close to her family.

Once we reconnected and I learned about all the details of the latest events I was glad she was at peace with the entire situation and we continued our communication either by mail or occasionally by phone. Time was taking us closer to the holiday season as she was slowly slipping into her new working environment and I coming to terms with the reality of an even deeper dimension to our relationship. Her decision to risk it all in order to escape the ever dimmer light of a decent life in Romania reinforced my inner conviction that our destinies were meant to eventually converge. Our on-and-off correspondence over the years and also her love for music that I remembered came as a decisive addition to the culmination of her latest attempt to freedom. The picture was now complete and it convinced me to take the next step in order to bring us together, and I did.

December 31, 1988

The holiday season was in full swing and we were all ready to enter a new year. As planned, I was getting ready to call Valentina on New Year's Eve while I had already crafted in my mind a unique ending of 1988. Moments before I was ready to make the phone call to wish her a happy new year, I filled up two glasses of champagne and I prepared my wording. It was a moment I will never forget. As the phone rang I did my best to stay calm although I felt a great sense of expectation for the imminent conversation. She picked up, and after we exchanged expressions of affection combined with the latest news, I asked her to get ready for an important question. Then I gently said: "Valentina, would you like to be my wife?" There was of course a short moment of silence and I felt that I had to make my presence noticed again so I asked: "So?" The answer came lovingly as if to confirm the certainty of our already often expressed feelings to each other: "Yes! I would love to be your wife!"

In the exaltation of that special moment I immediately suggested a toast and we vowed to enter 1989 with new resolve for happiness and with the determination to eventually be together. After we hung up I continued my celebration deep into the night with Silviu and we made more exciting plans for my newly motivated trip to Romania. It was already 1989 and we had no idea about the significance of that year first from a personal perspective and second considering the wide-spread Eastern European political transformation waiting in the wings.

17

Eight Years Later: 1981 - 1989

In early January 1989 I made sure to announce the new and important event to my parents and my sister. I tentatively scheduled my trip to Romania for that summer and we also contemplated having our wedding during my visit. The plan was to arrive there the first week of July and to return four or five weeks later. My school regimen in Austin allowed just for such a schedule since I planned to teach the first 6 weeks of summer school at ACC while the high school fall semester was supposed to start immediately after the middle of August.

The Big Plan

I spent some time thinking about the trip and I had to give deep consideration to a number of issues. I wasn't exactly making a lot of money even with my two jobs so I had to plan it such that the entire endeavor would be harmoniously optimized, and there was the security question once I would arrive in Romania. Since I had been keeping in touch with Sergio in Latina for all those years I thought it would be great if I could see him also. Consequently I contacted him and I presented my intention. Of course he was very happy for a possible reunion and he was even willing to help me with the second part of my plan.

With this in mind I planned to fly into Italy, spend a few days in Latina with Sergio, rent a car and drive all the way North through Austria and then East through Hungary on my way to Romania. As I was aware of the shortages of gasoline in Romania I asked Sergio to search for a diesel engine car, as diesel fuel was much easier to find than gasoline in Romania. He promised to help and I was very happy to find in him the same reliable friend that I was blessed with during my stay in the Latina refugee camp in 1981-1982.

The rest of the spring semester I focused on preparing for an exciting summer. We did play a few more volleyball tournaments and we traveled around Texas but I was definitely concerned about the financial burden the trip would impose on me. Consequently, I did my best to limit unnecessary expenses before the trip and I started gathering what I intended to take with me to Romania both as personal items and a variety of presents. By 1989 the shortages were very pronounced in Romania not only in terms of food and immediate necessities but also in electronics, recordable VHS videotapes and audio cassettes, coffee, batteries, chewing gum, and even cigarettes (famous brands, such as Kent, were a precious 'trade' item on the black market). Therefore, by June of 1989 I had two huge pieces of luggage almost full of stuff including a number of souvenir T-shirts and my regular clothes along with my volleyball attire. As far as I knew, at that time there was no strict weight limit imposed by airlines so I wasn't really worried about that, but I was limited to only two pieces to check-in. However, it seemed sufficient while I was thinking that if I would get more stuff in Italy I could just load it all up in the car, which I eventually did.

Reunion in Latina, Italy

By the first week of July 1989 I was ready for the big trip. By then Silviu had found a steady job as an electrician which was exactly in his field and he was also well-versed in taking care of the house. At that time I already had two dogs (a German Shepherd and a Golden Retriever) and a number of homing pigeons, so he was left in charge of the entire 'farm.' Knowing him, I knew that everything was in good hands and I was ready to leave without any hesitation. One early morning he took me to the Austin airport, we hugged as we were saying goodbye, he wished me the best of time throughout my trip, and I wished him a great rest of the summer in Austin.

The next day I landed in Rome and of course Sergio was there expecting me. Reconnecting with each other was a little bit on the emotional side since our friendship never faded in spite of the distance or time. I immediately placed on his head the large white cowboy hat I had for him and we laughed at his Texan look. About two hours later I read the highway sign "Latina" and a score of memories ran through my mind. Sergio felt my reaction and told me that the volleyball friends were anxious to see me again. We made plans on the spot for an evening of volleyball fun, but for the time being we had to secure a car for me so that I could depart for Romania 2-3 days later.

That wasn't to be an easy endeavor. We went to several car-rental places in Latina but as soon as we mentioned that I would drive the car to Eastern Europe, especially to Romania, it was like hitting a brick wall. Apparently no insurance company would cover the car for such a trip and the main reason they invoked was fear of theft. Consequently, I grew a little worried about my predicament: there was no way I could get plane tickets to Romania with such a short notice, so I wasn't really able to change my plans. However, Sergio came up with a solution that impressed me to the core of my being. He took me to an old friend of his who owned a used car lot, and he practically bought a car in his name. Then we obtained all the proper documents for me to drive it to Romania, including the European required insurance. It was an older Opel model running on diesel fuel which was exactly what I wanted. The owner inspected the car before we drove off and it seemed to run smoothly. In any case, there were two obvious problems with the car that neither Sergio nor I made a big deal of at that time: the car had been sitting on the lot for quite a while and the tires, although not completely worn out, were very old. I drove the Opel around Latina for a day or two and I had to get used to yet another thing: the transmission was on the back wheels which made controlling the car in certain situations slightly more challenging than with the more traditional front-wheels transmission.

In the meantime we took a 'virtual' tour on the map of Europe and we arrived at the conclusion that driving all the way through Northern Italy, Austria, and then Hungary was a very long proposition. Instead, Sergio suggested another route: cross the Italian peninsula in a few hours, embark with the car on a ferryboat from Pescara, Italy to Split, Yugoslavia, and drive from there through Yugoslavia and Hungary all the way to Romania. At least on the map this route seemed much shorter so we proceeded with it. Sergio's secretary was very instrumental in securing a next day reservation on a boat to Yugoslavia and I was ready for departure.

That evening, with all the excursion plans set, we did have our volleyball mini-reunion and we enjoyed every minute of it. After the game we went out as a group for pizza and drinks and I had the long-awaited opportunity to spend some time with the rest of the group. Of course, the question of the evening was: "So Irineu, how is your life in America, and how is volleyball?". I did my best to describe in details my life in Texas, while I was still 'rejuvenating' my communication skills in Italian. As all my friends were very nice and polite, I received compliments on my conversation ability that seemed to be still alive after all those years. I promised that upon my return from Romania we would get together again, and we parted ways late in the night.

The next morning I said goodbye to Sergio after we loaded up all my stuff for the trip in the car; I filled it up with diesel fuel, and I set myself on the road, a long road to Romania. Since the car was not equipped with a stereo, I had bought myself a small radio-tape-player boom-box that operated on batteries in order to have some entertainment for the trip. That evening I was supposed to embark on the ferry to cross the Adriatic Sea to Yugoslavia overnight so I could continue my drive from Split the next morning.

Across Italy

Not only was diesel fuel less expensive than regular gasoline but diesel cars were supposed to be much more efficient as mileage was concerned. My Opel did very well for a few hours on the Italian highways. After I left Rome behind, the road took me through beautiful countryside with rolling hills covered with fruit trees and grape plantations as you see in classical pictures portraying Italy. Many villages and small towns would line up on both sides of the highway and I was nearing my destination rapidly.

However, a problem arose. Although no warning lights appeared, I noticed the fuel gauge going down much faster than normal. Worried that something had happened with the engine, I pulled off the highway, I opened the hood of the car and I was shocked: the entire engine was soaked in diesel fuel. Not only that, but as I raised the hood now it was literally raining diesel fuel all over the engine dripping from the inside of the hood. I looked at it in disbelief and I said to myself: "If this were gasoline the car would have had exploded long ago!" Not deciphering the cause of the problem, I weighed my options and one thing was for certain: I had to take the car to a mechanic. I looked around and not too far in the distance I saw a small town on the right side of the highway. I closed the hood and I slowly drove into the town, obviously losing more fuel on the way. Soon enough I located an automobile repair facility; I parked, and I shut off the car immediately. The mechanic came promptly and I opened the hood. He was almost as perplexed as I was the first time I saw it, but he instantly understood the problem and explained to me. What had happened was that diesel cars had a double fuel line from the engine to the fuel tank: one line would take the fuel from the tank to the engine, but since there will be unburned fuel left, the second line would return that fuel back to the tank. He said that there was a certain screw that acted as an air-valve for the second fuel line and that screw got loose and was pushed off allowing the diesel fuel to shoot all over the engine. He justified it by saying that apparently the car had been sitting for a long time and some of the rubber hoses virtually disintegrated. In the end all he had to do was to replace the screw, and the problem was solved. He asked for very little money and after I thanked him I filled up again and I was on my way toward my destination.

In spite of this incident I made it on time to the Italian border port at the Adriatic Sea and all went well as I boarded the ferry to Yugoslavia. I spent the entire night on the ferry catching a few hours of sleep in an ordinary passenger seat, and in the morning I arrived in Split, Yugoslavia. I carefully drove off the ferry into town and I asked for directions to Hungary. Since the port of Split had constant contact with Italy, I was able to make myself understood in Italian and soon enough I was on the road again.

Rough Road through Yugoslavia

The sky over Split was cloudy that morning and I was wondering if rain was in store for me as I was facing a long day of driving. Per my communication with my parents in Romania I had to arrive at the Hungarian-Romanian border close to Satu Mare, a mid-size city in the Northwest of Romania, at 8 o'clock the next morning. We had relatives in Satu Mare who were friends with the supervisor of that precise entry checkpoint into Romania, so the idea was that we would meet at the border in order to prevent the usual abuse that incoming visitors would suffer at the hands of the border agents. The story was that cars and luggage were always checked extremely carefully and visitors would have to offer hefty bribes in order to pass through without having some of their possessions confiscated or unjustifiably taxed. In light of this arrangement, therefore, I had to do my best to make it on time, so I planned my drive through Yugoslavia and Hungary accordingly.

The first few hours went very smoothly but early in the afternoon it started to rain. Although the rain was more like a drizzle, at times it did force me to slow down especially driving on winding roads through hills and forests. Even so, having my mind preoccupied with the long-awaited next day's reunion, I didn't slow down enough. As I was taking this unexpected curve to the left, I realized I was going a little too fast so I stepped on the brakes. Even though I didn't really slam the brakes, it was enough to set my car on a slide off the road, over a few yards of wet grass, and into some bushes. The slide was cut short by a young tree which proved strong enough to take the shock. Apparently, my quick braking set in motion a series of factors that led to this outcome: most of the load of the car was in the trunk, the transmission was on the back wheels, the road was wet, and the tires were old enough not to keep the car on the road.

Obviously shaken by the incident, I immediately turned off the engine as I got out of the car and walked around it. Then I was really shocked: a couple of yards beyond the young tree that stopped the slide there was a deep slope going down in a valley. I almost wanted to hug that tree with gratitude: if it had not been there my car would have rolled over into the valley and that would have been an unimaginable catastrophe. I restarted the engine and I tried to move the car in order to get back on the road. However, the car was surrounded by bushes, the young tree was half way under the car, and the ground underneath was wet, so I wasn't able to move it. My only option was to walk back to the road to seek help, and I did.

It was already mid-afternoon and there was hardly any traffic on this road in the middle-of-nowhere. It was a wooded area and I couldn't see far enough to hope for any town or village. I waited, therefore, on the side of the road for a few minutes and unexpected help came. There was this large truck with three people on board going in the same direction as I was, and I waved desperately asking them to stop. They stopped with a squeal and when they came out of the truck I pointed to my car. They understood my precarious situation and also realized I was a foreigner. I tried to communicate in Italian and English but it was difficult to understand each other. However, they knew what to do. They immediately pulled a large chain from inside the truck, backed up their truck to the rear of my car, tied it up and in a few minutes my car was back on the side of the road. Then I realized that the impact with the tree actually bent in the frame between the two doors on the right side of the car, but the doors were still working. I started the car and everything seemed to be back to normal.

I turned around to the three men who were waiting for me to leave, I thanked them, and as a sign of gratitude I gave them a little Italian money I had handy. I took my seat behind the wheel and I slowly steered back on the pavement. I only drove 20 or 30 yards and when I looked up in the rearview mirror I saw the three gentlemen waving their hands desperately in the air signing me to stop. I stopped and I got out of the car while they were all running toward me pointing to a continuous trail of diesel fuel that dripped heavily on the road. I immediately stopped the engine and we all looked under the car to figure out the problem. What had happened was that during my slide off the road the bushes cut off one of the rubber fuel lines that were tightly secured on the bottom of the car (apparently it was the same return line to the fuel tank that I had problems with before leaving Italy).

It was obvious that I could not continue my trip without fixing this problem. Within the language barrier we experienced, one of the men was still able to suggest that I should leave the car there and they will take me to an auto mechanic about 6 miles down the road to search for a solution to my problem. I followed his advice, I took only my wallet and my documents with me, I locked the car and I joined them. In a few minutes we arrived at the mechanic; they explained the problem, and he suggested what to do under the circumstances. We quickly returned to my car with a little metal tube and some wire and one of the men performed the 'surgery': he inserted each end of the tube into the fractured fuel line connecting it back together. Then he used the wire to tighten the rubber fuel line around the tube and asked me to start the engine in order to check for leaks. It all seemed to work well, I thanked them again and I departed one more time, this time successfully.

A Night Through Hungary

The whole incident had set me back quite a lot on my tentative schedule and since it was already early evening I grew worried about my arrival on time at the Romanian border the next morning. The solution was not to take any breaks other than refueling the car. This worked, and in a few hours I crossed the Yugoslavian-Hungarian border and there I obtained a written statement indicating that the scratches on my car along with the bent door frame happened before I entered Hungary. That document was meant to prevent future questioning regarding the incident, which did work.

It was already dark and I had been driving nonstop for several hours. At around mid-night I started to feel really tired and my eyes demanded some well earned sleep. The last two days had not been easy and the little sleep on the ferry was obviously insufficient. Therefore, I decided to stop and take a short nap somewhere on the road. As I was passing through this little town, I spotted a street light; I parked off the road underneath the light fixture; I stopped the car and I dropped the back of my seat to its lowest position so as to resemble an improvised bed. However, I had a problem: what if I fall asleep and not get up on time to make my appointment at the Romanian border? The real problem was that I didn't have any alarm clock or any other way to wake up in an hour as I was planning to do. The only solution was to rely on my internal alarm clock, and before falling asleep, I repeated several times in my mind this request: "I will wake up in one hour." Then I let myself drift into a relaxed state and soon I fell asleep.

To my great surprise I woke up *exactly* one hour later; I looked around; I thanked my invisible alarm clock, I got out of the car; I stretched for a few minutes, and as refreshed as I could have been under the circumstances, I was back on the road. After several more hours of driving, the sunrise in front of me announced that I was getting closer to my morning destination. My map of Hungary showed only about 60 more miles to the Romanian border; the time was just past 6 a.m., and I noticed that within about 40 miles I would pass through the last small Hungarian city before entering Romania. Then a novel idea came to my mind: this city would be my last chance in Hungary to buy some last minute stuff for my trip. I was aware of the stringent shortages of food in Romania compared to Hungary, so thinking of yet another day of driving to my final destination, I planned to buy a variety of packaged meat, salami, and cheese that would not go bad over the rest of my journey.

With this in mind I entered the city and immediately I searched for an open store. I parked in front of a relatively small food market but unfortunately it was not yet open: according to the hours of operation posted in the window I had to wait until 8 a.m. The time was about 7:30 a.m. so I decided to wait, realizing that I would be already about one hour late for my border appointment with our relative. I still considered it worth waiting and as soon as the store opened I rushed in, loaded up a couple of baskets and I was ready to pay. However, that became a problem: I didn't have Hungarian currency and it took a while for them to figure out how much I should pay in U.S. dollars or Italian lire.

Soon enough I was back in the car, anxious to cover the last 15-20 miles to the Romanian border. That was when the anticipation of stepping again on Romanian soil took a hold of me. I was driving, thinking back over the eight years that had passed since my defection. Although I had a pretty decent idea about what to expect, since I had been keeping in touch with my family and with Valentina, I expected Romania to be drastically different, especially to experience it for myself. That proved to be very true!

Entering Romania

I was just a few hundred yards from entering Romania; I had yet to pass the Hungarian exit checkpoint, and my heart was pounding as I really did not know what to expect. After the necessary but brief formalities, the Hungarian border personnel wished me well as I was approaching the Romanian checkpoint. Within 30 or 40 yards, in front of me arose this rudimentary barrier meant to stop all incoming traffic. I respectfully stopped my car a few yards in front of it, awaiting its expected rising. It took only a few seconds and there it went: the greatest symbol of separation of the two countries was suddenly raised up seemingly in oblivion, to state at least for a few moments that, in fact, in the larger scheme of things, we were all one. In my mind, the raising and lowering of the border barrier embodied a clear man-made separation device meant to temporarily guide national destinies toward their chosen resolutions.

As soon as I crossed over into Romania and the barrier went down in my rearview mirror, I had a quick glimpse of freedom being shut off behind me, but the thought of holding an American passport calmed me down so I was able to face the Romanian border agents in a relatively relaxed manner. However, two unpredicted events were just about to unwind. First, I was directed to run my car through this low cleansing water bath that, as I found out later, was supposed to disinfect the tires of my car in order to prevent the 'import' of any bacteria and/or viruses from the 'West.' Second, as soon as I parked the car next to the indicated check-up point, my front right side tire went completely flat. I was perplexed. I asked myself "How come?" and the unspoken answer came right away: "A nail in the cleansing water bath." Since I didn't see anybody else around, I immediately checked the time and I asked the agents what time they had. I then realized that in fact I was two hours late to my scheduled meeting with our relative, due to the time-zone difference between Hungary and Romania that I completely forgot about. Preoccupied with all this, I neglected to ask the agents if anybody was waiting for me at the check-point, so I simply followed their instructions.

In the meantime, they demanded that I unload my luggage on the large benches situated on a covered patio and they proceeded to search the rest of the car. While I opened up my luggage they were roaming around the car like hungry wolves on a prey. Not knowing if our relative was still waiting for me inside, and to ease my way out of the border agents check, I selected a decent bribe for the two men, and they allowed me to reload my car. I then proceeded to replace my flat tire with the spare, when my relative appeared from nowhere; it turned out that he had been waiting in the supervisor's office all along. We shook hands as he welcomed me back to Romania, and in a few short minutes I was following his Dacia (the only Romanian-made car) to his Satu Mare residence.

Within a few minutes we entered the city, and for me, that morning would carve a somber testimony to the reality of 1989 life in Romania. We drove relatively slowly through the morning traffic of the small suburbs mostly populated with horse-driven wagons. Strikingly different from my experience in Hungary, I witnessed a depressing sad scenario of dirty streets, desolate people, and often run-down buildings. It was like an unseen hand had dropped a huge black curtain over the decent image of life in Yugoslavia and Hungary to create a deplorable version of Communism, Romania. I instantly realized that, yes, the descriptions I was provided by my family and Valentina, were in fact very generous. At least so far, the reality on the ground seemed to be much worse and remarkably worse than what I remembered 1981 to be.

With this contemplative image in my mind, the streets of Satu Mare took us to my relative's house. We parked in the street and as we got out of our cars my first remark was that we should find a place to fix my flat tire; I didn't want to continue my long trip home not having a working spare. He assured me that it wasn't a problem to fix it, and he said he had a big surprise for me: "Your parents are here, in my house, waiting for you! They came by train last night." That really blew me away; I didn't expect it, and despite all other difficulties, it made my day. I couldn't wait to walk in the house to see them; yes, my mother had visited me three years earlier but I had not seen my father in eight years.

Our relative guided me into the living room where my parents were waiting patiently in the company of his wife. The reunion was sweet. We embraced, then we looked at each other, then we embraced again. We sat down around the table and shared long-awaited impressions especially on my trip since I left Austin, culminating of course with my driving adventure. Our host had prepared a nice welcoming breakfast and as soon as we finished eating I requested a quiet place to rest for a little bit. We were planning to drive all the way home, which was yet another full day on the road. I took a short nap, then they made a strong cup of coffee and we were ready to take off.

The Way Home

On our way out of Satu Mare we had to stop at a garage to have the tire fixed which didn't take too long, and around noon we were on the road to Ucea de Jos. In spite of having gotten very little sleep for the last two days, I seemed to handle the driving pretty well. Of course having my parents with me in the car was a big help and a natural energizer. The subjects of conversation were geared toward the latest events in Romania in order to bring me up to speed by the time we made it home. My sister and her family with two small children had just moved from Northern Romania into my parents' home, so now the household was back to six people under one roof which reminded me of my childhood. On the political arena there was no real hope for change and consequently the standard of living was lower than in most other Eastern Bloc countries. In order to pay the national debt, the government exported virtually everything the country produced. Ceausescu's cult of personality was at its highest. The daily television program consisted of about two and a half hours, from 8 p.m. until about 10:30 p.m., and it was almost completely dedicated to the latest on Ceausescu's 'accomplishments,' meetings, and international visits. There were frequently scheduled breaks in the electricity service in order to save energy, and there was a massive shortage of gasoline, not to speak of other basic necessities. Several foods had been rationed and consequently the lines in and outside the stores were endless. Despite this reality, it seemed that there was no real hope for any kind of organized protest and I was completely familiar with the risks of partaking in such movements. Most people seemed to manage shortages and the frustration by coming up with inventive solutions and/or bribing their way out of misery. As always, the villages did better food wise, compared to the large cities, since they were not exclusively dependent on the market. I asked how our family dealt with the persistent crisis, and, not to sound too pessimistic, my parents seemed to paint the picture of a decent life in the small village of Ucea de Jos.

About halfway through our drive home I had to face once again a car problem. I noticed the gauge showing a faster than usual decrease in fuel level and I immediately suspected a re-occurrence of the problem I had in Italy. I pulled off the road, I stopped the engine, and I expressed my suspicion to my parents. I opened the hood and yes, the little screw installed by the Italian mechanic was nowhere to be found. The loss of fuel was less drastic than in Italy since I stopped quickly but I still had to solve the problem at least temporarily. We were on the road, far from any populated area so I had to come up with something that would work. Then I remembered the MacGyver series I used to enjoy watching in the U.S., where the hero would improvise in extreme situations simple tools or even machinery to solve complex problems. So with a smile on my face I silently thanked 'MacGyver' and I looked for a pen I knew I had somewhere in the car. I took the ink reservoir out; I trimmed the pen to the proper length; I filled it up with chewing gum and I pressed it over the little tube that had lost the screw: it fit perfectly and it stopped the loss of fuel. The gum fixed it in place and I was hopeful it would work. It did.

We continued our memorable trip home on less than decent roads and the night did not wait long. It was already 9 or 10 p.m. and the shortage of electricity in the country had dropped the roads in a pitch-black tunnel illuminated only by my car's headlights. Although there was hardly any traffic, I had to slow down drastically to stay in my lane especially due to lack of the directing white lines that usually mark the roads. It was a challenge. Tired, with the headlights covered by dust after two days of almost nonstop travel, I had a hard time keeping the car on the right side of the road. However, with lots of extra precaution we made it to Ucea. As we entered the village, there were no street lights working but we were home. I stopped the car in front of the familiar metal gate and we already heard signs of life from the inside. My sister, her husband, and their two small children had been waiting, anticipating the unique reunion.

It was about 11:30 p.m. when I pulled the car into the front yard and they closed the gate behind me. It was an emotional embrace: I had not seen my sister in 8 years and I was really impressed by her family. That was my first time meeting her husband and kids and all seemed like a well-balanced household of three generations living together. Of course there was a festive table prepared, and within a few minutes we were all sitting around it enjoying the moment with some food and a glass of wine. Since my parents and I were spent after the long day on the road and the kids needed to go to bed, we shortened the party and welcomed a good night rest, promising to continue the celebration the next day.

Valentina

The next morning I slept in, catching up on my rest, so I had a late breakfast. My sister and her husband were both teachers enjoying the long summer break, which made it easy for all of us to relax and savor that beautiful day of July together. Cristian and Irineu, my sister's kids, were playing with the little toy cars they received from 'across the ocean' and the rest of us had a great time socializing. As much as I enjoyed the late morning atmosphere, I couldn't wait to see Valentina. So, early in the afternoon I asked my sister to accompany me in search of her.

As a surprise, we first drove to Vistea de Sus, her parents' village, presuming she would be there, but she wasn't. We were told that not long before our arrival she had left by bicycle back to Victoria so we could most likely find her at her apartment. Ligia, my sister, guided me straight to the apartment and my heart started racing. We climbed up the stairs and rang the bell. A few seconds later the door opened and, crowning the moment, we ran into each other's arms under the compassionate watch of my sister. It was real. After all the letters and the phone calls from Texas, this time all we had imagined was actually happening. I saw in her eyes the shiny light of happiness that instantly confirmed all my expectations: we felt deeply for each other and there was absolutely nothing to stand in the way of our life together. It took a few seconds of spontaneous contemplation through tears of joy, and, with her hands in mine I said: "It is you. It is really you!" The revelation of 31st of December 1988, "Yes, I would love to be your wife," came back vividly in my mind. I was finally holding dearly in my arms my fiancé and that was all I wanted for the moment.

We spent the next few days planning the rest of my stay in Romania. I was introduced to her mother and her step-father (Valentina's father had passed away about 11 years earlier), and we visited places mostly around Victoria. She was still on house arrest so she had to periodically check in with the Victoria police department, and any time she wanted to leave town she had to secure a written permission from them. We were very aware that driving a car with Italian license plates attracted more attention than we wanted, especially as far as the police were concerned. Moreover, it was well-known that police would trace any socializing between Romanians and foreigners (especially Westerners). In this respect any family that would host foreigners had to report such contacts immediately. Even my parents in Ucea had to comply with this requirement since I was living in their home.

Aware of this situation I did my best to prevent unnecessary hardship on anybody. I knew Valentina's sister and her husband years before 1981 and I had just met their two young boys, Paul and Valentin. They all received me with open arms and I didn't want to bring any negative political cloud over their careers – they were both engineers with well-established places of employment. We would get together mostly in Vistea which was about 3 miles East of Victoria and still very close to the mountains. Their residence provided a more secluded place to spend time with the family. In fact Valentina's brother-in-law even helped me fix yet another problem with my car: the rusted exhaust pipe needed repair, so he took it to a near-by mechanic. It all had to work well since we had a lot more driving in store for my elder Opel.

Occasionally we would drive to Fagaras which was the closest city that offered one of the famous 'Shops,' the small government stores where one could pay only in foreign currency (mostly U.S. dollars or German marks). In spite of the heavy shortages in the country, these 'shops' were small islands offering a glimpse of the West. We would get items such as good coffee and spirits that could not be found in the regular stores. I remember one day in Fagaras when we had just finished shopping at the 'Shop' and we were returning to the car. Suddenly we noticed a large and noisy crowd in front of a small store. As the shortages were very pronounced, people would become border-line hysterical when certain items would be available. There was no orderly waiting line this time. There was just a huge mob wanting to get their hands on whatever they were selling, regardless. Out of curiosity, Valentina and I approached the group but we would never find out what people were competing for. As soon as we got close enough to touch the next person, one older lady jumped up in anger and screamed at Valentina: "Watch out lady, you will break my eggs!" Apparently she was holding a bag of eggs that she purchased earlier from another store most likely at the end of a similar experience, when inadvertently Valentina lightly touched her bag. Realizing how volatile the situation was, we gave up, returned to the car, and drove straight home.

We related the story to the rest of the family and it became a point of reference in many debates over the economical state of the country. In the meantime we had started to make plans for our wedding and, since we were contemplating a small wedding party within the family, the market was raising some questions regarding the availability of items we would need; the 'shops' would partially come to the rescue.

Trip to Bucharest and the Black Sea

In order for a Romanian citizen to marry a foreigner the policy in place required the couple to file a petition that was eventually submitted for the approval of Ceausescu's government in Bucharest. For that we had to travel to the capital, complete all the paper work, forward it to the proper office, and then wait for a response. Since we had no other option we made plans for a trip to Bucharest. Of course, first Valentina had to secure an official permission from the

Victoria police since we would be out of town for a few days, and she did.

The drive to the capital was about four hours, so we thought that we should arrive there in the evening and take care of the paper work the next morning. However, we needed a place to stay overnight. For that I appealed to the mother of a Romanian friend of mine from Austin, who lived in Bucharest. I called her ahead of time and she was more than happy to have us stay in her apartment.

The trip from Victoria to Bucharest went well and one late evening we arrived at her place. Parking became a problem since my car had Italian license plates. She was a little worried about finding a safe parking spot but in the end we parked on the street, further down from her apartment, under a street light. She was very nice and hospitable and promised to be our guide the next day since neither Valentina nor I was familiar with the big city.

The next morning all three of us went to the Department of State's office for marriage licenses and our friend was very efficient as we were facing long lines of people with a diverse range of problems. We filled out all the required forms and we handed them to the proper clerk. She took a long look at the file, checked to make sure everything was in order, and she told us that we will receive notice on the final decision. Then I anxiously asked how long she thought it would take, to which she responded: "For a case like this, it will take about a year and a half since the approval must be signed by Comrade President Ceausescu." We were perplexed: a year and a half? That was a long wait ahead of us, but again, we had no other option. We knew it wasn't her decision, so we thanked her, we said goodbye and left the building in total disappointment.

Since from Bucharest to the Black Sea beach was just about a 4-hour drive, we had made plans to spend a couple of days in Constanta, the largest Romanian city and port at the Black Sea. Moreover, we had contacted some friends of Valentina's family who lived and worked there and everything was set for us to spend a little time with them while enjoying the beach. Later that evening we made it to

Constanta and while searching for their apartment, I spotted an auto-service shop and I thought it would be a good idea to have them look at my MacGyver 'masterpiece' improvisation. They did and had fun with it, but in the meantime they fixed the problem for good. I paid while I thanked them and soon enough we made it to the apartment where we were received very nicely. I was the new face in the crowd but they made me feel at home. However, a big concern arose. When they found out that I was driving a car from Italy, they suddenly panicked. One of the members of the family was employed by the Port of Constanta which was an entry-exit gate of Romania and therefore, he was under close scrutiny by the Communist government. Consequently, they asked me to park the car far away from their apartment building so hopefully nobody would notice that they were hosting a foreigner. They explained that this way there was no need to report our presence to authorities. Of course, as I understood their concern, I did my best to find a parking spot a few blocks away from their place and we spent the rest of the evening socializing. It was great to know them and we quickly identified many common philosophical views of the world as I hinted at the down to earth Western ideas and my metaphysical understanding of life.

Valentina and I spent a couple of beautiful days at the beach visiting places we knew from our vacations as college students and soon enough we were back on the road to Victoria. At home there was great anticipation regarding our marriage license, but with the news on the table we all had to face the political reality and its implications, so we rolled with the situation as it came.

However, we wanted to do a little more than just wait a year and a half. The idea came: why don't we get married under the Christian Orthodox religious tradition first, since we were all together, and then wait for the civil approval from Bucharest as long as necessary. This came as a great idea but there was a problem: the tradition required the religious ceremony to follow not precede the civil union. Under the unique circumstances, my father did a little research and arrived at a conclusion that it can actually be done without breaking any laws. So we planned the great event for a special day, the 15th of August which was a major religious holiday and my parents' wedding anniversary also. In the meantime Valentina and I continued enjoying our time together and took a few more short trips around the region among which we included a quick visit to Seica Mica. It was fascinating to relive childhood memories of my many vacations at my grandparents' house, as they rolled back seemingly untouched.

Visit to Medias

One other memorable trip was to Medias, to see my cousin Marinela, her parents, and my other aunt on my mother's side, Pusa. Ever since I was a child I enjoyed our reunions in Medias which was a medieval city in the Tarnave wine country, rich with hundreds of years of history. Marinela, who I couldn't wait to see, was a Latin language

The last of my homing pigeons in Romania, Medias, 1989

teacher recently divorced who likewise couldn't wait to see me after eight years.

We had a great visit but at one point she pulled me aside and in strict confidence she shocked me with unexpected news. Some months earlier she applied to the Romanian government for a visa to visit West Germany at the request of some German friends within a religious affiliation. Amazingly, she did receive the visa along with the passport and she was planning the trip to Munich. However, under her unique personal circumstances, she was basically committed to leaving the country for good: to defect. When I heard that, I was, of course, surprised but as her cousin who had done it himself eight years earlier, I understood her motives perfectly. She expressed interest in coming to the U.S. but that would be a long road ahead; first she would have to find shelter in one of the Western European countries and then we would make further plans. Instinctively I was thinking of Italy, with the old pictures of the refugee camp in mind but she had a visa for West Germany so technically she would have to find some accommodation there.

However, her friends in Germany would not even consider her defecting from Romania under their umbrella, so we had to think of another avenue. She asked me when I had planned to drive back to Italy and we found out that our tentative dates for exiting Romania were pretty close to each other. Moreover, her best exit point coincided with mine since we both planned to appeal to our relatives from Satu Mare to facilitate our encounter with the exit border agents. Our plan was made: she would enter the checkpoint on foot and I, as a gentleman, out of the blue would offer her a ride into Hungary toward her destination, West Germany. Therefore, she would take a train to Satu Mare, spend the night with our relatives, and we will synchronize our arrival at the exit checkpoint for the following morning.

After our short visit to Medias, Marinela and I were supposed to communicate by phone but carefully enough not to reveal our plan. The secrecy of such a plan was as important to her now as it was to me in 1981 and we were just hoping it would work.

The Religious Wedding

The 15th of August was drawing near. Valentina and I had been making plans for our religious wedding and since the civil union had not been performed, we were under obvious pressure to keep it confidential. The only people who knew were our families and we decided to have it performed at Valentina's parents' residence in Vistea de Sus.

That special day did not start well. I had spent the night with Valentina and, as I was driving to Ucea to pick up my parents for the unique event, I had another flat tire. Apparently, the well-aged tires of my Opel were sick and tired of the under-standard Romanian roads and they wanted to remind me of that. I quickly installed the spare but I was anxious to fix the flat as soon as possible, just in case there would be more such surprises in store.

However, I was in Ucea de Jos on a big holiday morning and there was no auto-service around. Then my parents reminded me of a good friend of the family who lived down the street and who had been a professional driver. "He might be able to help" they said, so I immediately drove my car to their gate. He was very happy to help but at that exact moment he was about to leave the house. He and his family had planned to join a huge crowd of people who would attend the special religious mass at the monastery of Sambata, about 15 miles away. He said he would fix the flat the next day, but under my fear of driving the car without a working spare tire I respectfully insisted, and in the end he and his son fixed my flat on the spot. I felt horrible causing them to be late to the monastery mass but they understood and all ended well. I was extremely grateful to them and I expressed it many times since then.

As soon as my father finished his traditional religious service in Ucea we embarked in my Opel and drove to Vistea. My sister Ligia joined us but her husband stayed behind with the kids. When we arrived in Vistea everything was already prepared for the big event. The yard was full of flowers, which was and is Valentina's mother's forte, as was a huge festive table set for the ensuing celebration. Valentina's room was impeccably furnished and decorated to suit the event. We were all very impressed and couldn't stop complementing her entire family for their efforts to make it all so tastefully special.

Valentina's sister and brother in law were obviously instrumental in the entire process and, since the ceremony was set to be a closed family affair, they joyfully agreed to be our best man and woman according to the Romanian tradition. My father, accompanied by my mother, performed the standard Orthodox wedding mass. It was all surreal. We were just a handful of people but it felt like a grandiose event; in fact it was. Everybody participated fully as if the whole world was watching. We documented the entire event with an impressive set of pictures and I couldn't stop marveling at Valentina's beauty: in a tastefully chosen dress and with the unique flower arrangement she lighted up the room as well as my life.

As soon as the congratulations and good wishes came to a close we moved to the table on the porch to celebrate with a much anticipated wedding menu. Despite the shortages, Valentina's family managed to put together a magnificent wedding party. Valentina's sister's kids, Valentin and Paul, were part of the proceedings and, as it turned out, they would be a big and important part of our lives.

The wedding party lasted well into the evening and after I took my parents and my sister home I returned to Vistea to be with my lovely wife and her family. On the way back I had a strong feeling that in fact I was actually going home, my new home to be. They went out of their way to make me part of the family and I deeply felt a genuine attachment between all of us. It was as if we had just been waiting eight years for this fantastic union and it did finally happen. Carmen and Olimpiu, Valentina's sister and brother in law, were not just my sister and brother in law but they had just become our best man and woman. We had so many things in common and so many stories to tell, since we grew up virtually in the same town. That evening would remain an unforgettable time we spent together, the evening that crowned one of the most beautiful days of my life.

Leaving Home

However, as many of our life's avenues lead us to less desired decisions, the time for my return trip to Italy drew near. I had to get ready for a long drive all the way to Latina, but this time I had to take the route through Hungary and Austria to Italy for two reasons. First, from Romania it was almost impossible to book a pass on a ferry to cross the Adriatic Sea from Yugoslavia into Italy. Second, it was the unexpected development involving my cousin Marinela's wish to escape from Romania. She had a visa to West Germany but she didn't really want to stay there.

Overall, I looked at this prospective trip as a new adventure more so thinking of passing through Austria which I had never seen before. In the meantime Marinela and I established the exact date of exit from Romania so we could synchronize our trips to Satu Mare. It seemed to be no problem with our relative from Satu Mare joining us *independently* to the exit checkpoint, so we orchestrated our departures from home such that we would both be there at about the same time one early morning.

I had never expected that saying goodbye to my family and Valentina would be an easy thing, and it wasn't. The inner pain I felt during the last few moments together was excruciating. I did my best to keep it inside but knowing that obviously they all felt the same, cracked me up and in the end I couldn't stop the river of tears that washed my face as I was driving away. I think that most people can testify to the unmistakable pain/knot in the throat and chest that accompany such moments. With great reluctance my being absorbed this pain along with the tears of the next few minutes since I had to focus now on the new task: to drive all the way to Satu Mare and hope for a swift transition at the border.

In the meantime, the one and a half years wait for the Romanian governmental approval of our marriage occupied my mind, but having no actual control over it, I made a conscious effort to put it aside. That was yet another brick in the wall of anti-communist conviction that I had been building ever since I remembered. To help myself cope with the entire situation, my feelings for Valentina came to the rescue. I really felt that after all we had been through, we could wait that long and I had no doubt that she felt the same. After all, we considered ourselves married at least under the religious Romanian tradition and, along with the memories and the wedding pictures this would sustain our resolve to wait it out. Little did we know at that point that things would soon change for the better.

At the Border

Early the next morning, I was slowly pulling into the Romanian exit checkpoint to Hungary when I saw at a distance Marinela. The border agents had just finished checking her luggage, so she was almost ready to cross the border into Hungary but she was on foot and there was no public transportation available from the border to any Hungarian city. It was obvious that at least up to that point no border agent had any idea of me and Marinela being related. This played very well into the plan we had conceived and I was pretty confident that we would not have to give any extra explanations.

Our relative from Satu Mare was once again busy inside as he was visiting with the border checkpoint supervisor. The two border agents inspected my car as they checked my documents and at the end of the required inspection our relative came out to say goodbye. We shook hands and he wished me well, when one of the border agents approached me by saying: "Excuse me sir, but there is this lady who needs transportation to the nearest city in Hungary. Can you offer her a ride?" I answered quickly, almost without hesitation, trying to make a joke: "Of course, if she pays well!"

That was how we both exited Romania. Marinela threw her bag in the car, took the passenger's seat, and we entered the Hungarian checkpoint where, of course, we didn't have any problems: she had a visa for West Germany and I had one for Italy.

On the Way to Italy Via … Munich

As soon as we embraced the much better Hungarian roads even my car seemed to give out a sigh of relief. We were facing a long ride ahead, so Marinela and I had plenty of time to plan our next step. The itinerary we chose would take us through Austria and then … Italy. Marinela had vehemently decided not to return to Romania and at the same time, she did not see any possibility of emigrating from West Germany due to the presumed reluctance of her German friends to assist her in such an endeavor. Consequently, the only way to go forward was for her to join me on my trip back to Italy and hope for a solution there.

However, as soon as we entered Austria we decided to take advantage of her visa to West Germany and visit Munich which was pretty close to the Northern Austrian border. We arrived in Munich late in the evening and we followed the main streets to downtown. It was a nice view of the night life of a German city: there were scores of young people enjoying the cool night with guitar music and ice cream in a large plaza overseen by two impressive cathedrals lighted up by generous reflectors. I parked the car for a few minutes, we had a couple of ice creams, we took in the unique atmosphere, and then we left, decided to make it to Italy the next day.

There was no problem entering back into Austria since we both had transit visas. We drove the night away toward Italy but early in the morning the many hours of driving took their toll on me so we had to stop for a rest. The good thing was that one could find rest stops pretty often along the Austrian highways. We took a well deserved rest and soon after that we entered the mountainous region that marked the transitional territory from Austria to Italy.

It was late in the afternoon and the views were magnificent. The Alps were every bit as grandiose as anybody would describe them to be. Most of the pictures I had seen up to that point would not do them justice. It was a breathtaking beauty: massive mountain chains were guiding the impeccable highway as it was winding its way deep into the heart of such pristine scenery hard to describe in words. It seemed that the wild high peaks marked by their lack of vegetation were the overlords who allowed in their great generosity the human hand to carve this highway as a symbol of connectivity with the other side. The few well-kept houses with shiny red roofs spreading on the side of the mountains were the only testimony to the fact that people did live in this area. There were very few actual clusters of homes to be called villages or towns and this appeared to support the natural beauty all around.

Within this dream-like scenery we were rapidly approaching the Austrian-Italian border. I was aware that Marinela did not have a visa to enter Italy, but I was hoping that with my American passport and my car with Italian license plates we might be able to sneak in. It wasn't to be. As soon as the border agent checked her passport he pointed back toward Austria and advised us to get a visa for Italy at the Italian embassy in Viena.

I had no choice but to turn around and we headed back on the highway thinking of what to do. There was no time to drive all the way back to Viena since I had a limited number of days left until my flight back from Rome to the U.S., so I had to find another solution. Suddenly I noticed the first highway exit sign and it indicated a town with an Italian name. Out of instinct I took that exit and the road guided us in a loopy U-turn under the highway heading back toward Italy. I carefully followed the road and in a few minutes we arrived to a small village where, of course, we had to pass through another checkpoint. As we came within a few yards from the simple red-and-white wooden barrier, I was thinking of how I should approach the border agent, when he showed up from the adjacent building waving to us with a friendly gesture to go on while he raised the barrier. Apparently, the Italian license plates on my car inspired him to assume that we were Italians returning from Austria. I waved back as a sign of gratitude and I drove on, searching for a way to get back on the main highway toward Rome and eventually Latina.

Driving Through Italy to Latina

Under normal circumstances the day and a half drive to Rome would be a great experience. However, our condition was not even close to normal. The lack of sleep and no resting out of the car, made the excursion pretty tough. Since Marinela also had a driving license we did switch places once on the following morning. We were desperately trying to make it to Latina before dark so I wanted to get some rest in the passenger seat. Soon after I woke up I noticed that something was not right with the car. My cousin also felt something different with the steering, so I immediately asked her to pull the car off the road. It was what I expected: another flat tire. I quickly replaced it with the good spare and we were on the road again, with me driving.

Within a few miles I located a small town off the highway and I took that exit. It didn't take us long to find an auto mechanic, and for a small amount of money he replaced the useless tire with a used one that was in good condition. Under the 'protection' of having a good spare tire again, we continued the drive to Rome.

Since I had left the little boom box in Romania, we didn't even have music or a radio to listen to so we did our best to keep us awake by engaging in conversation while making plans for the near future. The idea was that, as soon as the next morning, Marinela would turn herself in at the refugee camp and start the process of emigration to the U.S. Of course I would be her sponsor so we didn't envision any problems with the ensuing process. However, we were in for a surprise.

That evening we did make it to Latina and, although surprised that I wasn't alone, Sergio received us with open arms. My cousin and I were exhausted but we still spent some time with Sergio as we made plans for the next few days. After all, I only had a couple of days until my flight back to Texas, and in the meantime we had to settle Marinela in her emigration procedure.

However, the next morning offered us a shocking surprise. As we entered the old refugee camp of Latina, we received notice that in fact they did not accept refugees anymore. At that point in time they were only providing assistance to refugees already in the system but who had been placed there via a refugee office in Rome. Under a closer scrutiny I realized that I probably should have investigated the status of the refugee camp upon my arrival from Texas, but at that time I was just passively drawn to the place so I only passed by briefly, in the memory of my stay there eight years earlier. Moreover, as I was preparing my trip from Latina to Romania, I had absolutely no idea about my cousin's plans to defect; had I known that, it would have been a different story.

The solution came once again from Sergio: "We should go to Rome to seek approval for your cousin's emigration request" he said promptly. He drove us quickly to Rome, we filed the proper documents, and we were told that due to the high volume of such cases it will take a while to schedule Marinela's interview, but they promised to contact us as soon as they had a date. That was the best we could have done at that point so we returned to Latina to prepare my imminent departure to Texas.

A couple of days later Sergio and I took another trip to Rome, this time to the Rome International Airport. We had a nice conversation all the way there as I was expressing my sincere gratitude for everything he had done to help me with the entire trip. Not only had I left him with a car in need of repair, but he also promised to see that my cousin would advance her case and eventually join me in Texas. I had always appreciated his compassion and generosity, but this was more than I could have expected even from him, my best friend (upon my return to Texas, I did send him some money to offset part of the cost, but despite all our efforts, Marinela would remain in Italy for many years to come). Sergio and I made it on time to the airport terminal; we embraced each other and said so long as I was heading toward my gate. I had always expressed to him my burning wish for his visit to Texas and that time, once again, it was left to the realm of a distant possibility; although it has not happened yet, I am still hopeful, since I am certain that our friendship will never die.

Back to Austin, Texas

The long flight over the Atlantic offered me the time to rest and to play back the entire film of memories from my wonderful summer vacation. It all seemed orderly, like an unseen hand was at work. Even the unexpected and often undesired events seemed to fit in perfectly. I was at 30,000 feet above Earth and I couldn't stop marveling at the beauty of the entire adventure called life. Seeing things from that perspective brought me an apparent calm and a deeper understanding of our existence. Of course, unconsciously I was relying on my years of reading about and exploring the meaning of our life on Earth and names such as Erich von Daniken, Einstein, and Shirley MacLaine came to my mind as I was wondering what they would say about the last month's sequence of events I went through. In the back of my mind I already knew the answer. I could even envision it in a multiple voice in unison: "You see? It is all in order!"

Soon enough, though, a real voice said just about the same. It was Silviu waiting for me at the Austin airport. I couldn't wait to share with him my experiences and neither could he. On the way home and long after, we ran through most of the stories that had colored my vacation so beautifully. It was good to have a friend who was genuinely interested to listen and express his opinion about the twists and turns of my summer adventure. After all, he understood it all perfectly and was able to relate to it since he himself came to the U.S. from that same environment.

However, there was one problem that we both agreed to do something about: one and a half years of waiting for Valentina and I to receive the civil marriage license approved by the Romanian Communist regime was way too long. Silviu and I explored every avenue we thought of in order to come up with a solution but nothing seemed to hold water. In the end the 'solution' appeared from nowhere as soon as the 1989 fall semester started.

Appeal to the United States Government

The first day of school at Kirby Hall was full of expectations. Obviously all my colleagues were curious about my vacation in Romania so I was happy to share brief thoughts about it. But one in particular, Julio, who had been teaching Spanish there since 1984, was especially interested to hear more details. Julio and I had become good friends immediately after my arrival at Kirby Hall in 1985 and we always have found ourselves on the same page not only on academic issues but also on administrative concerns. Under the directives of Mrs. Rase, for several years he assumed the Principal responsibilities at the school, so I was widely aware of many of the positives and the negatives our school was facing as it tried to provide the best and affordable private K-12 education in Austin.

So one day, after I expressed once again my frustration regarding the long wait for a marriage license under the Communist rule of Romania, Julio suggested that I should appeal to the American government for assistance. That took me by surprise and I responded: "Wow! That sounds great, but how do I go about it?" Then we came up with a plan: we were supposed to meet one evening at his house and brainstorm to put together a letter of explanation addressed directly to President Bush. Of course, the letter would ask for assistance in speeding up the slow process of granting approval that so well characterized the Communist regime of Romania. As we parted ways that day he said: "I am sure my wife can also help us craft a nice letter, so let's do it!"

The evening we agreed on came quickly and I was approaching Julio's house with renewed hope that the one and a half years wait would be shorter. We sat down for a couple of hours and, with a pen on a note pad, the three of us finalized our project. The result was a concise letter that explained the situation and also asked respectfully for assistance. The next day I typed up the letter and I mailed it to the State Department in Washington D.C.

Not too long after, my ardent anticipation for a response was nicely met. I received an official statement that my request had been forwarded to the proper office which will send a copy to the U.S. embassy in Bucharest, Romania. Although the general flavor of the response was relatively positive, it did indicate that as a norm, even the U.S. embassy could not really interfere in the decision making of the government of the host country. In spite of this, I was content to have done whatever I could to help our cause and I also communicated that to Valentina.

A few weeks later, one of my phone calls to Victoria, Romania would find Valentina in more than a happy mood. She held back the news but only for a short while. With great excitement she told me that she had just completed the one year of home arrest to which she was sentenced after her failed attempt to defect from Romania a year earlier. Now she was free although she would never be able to continue her teaching career, so she was looking for another job. That was very good news in the mid-Fall of 1989, and more extraordinary good news was on its way.

Eastern European Communism Collapses

Although after the Second World War the Communist dictatorships of Eastern Europe developed according to the specific conditions in each country, they had one essential common trend: they oppressed their populations up to the point of no tolerance. That point became imminent starting with the summer of 1989 and materialized fully during that Fall. Starting with Poland and spreading to Hungary, East-Germany, Bulgaria, and Czechoslovakia, the liberation movement from Communism is best remembered as the 'Fall of the Berlin Wall.' While in West Berlin, facing the division wall, the U.S. president Ronald Reagan said it best: "Mr. Gorbachev, tear down this wall!" The Fall of 1989 brought that powerful invitation to fruition and the general consensus is that Gorbachev's new policies in the old U.S.S.R. were instrumental.

We, as Romanians who had lived for many years under the Communist regime of Ceausescu, were watching the news from Texas, but could not bring ourselves to believe that it would also happen in Romania. Silviu and I had many evening discussions on this theme and we were just hoping that Romania would not remain the only sad island of political oppression in Europe. Both of our schedules were pretty demanding. Between his long hours at work and my two teaching positions, we basically had only late evenings and weekends to socialize and occasionally to play volleyball.

In the meantime we were keeping in close contact with our families in Romania but, of course, that wasn't a safe source of political information since we didn't want to cause them harm at the hands of the Securitate. Virtually all international phone calls were recorded; wiretapping had been a powerful instrument in the hands of Securitate ever since telephones became a popular means of communication. Even my conversations with Valentina dealt mostly with general subjects remote from the political arena. For the time being, and especially with no news from the U.S. embassy in Romania, we were still contemplating waiting at least one more year for the release of our marriage license.

However, one early morning of December 1989 shattered our entire skepticism. It was about 5 a.m. when the telephone rang. Silviu picked up and almost as quickly as he answered it he came running to me, waking me up with the news: "Ceausescu is down!" In fact a friend of Silviu's who lived in Canada happened to watch the news and he was anxious to be the first to let us know. I jumped out of bed and I immediately turned on the television set. The latest CNN news confirmed the telephone call. From that moment on, as long as we were at home, the news channels were on non-stop. We followed the developments in Romania hour by hour and we were sad to know that out of all the Eastern Bloc countries only the Romanian revolution was the violent one. It seemed that the Securitate had a strong hold for a while, hence some hope to restore the totalitarian Romanian brand of Communism, but as soon as the military sided with the people's revolution, it was just a matter of days until the entire regime would collapse.

The Romanian Revolution

For weeks, a Calvinist pastor from Timisoara, Laszlo Tokes, had been summoned to leave his parish for a marginal one due to his open opposition to Ceausescu's regime. Under this threat, people in the city rose in protest to protect him. On the 16th of December the protests escalated and masses of people demonstrated in the streets of Timisoara burning cars and braking windows. That evening, larger crowds gathered shouting anti-Ceausescu slogans as they were approaching the Communist Party headquarters. The army and the Securitate brought armored cars and tanks but they did not start shooting. In the meantime Securitate arrested Tokes and his wife and kept them isolated.

On the 17th of December Ceausescu received reassurance that the army and Securitate will start shooting if need be, so he left on an official visit to Iran. He never gave credit to the anti-Communist movements in the rest of the Eastern Bloc countries, attributing the riots from Timisoara to some isolated foreign spies and agents–he had been fed this kind of information all along. Meanwhile in Timisoara, at about 6 p.m., the Securitate started shooting as the demonstrators were raising barricades. Numbers later published indicated that there were 97 dead and 210 injured.

Between the 18th and the 20th of December more people were shot and several children seeking shelter on the stairs of a cathedral died. At the same time more riots had started in other cities such as Cluj and Iasi. On the 20th of December, in front of 150,000 demonstrators, Timisoara was declared the first free city of Romania. The army refused to shoot, even at Ceausescu's direct order! He had just returned from Iran. Moreover, the movement spread to other parts of the country. Riots started in Arad, Sibiu, and Brasov and they were all marked by casualties.

On the 21st of December Ceausescu ordered a rally in Bucharest to support his cause. More than 100,000 people were bused in, but it proved to backfire. Soon after he started his speech, the crowd in the back started shouting: "Timisoara! Timisoara!" Banners came down quickly and he lost his grip.

For the first time people detected a powerless and disoriented Ceausescu as he and his entourage retreated inside the Central Committee building. After a second failed appearance on the balcony, Ceausescu, his wife, and a few confidants climbed on the top of the building and embarked on an overloaded helicopter heading to a selected military base. Upon an emergency landing and the cooperation of the driver of a car they hijacked, the small group was turned in and detained by revolutionary representatives.

Although the army had already sided with the revolution, the Securitate still believed in a return of Ceausescu so they kept fighting all around the country. The city of Sibiu witnessed some of the most deadly opposition. Even today some of the buildings stubbornly preserve bullet holes in their walls to testify to the atrocities of December 1989.

By the 24th of December a transitional government was formed and it was called the National Salvation Front. However, since it was quickly made up of former Communist dissidents, writers, and poets, they had been eventually accused of hijacking the Revolution. Nevertheless, two years later they won a democratic election and held power until 1996.

On the 25th of December 1989, the first Christmas in a free Romania since the end of the Second World War, Nicolae and Elena Ceausescu were tried by a court of the National Salvation Front. In less than an hour they were found guilty of crimes against the country and the Romanian people, and were sentenced to death. A firing squad executed the sentence immediately, in a cloud of controversy. However, the news of the death of the dictators diminished considerably the violent efforts of the Securitate to regain control. The entire country was engulfed in euphoria and jubilation as a new era had arrived.

But the celebration of freedom was relatively short lived. Soon enough people realized that the new government would still be made up of totalitarian ex-communists who had basically only changed nomenclature; as the old Romanian saying goes: "The wolf only changes fur but not habits." Consequently, the economic progress registered in the following years was far behind that of other former Eastern Bloc countries, and that trend continues even today. On this theme I remember my father's comment when I told him over the phone that some people say that now Romania will catch up with the West within five or ten years. Here was his answer: "That's a fairy-tale. It will take us generations to get out of the mud of Communism." This far he has been right. Although the quality of life in Romania is improving via the freedom gained after the revolution, true progress is undermined by high levels of waste and corruption within the elected government.

End of an Era and its Implications

It was obvious that the law of the land had to change as an outcome of the revolution. With an estimated 1,100 dead, most of which died during the provoked chaos ensued presumably caused by Securitate still fighting for their reign *after* Ceausescu had been ousted from power, the interim government had to make drastic changes so they could legitimize their position. Consequently, the freedom to travel abroad was quickly institutionalized, among other civil rights that people begun to exercise.

In our almost daily phone conversations, Valentina would keep me posted on the latest, so as soon as I learned about the new right of Romanians to request passports for international travel, I collected the proper information regarding the next step we needed to take to be together. The step was clear: I had to file a "fiancé petition" at the American embassy in Bucharest. Valentina would have an interview there in order to confirm the legitimacy of the entire process and then she would receive a visa for the U.S. To avoid any delay I quickly completed the required forms and sent them over.

However, as probably expected, the process was not as smooth at the other end. Valentina had to get her Romanian passport before her interview at the American embassy. It was January 1990, the first month of true freedom for Romanians in 45 years, so it was expected that scores of people would storm the passport offices in order to make their long-term dreams realized. This was quickly confirmed when Valentina and her brother-in-law, Olimpiu, went to the passport office in Brasov. Taken by the prospective of traveling abroad, the entire building was basically flooded by people. Not only that, but civility was almost non-existent since every person wanted their passports *immediately*. She was fortunate to have Olimpiu by her side; he was able to find his way through the crowd, which wasn't an easy physical fit.

With the passport in hand Valentina was ready now for a trip to the American embassy in Bucharest to continue the process. It all went well there also and we started making plans for her coming to the U.S. At last the one and a half years of waiting for the marriage license was about to turn into just a few months.

Hole in the flag, Berlin

18

Raising a Family

On the 17th of March, 1990 I picked up Valentina from the Houston international airport. She was at the end of an exhausting long flight and we were facing a three-hour drive to Austin. These were three long-awaited hours of conversation and joy to be together, this time on American soil. While we were recounting the latest in our lives and the ousting of Ceausescu, we also touched on plans for our near future.

Kirby Hall School Opened its Arms

As soon as I expressed my obvious joy to my friends and colleagues at Kirby Hall, and since she knew about our wedding plans, Mrs. Rase, the Director of the school, suggested without hesitation: "Why don't you have your wedding here at the school? The library, in front of the fireplace, can be a nice setup for the ceremony." I was amazed. What a great idea. Of course Valentina and I said yes, and we went on with the planning. Mrs. Rase and a few Kirby Hall teachers took care of most of the preparations. That really helped, since we were not really familiar with wedding procedures in Texas. In retrospect, we probably needed to be more involved and appreciative of the efforts behind the scenes but we were so moved and overwhelmed by the entire process that we just went with the flow.

The day was the 5th of April (my mother's birthday) and the ceremony was a sensitive one for both of us. Beside the teachers from Kirby Hall we invited some Romanian friends, and from Austin Community College, my other place of employment, only my supervisor participated. We said our vows in front of the nicely decorated fireplace, followed by a small reception in the library, and we continued with a reception at one of the teacher's home which was another unexpected act of kindness that marked our special event. In the end we also had a reception at our house mostly with the Romanian friends, and this time it lasted deep into the night. We were so grateful to all who made that day so unique and a special "thank you" goes to those who came up with the idea of tying up a bunch of empty aluminum cans in the back of our car, dangling on the pavement as soon as we drove off. That 'collection' of cans is still stored away at our house in remembrance of that special day.

And the Kirby Hall 'embrace' did not stop there. Valentina was offered a part-time teaching position in German and French, while we were looking into her starting a doctorate program with the University of Texas at Austin. Soon she took her driving license tests and we purchased a second used car. Now she was able to commute more freely to Kirby Hall since her schedule was not really matching mine. Besides, she would start the doctorate program and, Kirby Hall being in the proximity of the university, she would be able to park at the school and walk to the university. This combination was really helpful to us and we were very grateful to Kirby Hall and Mrs. Rase for making it possible.

Financial Crisis

That same year, due to a set of very complex economical factors, Kirby Hall, a private school that sustained itself only on student tuition, suffered a drastic drop in the number of students. Consequently, Mrs. Rase came to all of us full-time teachers with this proposition: under the new circumstances of financial strain the school was not able to pay full-time salaries, so we had to make the choice of accepting pay by the hour (at the part-time rate) or be let go. However, the promise was that as soon as the number of students increased back to the necessary level, we will be restored to our previous status for the following year. Julio, the Spanish teacher, I, and a few others chose to stay and be paid hourly hoping for the situation to improve the following year.

In parallel, since we had to make a financial adjustment of our own, Valentina and I decided to sell the house and look for another one with lower monthly payments. This would also give us a chance to start anew in a house of both our choosing. Soon enough we located a comparable home in the same part of town but at a much better price, hence much lower payments. We signed the paperwork and not too much later we sold the old house at a very small loss.

The moving process went well as far as the contents of the house was concerned since we had great help from our Romanian friends, but it raised some problems when it came down to moving my homing pigeons – with the two dogs we had there was obviously no problem. Silviu and his family were already living in their own house so they helped as much as they could, but with respect to the birds, there were sensitive issues. Homing pigeons live and die by their strong instinct of returning home, to the place of their first few flights that is. So to move my 30 pigeons from their old house to the new was a challenge. Silviu and I worked hard to first move the old 8-by-8 pigeon coup to the new house and then we moved the birds. However, from that day on I had to keep them locked up since otherwise they would have gone to the old place. At that point I applied an old trick hoping to still settle in the new house as many old birds as possible even if I had to lose some – the thought of keeping them locked up for the rest of their lives was not appealing to me. I waited for them to raise a generation of young chicks which I separated in one half of the coup, and after the young ones flew out and settled in the new house, one day I released the old team. As soon as they regained their freedom, they did fly away, so they did go back to the old house, apparently, but since there was no pigeon coup there anymore and no food, and since the two houses were only about two miles apart, most of them came back to the new house. In their innate wisdom apparently they understood that in order to survive they were better off adjusting to the new home, and they did very well at that.

With all of this having been accomplished within a few months, we examined the prospects of the following year. We were content in the new house (especially with the much lower monthly payments) and we really liked our neighbors. In fact we received much needed help from them when we had to leave town: we always knew that the house and our little 'farm' in the backyard were in good hands. In the meantime we were expecting good news regarding the financial status of Kirby Hall. Indeed, that came toward the end of the school year. The estimated student enrollment for the following season looked very promising and Mrs. Rase announced a return to the previous full-time faculty status for many of us and we were very grateful and relieved. Julio and I were proud of the way Mrs. Rase handled the situation. We also remembered the 'complot' of a few years earlier when a group of teachers led by an administrator attempted to take Kirby Hall on an undesirable path. We and a number of other teachers sided with Mrs. Rase who was totally opposed, and we managed to keep the school on the path of academic excellence in service to the larger Austin community. I am convinced that Mrs. Rase appreciated our commitment to the school, and over time we remained very good friends.

The New Romania

In the meantime, on the other side of the Atlantic, in Romania, free enterprise was now a viable option and much of the state-owned land and factories had been offered for sale by the government at auctions all around the country. Moreover, the private agricultural land once nationalized by the Communist Party (like the land my grandfather owned before 1962) was now released back to the rightful owners. The crucial problem though, was that by 1990 most of the people who used to work that land were now much too old to keep working or they were already dead. Even worse, the new government passed a law that would allow the state representatives to fine those land owners who were not working their land. However, most people found ways around this problem by leasing their land to those who could work it. That was how many families around the country found a new line of profitable business by working large plots of land. In fact my parents also had to lease out their land to avoid governmental fines.

When the holiday season of 1990 drew near we made plans to spend the winter vacation in Romania. Although we were well informed about the changes incurred after the Revolution, we were curious to see them for ourselves. Valentina's sister's family had opened a business immediately after she left Romania and it proved to be a promising endeavor. Therefore, we were all looking forward to being together in Romania for the holidays which would have been my first winter time spent in Romania since 1980.

Consequently, we booked an economical December flight on the Romanian airliner Tarom that connected New York to Bucharest as a routine route. We filled up four suitcases that included many presents for our families in Romania and we arrived to New York to make our connection to Bucharest. At the time of departure we received the shocking news: our flight was delayed due to a strike of the Tarom employees in Bucharest. Since there was no other connection available, we had no choice but to wait in the airport for news from Romania. However, we were told that the strike could last more than 24 hours, so we had to find a place to wait. My old Romanian friend, Gerry from Austin, who had also spent time in the refugee camp in Italy, was now living in New York so I called him from the airport. He was more than happy to take us into his home and be our host while waiting for the flight to Romania. We spent three days together, we had a great time, but the strike in Bucharest did not end there. At that point we decided to return to Austin, so we booked the first flight we could find.

We arrived home on Christmas Eve late in the evening and we were obviously unprepared for the holidays. We rushed to the store and grabbed a few things; in a parking lot I found an abandoned Christmas tree; we went home and decorated the tree, and we managed to have a decent holiday anyway. Beside the inconvenience it caused us (including not refunding the cost of the tickets), that vacation stood out as evidence of the new gained freedom of Romanian employees to declare a strike, which was unheard of in the days of totalitarian communism.

Car Trip through the U.S.

Our life and regimen in Austin really required a dependable means of transportation, so during the spring of 1991 we sold my old car and started payments on a new Toyota Corolla. That summer we planned a vacation trip by car to the famous Niagara Falls. Since this would take us close to Cleveland, Ohio, we contacted our good Romanian friends who lived there and we announced our visit. They were thrilled.

Soon after I finished my first short summer semester at ACC, we set ourselves on the road to Cleveland. We exited Texas through Texarkana and we took a break in Memphis. As avid music lovers, we visited Elvis Presley's estate and I couldn't help but remember the many rock-and-roll stars who died, we say, prematurely due to choices they made during their stardom. Names like Jimmy Hendrix, Janis Joplin, and Jim Morrison came to mind as I mentally ran a quick 'inventory' of my almost 700 vinyl record album collection. Should we feel deprived of more quality entertainment had they lived longer, or should we just treasure what they provided while alive? I think this becomes an issue of understanding and accepting destinies the way they are, including our own, all the while realizing that our choices are decisive. While in Memphis, I was stepping on the ground where one of the most influential rock-music legends lived, and I know that before 1989 this possibility didn't even cross my mind. Yet, it became reality. Was that part of my persistence-driven and choice-driven destiny in the unfolding of significant events in my life?

We stayed overnight in a hotel close to Memphis and continued our drive to Cleveland the next day. That leg of the trip revealed the natural beauty of the U.S. The highway would take us through hundreds of miles of virtual virgin land, where only the highway itself stood proof to the human intervention. The forests of Arkansas and Tennessee were pristine and as we were advancing deeper into the Northern half of the country the climate and the signs of four seasons became gradually more visible. The summer colors were reminding us of those of our native country since we were approaching the invisible mark of the land, namely the 45th parallel which 'passes' through the southern half of Romania and crosses the Great Lakes of the U.S. and Canada.

That evening we arrived to our friends' house in Cleveland and the reunion was magnificent. Many memories engaged us in a long after-dinner chat. Romanian realities from the pre-1989 homeland came alive as we sipped on some red wine, but we also made quick plans to visit Cleveland and eventually Niagara Falls.

The following day was a revealing visit to the downtown Cleveland area including the famous Rock-and-Roll Hall of Fame. It was out of this world for me. I was visiting the most prestigious museum in the world that underlined some of the greatest names and accomplishments in rock-and-roll. Of course I left the museum with the hope that some of the artists I loved who were not yet inducted would eventually be, and the hope is still alive as far as Rush and Deep Purple are concerned.

We said so long to our wonderful hosts and we left Cleveland for Niagara Falls with the plan of returning to Texas via the East coast. I have always been impressed by human marvels ancient or modern but I am also deeply taken by wonders of nature. In this respect Niagara Falls needs no description; one image is plenty, let alone being there. The grandeur of the entire scene followed us as we left the Falls and headed South-East. I was very excited at the possibility to visit Virginia Beach, the home of the greatest American psychic Edgar Cayce. While I was sharing the information I had about him with Valentina, she became interested, so we ultimately found the place. Also called 'the sleeping prophet', Edgar Cayce was active during the first half of the 20th century when he dedicated his life to helping others. He had never requested payment for his readings (only accepting donations) and he left behind about 14,000 mostly accurate and beneficial readings for people from all over the world.

From personal readings on health issues, and the origin of Christianity, to some that concerned the future of the planet, Edgar Cayce covered a wide spectrum of topics of interest. The Cayce family, helped by some of his contemporaries, preserved the readings in printed form as an impressive library within the educational institution they founded called The Atlantic University. To see and touch some of these unique files became a dream of mine ever since I read my first book on the life and achievements of Edgar Cayce and that dream had just become true. We left Virginia Beach with a great sense of accomplishment but we didn't take the road until we experienced a few minutes of sunbathing on the pure and clean white sands overseen by the Atlantic Ocean.

With such nice memories stored away in our minds we drove through some of the Southern states to make it back to Austin. The rest of the trip was definitely marked by the realization that if a human being such as Cayce could perceive outside of ordinary reality, it was most possible that more of us could tune in, into the deeper levels of our existence in order to find answers to some of the ardent questions set forth with respect to the human race. This realization has followed me ever since and has helped guide my thinking to entertain all possibilities.

We made it home refreshed and enriched by the experiences of a wonderful trip and we were ready to start the school year within a new frame of mind. We were prepared to embrace our future with optimism regardless of the circumstances.

Our Family Expands

The early days of January 1992 brought great news for all of us: Valentina became pregnant. Her mother was visiting from Romania so we celebrated the event together. In the meantime we decided to have a natural birth so we contacted a midwife place in Austin, we signed up, and participated in all the required training. It was all very interesting and educational. Valentina's mother, who had been a medical assistant all her life, was also instrumental in our preparations. However, during the summer months she had to return to Romania, and Valentina's sister, Carmen, joined us in Austin to offer her help when the baby would be ready to join the world.

All went well up to the final day when we drove into the midwife's well-equipped location. We followed the instructions the best we could but something slowed down the natural dilation process and the birth was delayed. After many hours of most dedicated effort, the midwife decided to take us to the hospital where we spent almost the entire night in continued labor. Finally, with careful medical assistance, during the early hours of September 14th our healthy boy was born.

That was the greatest moment of my life. Carmen and I accompanied Valentina throughout her efforts of giving birth and we were next to her as our son made his entrance into this world. To watch the doctor and nurses deliver a baby while you are just a few feet away is a life-changing experience. If the baby being born is your own the experience becomes life-defining. David-Sergio opened his eyes in the hospital delivery room under the care of a professional team and I was flabbergasted. It is almost impossible to put in words the depth of the feelings that hijacked my mind in those moments. However, as I was holding Valentina's hand, she was the first to read the emotion that overwhelmed me, and she described perfectly later: "You almost fainted!" Since all went very well, that same evening we took Valentina and our son home, and Carmen was basically in charge of taking care of both.

Due to her commitment to the family business, soon after Valentina and I were able to handle things on our own, Carmen had to return to Romania. During the next few weeks though, Valentina, Carmen, and her mother decided that we did need extra help especially since we both had to work. Consequently, my mother-in-law came to live with us for a longer period of time, and that changed our household for the better. Not only was she a great cook, but with her life-long experience we knew that everything was in good hands and we were very grateful.

The following year, as our son Sergio turned one year old, my mother took the trip to Texas to help us while my mother-in-law returned to Romania for a few months. In addition, over the last month of her stay in the Fall of 1993, we insisted that my father should come for a visit since he had never left Romania up to that point.

To make his trip even more fulfilling, we arranged that he would fly into Chicago, spend a few days with an old friend who was now a Christian Orthodox priest for a Romanian community there, and then join us in Texas. My father's visit to Chicago was remarkable since he had been very curious about the fate of his native religious faith overseas. Together with his friend, he even performed a few religious services which became a unique and forever treasured experience for him. While in Austin we did the best we could to visit places of interest such as Dallas with the Kennedy memorial, San Antonio, Houston and NASA, including the port of Galveston at the Gulf of Mexico. We spent the rest of the time around Austin including Sunday masses at the Orthodox Church in Austin, which my father enjoyed, as well as, of course, being around the house with my parents' new grandson.

One sensitive moment developed while, at his insistence, my father was performing a traditional Orthodox blessing ritual in our home. At one point during the hour-long service, tears came down his face as his voice trembled with emotion. Of course I inquired afterwards and my expectations were confirmed. It was all based on his disappointment over my questioning of some dogmatic and doctrinal teachings of the traditional Christian Orthodox Church. Although over the 12 years of my life in the West I had not been interested in renouncing the religious tradition into which I was born, I did change some of my philosophical views on life and religion.

In fact, ever since high school I felt that there was much more to life than what traditional science and established religion were able to explain. Over my four years of university studies I read a variety of materials consistent with my questions and my feelings. While I was employed as a computer analyst in Victoria I even wrote my thoughts down in an attempt to describe my views on the limited understanding humanity had on its own condition– I actually paid one of the secretaries in our building to type my manuscript since no individual could own a typewriter unless it was registered with the Securitate (they very much feared the printing of anti-communist flyers). Some of the ideas were about the mysteries of Easter Island (its shape being a perfect right triangle) and the life of Jesus where I specifically focused on the missing 18 years of his life as it is reported in the four gospels of the Bible. As soon as I arrived in Austin, my life in the U.S. opened new horizons in this respect and the abundance of printed materials, videos, and audio tapes helped me expand my views. I researched many concepts with respect to life after death, life beyond Earth, and most specifically, the human condition. Consequently, I had been gradually building a foundation of thought that allowed me to question and debate some of the 'established' human beliefs at least as far as traditional science and religion were concerned. I systematically included metaphysical ideas in my repertoire and I even completed some independent courses of study in this field. Soon I discovered that many established physicists of the 20th century were supporting the idea that the universe is not a big machine running out of steam, but in fact it is a big thought manifested in physical form. Moreover, quantum physics strongly indicates that the entire universe is just that, a uni-verse, a 'verse' composed and played in unity by *all* its components. It is suggested that everything in the universe is energetically connected so that we cannot study one phenomenon excluding its intrinsic dependence on the rest, most importantly, its dependence on the observer. There were scientists who clearly underlined the similarities between Eastern philosophical views (Hinduism, Buddhism, and Taoism) and the 'new physics,' quantum physics. That was a huge revelation to me: finally the world of science had found common ground with that of spirituality. Based on this, we can now debate the meaning of life and the future of the human race from a more unified and reasonable platform of thinking.

This kind of thinking was not yet entertained by my father, hence the split between our points of view. I was certainly sad to see him unhappy and I did my best to convince him that one can definitely be a good person without necessarily having to adhere to a dogmatic doctrine. In some respect he agreed with that but most of his disappointment remained and it was basically related to the fact that my family did not 'practice' the traditional Christian Orthodox routine–going to church, praying, etc. Over the rest of my parents' stay in Austin we had a great time and we did well to put aside themes of disagreement such as this.

My New Love: Tennis

Beside debates on philosophical and religious themes I kept entertaining one of my other hobbies, namely my love of sports. I was playing less and less volleyball, but since Valentina had started some tennis training back in Romania, I also picked up tennis and we started hitting tennis balls together with every chance we had. In the meantime, the father of one of the best students I ever had at Kirby Hall was an avid and experienced tennis player. Milosav and his wife Lena were originally from Yugoslavia so we quickly found the common grounds on which we developed a close friendship. Not only were we playing tennis together almost every week (which helped me improve significantly) but Lena was very kind to babysit whenever we needed trusted help with Sergio. Moreover, Milosav and I found ourselves in synchronicity as we were both on similar paths of self-growth and self-discovery. We exchanged many books and video and audio programs on these themes, and our extended late-night discussions became invaluable learning experiences I will treasure forever.

In terms of my tennis skills, I was relatively a novice at the time, but I wanted to improve so much that the many hours Milosav and I played together became my main training, especially since I had never taken regular formal lessons. Beside tennis I was and I am also very grateful for the innumerable times our families sat around the dinner table offering great company to each other. The depth of our conversations was remarkable and I believe it could be attributed to having lived our lives on two continents. In any respect, tennis helped us connect on one level and our relatively common origin completed a picture of mutual respect and understanding that helped us enjoy every minute together.

Change in Employment: ACC

The fall of 1993 marked the 10-year anniversary of my first appointment as a part-time mathematics instructor at Austin Community College (ACC). Since I very much liked teaching there I had set my goal to eventually become full-time. Consequently, as new full-time positions opened in 1991-1993, I forwarded my application with high hopes of success. I was a finalist two times and at the end of the third selection process I was offered a full-time position at the Riverside campus. The opening was for January 1994 while I was still teaching full-time at Kirby Hall School, so we had to make schedule arrangements such that I could fulfill my obligations at both institutions; in fact, that spring semester I held two full-time teaching positions. In parallel to teaching I was determined to find a high-quality replacement for me at Kirby Hall so I entered that process with the help of Mrs. Rase and Julio, but the Fall of 1994 proved that our hopes were not matched by the availability of qualified candidates, at least for the time being. In the end Mrs. Rase temporarily solved the problem by hiring part-time instructors.

My new teaching position at ACC was every bit as rewarding as I had expected. Not only did it make a financial difference to our family but it also included retirement and health insurance which, as a small private school, Kirby Hall could not afford to offer. In addition, it also encompassed a supervisory component which was challenging and educational at the same time. In that respect I had a great chance to utilize my self-growth efforts as it came down to relating to students and faculty in a variety of situations. I couldn't ask for more.

Our Household Grows

Aside the positive developments in my professional life, along came good news from Romania. Since Valentina's sister and her family increased their business over the last year, my mother-in-law was instrumental in taking care of Carmen's two sons. In the meantime we in Austin could use similar help, so the plan was that the two boys would join Valentina's mother in Austin. Their successful business in Romania permitted the family to cover basically all the costs involved and the plan was that as soon as Paul and Valentin would make it to Austin they would attend Kirby Hall and eventually the University of Texas at Austin.

The next hurdle was securing student visas for them from the American Embassy in Bucharest. They applied once during the spring of 1994 but, for some reason, they were denied. That summer we took a vacation trip to Romania and during our stay there we made another trip to the embassy, this time all together; there was no problem and we returned home to Victoria with the visas in hand. Consequently, upon our arrival to Austin, our household included all six of us: the two nephews, our son, my mother-in-law, Valentina, and me.

Once again Mrs. Rase and Kirby Hall School extended their loving assistance as Paul and Valentin joined the sixth and seventh grade respectively. The first few months were challenging since our nephews' proficiency level in English was very low. However, with patience, hard work, and the professional cooperation of all Kirby Hall teachers, our nephews were able to adjust and from then on all went well.

Memorable Years

Later on, our son's first day of kindergarten was marked by an unusual display of affection. Naturally, Sergio joined the Kirby Hall kindergarten program and as soon as we entered the building that day, his expected group of classmates happened to be lined up in the hallway. As the teacher made the introductions, one boy stepped out from the group, ran toward Sergio with open arms, and, although they were seeing each other for the first time, he gave him a friendly hug saying: "Welcome Sergio!" This was Kyle and to me it sounded more like: "Hey, Sergio. Where have you been? I have been waiting for you all this time!" That encounter seemed to be a recognition of sorts or an unexpected reunion of two old friends who finally were together again. Kyle and Sergio have remained best friends, so that turned out to be an unforgettable trip to Kirby Hall.

Another early morning drive to school reminded me of the reality of cause and effect in our universe. I was taking our three boys to Kirby Hall and we were heading East with a strong rising Sun in my windshield. Valentin was on the passenger seat and Sergio with Paul were riding in the back. As we stopped at a stoplight listening to the radio, we were shocked and shaken by a huge 'bang' in the back of my car. Sergio instantly started crying, scared out of his mind by the incident, and his cousins did their best to comfort him. What happened was that a university student rushing to school was blinded by the Sun and was not able to stop his car on time. I got out of the car and checked everything. The student behind us was not hurt but both cars were in bad shape. Eventually my Toyota Corolla was declared 'totaled' and I had to get another car, of course, compensated by the other driver's insurance. My next vehicle was a used Toyota Camry and I treasured it for many years.

In parallel with all these developments, my love for sports translated into tennis training for the rest of our family. In this respect our nephews and Sergio took tennis lessons almost regularly and over their high school years Paul and Sergio became avid players qualifying up to the ranks of Texas Junior Champions, while Valentin in the end embraced volleyball. In the meantime, Valentina and I established a pretty constant routine of playing tennis every weekend which we follow even today.

However, my passion for volleyball was almost instantly rejuvenated when I received an invitation from my old friend David Olbright who was now living in California. He had put together a strong volleyball team still called "Texas Stars," composed of great players from different parts of the country including several from Texas. Consequently, he wanted me to be on his team as we were preparing for the National Finals tournament of 1996 in Dallas, Texas. This was the most prestigious annual open volleyball tournament in the U.S.; it was including hundreds of both men's and women's teams from the U.S., Canada, Central America, even Brazil, and it was organized by age-groups; we were playing in the "40s or over" group. At the end of three full days of heavy competition David managed to lead "Texas Stars" to victory in a dramatic final match against an experienced team from Brazil; our excitement was indescribable: we had just become U.S Open volleyball champions! That was one of the greatest volleyball accomplishments of my life and I will treasure the gold medal we each received forever. The next year, we would follow up with another good performance, this time in Kansas, when we won the third place, hence the bronze medal.

Beside school and sports activities that engulfed our entire family, one other significant event would mark those years, this time on the world-wide scene. On September 11th, 2001, I drove Sergio to school, and as we were walking toward the building, his best friend Kyle came running to us with the big news: "Have you heard? An airplane just hit a tower in New York!" I couldn't believe it; "of course it was an accident," I said to myself, but as soon as I arrived at ACC, the reality of the event shocked me as it did everybody else around. Consequently, that particular trip to Kirby Hall School the morning of 9/11 became yet another remarkable one for me and our family: the morning that changed the world.

Valentina's Search for Employment

As soon as she received her doctorate from the University of Texas at Austin, Valentina had started her search for a university tenure track position as an instructor of German. In 1999 she accepted a two-year offer at the Ohio State University in Columbus, Ohio, with the possibility for tenure, and she, Sergio, and her mother moved to Columbus. I stayed back in Austin and I was commuting to Columbus basically every three weeks. With special occasions I would drive (a two-day drive that is) but most of the time I would fly. Of course, for the longer vacations they would rejoin me in Austin, and this way we managed the separation from month to month.

Beside Valentina's professional accomplishments, those two years offered us many opportunities to experience both joy and sadness. Our time together in Columbus was great. The weekends I would fly in would be filled with fun time ranging from picking our own apples in orchards around Columbus, Sergio and I playing on the banks of the river behind their apartment or in the snow, to just playing games inside when the weather would not cooperate. However, deep sadness would overwhelm us at the moment of my departure. As we would say goodbye and I would be heading to the plane, I would be overtaken by the well-known deep pain/knot in the chest. In those moments I would appeal to all the strength I gathered from previous experiences and my self-growth efforts. The pain would be amplified also by the realization that Sergio and Valentina felt exactly the same, as I was looking back from the long walkway that was taking me away from them. In the end, the two years in Columbus helped us grow and we all benefited from that complex experience which, overall, enhanced our lives.

In addition to all this, over about the same period of time, I joined a small group of ACC faculty and I took a 'visiting lecturer' position with the undergraduate department of mathematics at the University of Texas at Austin (UT); this was in parallel to my full-time responsibility at ACC. The teaching at UT was very rewarding but unfortunately it only lasted for three years. Apparently, due to the university's fiscal burden, the financial status of the department determined the change of course.

For similar reasons having to do this time with the Ohio State University, Valentina's position did not turn into a tenure track so we all reunited back in Austin. Her search for work uncovered a part-time teaching opportunity at Texas State University in San Marcos, which was just about 30 miles from Austin. In the meantime our two nephews, Paul and Valentin had graduated first in their classes from Kirby Hall High School and had started college at the University of Texas in Austin; to ease up their commute to school, they moved into an apartment in walking distance of the university campus. Sergio, our son, rejoined Kirby Hall School, hence the remarkable morning drive to Kirby Hall School on 9/11, but we were all in for another major change in our lives.

Still searching for a tenure track position in German, Valentina applied for an opening at Texas Tech University in Lubbock, Texas. She did receive an offer. This was more or less the opportunity she was looking for, so we made all the preparations to move at least her and Sergio to Lubbock. Since Paul and Valentin were basically on their own, Valentina's mother had decided to rejoin Valentina's sister's family in Romania. So in the Fall of 2002, after a laborious process that included several trips to Lubbock, we bought a nice spacious house in Lubbock, within walking distance of the university and the middle school Sergio would attend. It really seemed to be a great setup. Consequently, I started searching for a teaching position in mathematics with the colleges around Lubbock, with the idea to relocate our entire family there.

In the meantime, the undergraduate mathematics department at Texas Tech University did offer me an adjunct position but at a substantial reduction in pay compared to my full-time salary at ACC. Consequently, I sent my application for a full-time opening at a community college close to Lubbock, but for some reason they did not show any interest in hiring me. Since I did not want to give up my ACC long-time affiliation, we had decided to go with the flow for the time being.

So I started commuting to Lubbock every two weeks, while Valentina and Sergio would visit Austin the other weekends. For the most part the drive was actually on the nice scenic roads of the Texas hill country. It took about six hours one way and Valentina and I became relatively accustomed to the route. Since they anxiously wanted some pets, Valentina and Sergio got an indoor cat, and I bought two certified German-Shepherd puppies bred by a German lady who lived on a ranch off the road somewhere from Austin to Lubbock. With this acquisition we had now four dogs, two in Austin and two in Lubbock which was a little more than we really needed, but under the circumstances, we had to manage.

That academic year a tenure track position in German opened at Texas State University in San Marcos and we decided that Valentina should apply, with the hope to keep our family in Austin. She was offered the position and almost immediately we started the process of selling the house in Lubbock while we were contemplating moving from North-central Austin to the South side for an easier commute to San Marcos. We accomplished all of this in the spring and summer of 2003 as we had offered our Austin home for sale and had started building a new one on a larger lot in South Austin.

We spent the second half of the summer in Romania and Deborah, our wonderful real estate agent, kept us posted on the new developments on both fronts. She would send us photos of the new construction so we were able to see the progress step by step. In late August Valentina started her new job, Sergio joined a new middle school in Austin, and on November the 15th we finally moved into the new house after we sold the old one. So 2003 was a pretty significant year for our family and all went well as we settled into the new place. We now had much more room in the backyard for our four dogs and my birds. I immediately made our vegetable garden ready for the following spring, and we planted as many trees, plants and flowers as possible to fill up our completely bare lot. In the process of it all I also had to accomplish the relocation of my homing pigeons one more time which was very successful. At the end of this chain of complex changes we were all happy to finally be together at our new place and we were looking forward to a future of significant professional and personal accomplishments.

19

Life Goes on

Business Expansion in Romania

On the other side of the Atlantic, in Romania, after many years of diligent work, Carmen and Olimpiu had gradually expanded their business and they were able to offer work now to several hundred employees. In 2004 they came to Austin for their sons' college graduation as Paul and Valentin received their Bachelor degrees from the University of Texas. With the diplomas in hand they decided to return to Romania to join the effort of making the already expanded business a lasting success. Indeed they did. Starting in the fall of 2004, Paul and Valentin had made themselves a driving force in assuring positive developments in their family business despite the signs of weakening economies throughout Europe.

Of course the success of our extended family in Romania had also a positive influence on our family in Austin, Texas. Not only were we all able to cross the ocean more often but our summer stay in Romania became gradually more comfortable. They would always provide us with a car to ensure easy and flexible transportation, and we would be able to visit different parts of the country that we had not seen for a long time. Most importantly, our time together was a real joy and we treasured every minute of it.

However, as far as the post-1989 Romanian economy was concerned, the state of the country was not helped by the constant competition between different political parties that succeeded each other as they were voted in and out during general elections. It seemed that as soon as they would be in power they would forget the true purpose of their reign and focus only on personal gain at the expense of the population. Even freshly created businesses would suffer by constant changes in the laws, which in parallel discouraged foreign investors due to the uncertainty of the immediate future. Moreover, it seemed that the general philosophy entertained by large masses of Romanians was marked by two conflicting views: on one hand they were anxious to take advantage of the long-awaited freedom gained after the 1989 Revolution, but on the other hand they were not willing to do what was necessary to reach their goals. One major barrier was psychological, as many were still expecting the government to solve their problems, which continued the feeling of dependency indoctrinated so powerfully by the totalitarian communist regime for 45 years. Another obstacle was an exaggerated and misplaced spirit of nationalism that caused many to recite slogans such as "We are not selling our country" whenever foreign investment was knocking at the door.

As far as our extended family's business in Romania was concerned, since my sister- and brother-in-law worked so hard to succeed, it arrived to a point where it was able to survive most of the bumps in the road, while many other free enterprise efforts failed. The new and significant boost came due to the expansion of the European Union. Suddenly European funds became available as the Union encouraged local businesses into 50-50 financial investment partnerships. Some businesses took advantage of this early in the offering and they are better off for it today. I was impressed by the promptness with which our extended family acted as they embraced the opportunity and I am sure it was all worth the gigantic efforts and persistence involved.

Trips, Trips, Trips

It has been said that the best education is traveling. I cannot agree more. Every time we step out of our immediate and usual surroundings new experiences await. As a mathematics professor I attended many math conferences outside of my home campus at Austin Community College in Austin Texas. Over the years I made a point of imparting my pedagogical experience via presentations at such conferences and workshops. Some of my favorite themes in education spring from my long-term academic experience both in Romania and in the U.S. and with my infatuation with self-improvement. I do believe that we owe it to ourselves to improve, since our philosophy of life is based on the totality of efforts we have put into finding answers to ardent existential questions. In fact these answers in large measure determine our choices, hence our future actions.

Regarding teaching, I have taken every opportunity to share my ideas with interested audiences at conferences in the U.S., Canada, and Romania. Not only have I presented my suggestions for better teaching, but in parallel I have always been interested in learning other professionals' points of view. Conferences in Austin, Houston, Dallas, San Antonio, Chicago, San Francisco, San Jose, Washington D.C., Toronto, and Brasov (Romania) have been suitable avenues to share ideas. However, after a while I was surprised to find that most of what I was interested in presenting was out of the ordinary. Rarely would I find other educators conveying ideas similar to mine. It seemed that most developments in education were geared toward use of technology, group work, and efforts aimed at erasing the long-term negative effects of discrimination. Although these are noble issues in modern education, I think that other avenues are also worth exploring, and examples abound: improving personal relationships between teachers and students via story-telling, raising the personal responsibility level in both students and teachers, bringing humor in the classroom, teaching non-traditional methods, comparing educational systems from different countries, and so on.

In parallel to mathematics gatherings I was also blessed to attend many of Valentina's conferences. Most of these became basically family mini-vacations since we would take our son, Sergio, and Valentina's mother along. San Diego, Atlanta, and San Francisco are just a few examples of places we traveled to. In most cases we would make a point of visiting specific sites of interest and of course we would immortalize them in pictures and videos.

Our collection of such memorabilia increased considerably once our extended family from Romania started joining us. Since the financial burden of traveling was lessened due to their business success, we took several trips together. A memorable one would be a cruise to Alaska which offered us a chance to see that part of the U.S. for the first time. It was impressive. Not only would we savor the grandeur of some of the age-old glaciers, but we also had a good taste of the living style in small towns on the shore, such as old settlements built during the gold rush on the West Coast.

On the other U.S. coast, the East Coast we had the opportunity to visit the Washington D.C. area several times. Beside the White House and other famous landmarks and museums we visited over the years, one special place will remain in my personal memories. This is the Romanian embassy. A particular reason for this is that in 2009 I had to take two trips from Austin, Texas to the Romanian embassy in Washington D.C. in the process of regaining my Romanian citizenship which would restore any inherited right I had lost because of the fear of perceived totalitarian communist retribution. Since I had renounced it before 1989 as a precaution for my intended trip to Romania, and since in December 1989 Romania became a free country out of the jaws of communism, I presumed it would be a simple formality. However, it was not. The amount of paperwork involved was out of this world. Moreover, fees, police and criminal records, and even employment verification were supposed to be hand-delivered, hence one trip to the embassy. The file would then be sent for approval to the state department of Romania in Bucharest and if affirmative, the decision would be published nationally in Romania, while the Washington D.C. embassy would invite me one more time for the final step, the official oath ceremony. It blew my mind: the old Romanian ways to handle such problems did not change despite the almost 20 years that passed since the Romanian Revolution. However, it all went well and I was happy to accomplish my goal which was to go on with my life under double citizenship.

As far as international travel was concerned, ever since her return to Austin we took advantage of some of Valentina's conferences in Europe. We therefore made a point to visit modern and historical sites in Florence (Italy), Paris, Munich, Prague, Rhodes and Athens in Greece, and of course Bucharest (Romania). One of the most notable such trips took place in the summer of 2007 to Paris, France. Both Valentina's mother and my mother joined us and we had a blast visiting the Eiffel Tower, the Notre Dame cathedral, the Versailles museum and gardens, and several other sites.

At the Berlin Wall

After we helped our mothers board a plane back from Paris to Romania, we continued our 2007 trip flying to Berlin. This was a long awaited project for obvious reasons. The famous Wall that separated West Berlin from the East was the greatest and the most depressing symbol of the obstruction of freedom practiced so vehemently by the Eastern Bloc Communist regimes. I had never fully understood how this was made possible within a city like Berlin, until I saw it with my own eyes. The tall concrete Wall, heavily reinforced with barbed wire and in many places doubled-up as it was permanently guarded by armed East German soldiers, literally closed in a piece of freedom in the middle of East Germany's Communist oppression. The 100-mile-long Wall was basically raised overnight in august 1961, so anyone caught on the wrong side of it that morning was stuck there for decades. The well-known Brandenburg Gate and the notorious Checkpoint Charlie are impressive attraction sites. Tourists from all over the world flood the streets around them as to take in the message: "Never allow this to happen again." The small Check-Point-Charlie museum speaks volumes. Both video and audio testimonies depict the desperate efforts of thousands of East Germans trying to escape to the West. Many died. The crimes committed around the Wall can fill many books and some have been also presented in compelling video documentaries. On a larger scale, it has been documented that Communism killed more people around the world than all the wars of the 20th century combined.

To us as a family, our visit to Berlin took a greater meaning. Sergio, our son, had a unique chance to understand some of the cruelest outcomes of dictatorial Communist regimes. Although Berlin was magnificently rebuilt after its virtually complete destruction by the end of the Second World War, the Communist Wall threw a dark and sad veil over the entire city. This somber memory is kept alive today all around the Wall on informative posters and explicative illustrations. In fact in many places around the city, different sizes of Wall pieces are still in place; they serve as vivid testimony of what it once was. Most of the Wall had been removed after 1989 and in its stead a concrete brick stripe of a notable color was implanted in the street pavement. To immortalize this, at one point I took a picture of Sergio as he was standing on top of the meaningful stripe, one foot in the East and one in the West. To me, that picture symbolizes the triumph of human freedom over any super-imposed cruel and ignorant separation, and I believe freedom should be proclaimed all over the world.

Another impressive attraction site in Berlin is the Holocaust Memorial, built to commemorate the atrocities committed against the Jewish population of Europe before and during the Second World War. I was walking through the *uneven* (weaving) alignment crafted meaningfully between the 2,711 *uneven* large prism-shaped slabs of stone which were anywhere between 1-2 feet to 7-8 feet tall, and I was deeply moved by the grandeur of the monument. By means of the uneven yet ordered assembly of stones over an area of 205,000 square feet, the monument suggestively conveys the never-to-forget message: millions of children, women and men, young and old were 'orderly' murdered simply because they were Jewish. Also significant is the location of the monument since it is set in the proximity of the ruins of Hitler's buried bunker and also close to the famous Brandenburg Gate. It seems that it was meant to say: "Learn from history rather than repeat it."

The Holocaust Memorial, Berlin

Since the Holocaust has been a major theme of research for my wife Valentina, a life changing trip we also took one summer was to Prague which gave us the chance to visit the Terezin Memorial. After Valentina's conference in Munich, we rented a car and drove first to Dachau, were we walked among memorial buildings of the first concentration camp the Nazis had set up in Germany. A few days later we entered Terezin, in the Czech Republic and I was completely taken by the similar message sent unmistakably by both sites: human philosophy of life and the society can degenerate so much as to cause incredible massacres such as the unforgivable extermination attempt of the Jews by the Nazis. That trip encompassed two views of modern life. On one hand we admired the beauties of modern Munich and the smooth transition of the ex-communist Czechoslovakia to the free world. On the other hand we had just been awoken to the possible dark side of life were humans can adopt dangerous views that could set up massive atrocities such as the Holocaust. Personally, I concluded that trip with a renewed inner hope for a better world, since the past should not be repeated but should offer lessons for a peaceful and happy future.

Several of our other trips were also significant, and this from different personal perspectives. Here are some:

Canada. During the summer of 1997 the three of us adventured on a car trip through the U.S. and Canada with a final goal: to spend four days on a resort about 40 miles north of Montreal. The resort, impressively surrounded by wooded mountains, was strategically built near a surreal lake on which one could ride a small pedal boat, and it was decorated left and right with large stones that seemed to offer majestic protection to beautiful though fragile colorful flower arrangements. The entire scenery appeared like something close to a dream state. We took long walks, taking in the fresh mountainous air and admiring the breathtaking views. Although Sergio was still very young, we managed to hit a few tennis balls on the adjacent tennis courts before we would settle down for the long dinners. The food was exquisite. A four-course French-style dinner was served every night and we all had to polish our manners to successfully last through it. On the morning we left the resort, we visited Downtown Montreal and we made a point to see the famous Olympic compound that forever put Romanian gymnastics on the world map in 1976: Nadia Comaneci received the first perfect 10 in history! We were both humbled and proud to be able to set foot on the grounds where such distinguished marks had been committed to history. From the Olympic site, our love for sports guided us to our first ever professional tennis tournament where we saw several of our favored world-class players. The very cool night took us by surprise as we were freezing in the stands of the Montreal stadium, but with that occasion we accomplished a virtually unattainable goal: to see the freshly new crowned French Open champion in live action, Gustavo Kuerten (Guga). After such a moving event, we stopped for a welcomed visit to my cousin Monica who by now was living with her family in Montreal. We had a great time together and our sons took full advantage of their first chance to meet. On our trip back through the U.S. we made sure to stop for an afternoon of more tennis in Cincinnati, Ohio, where we had a second opportunity to watch some of the best tennis players in the world compete. This was the following international tournament after Montreal, as they were preparing for the U.S. Open grand slam in New York. This time we collected autographs and we even took some memorable pictures with tennis superstars like Alberto Costa and Michael Chang. With all the memories of that long and fulfilling trip we couldn't be happier to return home to Austin to enjoy the rest of that summer and of course to watch on television the U.S. Open tennis grand slam tournament.

London. One year after the tragic death of Princess Diana we visited London. Naturally we walked by the Kensington Palace and we were sadly and in the same time pleasantly surprised to find hundreds of different flower arrangements guarding the gates. In my view, this was a sensible tribute to a distinguished and honorable life cut short in such mysterious ways.

France and Germany. On our way to Romania, one summer of the late 1990s, we made an ambitious plan. We stopped in London, left our luggage in the airport for a few days, and we took a speed train to Paris, France. The ride was unique. The train took us through the tunnel under the English Channel for a good 20 minutes before we made it to Paris. In Paris we rented a brand-new Renault (it had 8 km on the odometer), we visited the impressive European Disneyland outside Paris which became the highlight of the trip for our son Sergio, and then we headed to Germany. Our plan was to visit Christine, a good friend of ours from Austin who was vacationing in her home town close to the Swiss border. In fact, despite a terrible flu-like virus I picked up along the way, we took a nice car ride to Basel, Switzerland and to the Bodensee-Constance Lake. In the end our last evening in Germany became most memorable. Since we had just found out how close we were to the Black Forest Mountains, and since we knew that the springs of the Danube, one of the largest rivers in Europe (the largest of Romania) were close by, we expressed our desire to find them. It was already late afternoon but we insisted we could make it if we drove as fast as we could. The German no-speed-limit autobahn and our new Renault became a perfect team. At Christine's encouragements I pushed the pedal to the max. That was the fastest I have ever driven a car: 198 km per hour; I intended to get to at least 200 but the autobahn had just come to an end. However, we made it to the springs at dusk but we had enough daylight to enjoy the place. It all looked like a page from a picture book. The mountain peaks were guarding the scenery with their majesty as if they were protecting it from mal-intended intruders; we were not. We found the springs, and our adventure suddenly became an emotional experience to me. There was right there in front of my eyes a small pool of crystal-clear cool water, about 3 feet by 3 feet, coming out from the heart of the mountain and instantly conceiving the heart beat of an impressive river that connected Germany, Austria, Hungary, Yugoslavia, Bulgaria, and Romania. While we all had a quick drink and we splashed some fresh Danube water on our faces, I pictured myself traveling all along the river to reach its delta in Romania as it flowed gently into the Black Sea. Wow: 'born' in the Black Forest Mountains to 'die' in the Black Sea! What a life! I know we will treasure the pictures we took there for the rest of our lives.

Muir Woods. Over the years, we have been happy to take two trips to one of the greatest natural monument I had ever seen: the Muir Woods (the Sequoia National Park) near San Francisco. The entire site seemed to have one purpose: to remind humans of the grandeur of our natural habitat; to point out what humility really means and what our role to preserve such treasures is. To walk in the fresh cool air of the reservation on trails protected with such stoicism for ages by giant straight up seemingly endless trees, was one of the greatest experiences of my life; to stand at the foot of one such tree really sets things in perspective relative to what we really are in the larger scheme of our world. Those moments helped me reconfirm my love and attachment to nature and to our environment, that environment that ensures our existence.

Pikes Peak, Colorado. One other natural wonder we found amazing was the Colorado's "Garden of the Gods" which is divinely set at the foot of some of the tallest mountains in the U.S. guarded by the Pikes Peak. The summer of 2004 we did not make our regular vacation trip to Romania, so we decided to treat ourselves with four days in the cool climate of the Colorado Mountains. That was our chance to climb the highest mountain peak so far: Pikes Peak, 14,110 feet. We took the cog rail all the way to the top and we savored the fresh and rarefied air blowing in the high altitude wind. I felt it. At one point I felt a little light-headed but the views all around were magnificent. We came down the mountain happy about our accomplishment, but there was more in store. First was the Manitou Springs Cave of the Winds, with its pristine entrance set near a great canyon, and then The Garden of the Gods. The giant red stones that over millennia came out from the depth of Earth's crust were breathtaking. The geological explanation we received did not diminish the grandeur of the place, and our long walk on the many trails of the 'garden', guarded by gigantic fire-red stone clusters was indescribable. The memory of those four Colorado days we spent surrounded by such majestic natural wonders will stay with us forever.

My Books, Music, Film, and New Friends

Motivated by my extensive traveling combined with my other research I felt an inner calling to publicly express my thoughts about the world around us. In this respect, ever since I remember I found myself in search of answers to questions that might shed some light on the path humanity should take in the new century. My high school and college years in Romania were bursting out with such questions to which I was able to find only partial answers due to the heavy censorship imposed over the entire country by the communist regime. The lack of full access to pertinent information available in the West became, therefore, one brick in the wall of my drive to true freedom. For a long time I felt that there is much more to the picture of being human than just to make a living. Even before 1981 I had an inclination toward writing down my ideas, so I had left behind a number of short articles that most likely were lost within the large volume of my father's library.

Once I left Romania and I was engulfed by freedom and opportunities, I again realized this important prerogative in my life. My hunger for everything that pertained to finding answers to my questions had led me gradually to books, videos, tapes, conferences, and workshops that contributed immensely to the fulfillment of my goal. The culmination came in the mid-1990s when I enrolled in some graduate studies in education that also required a thesis. I proposed the theme for my thesis to be "the need for a new model in education, a shift from the paradigm of separation to the one of union," and it was warmly accepted. I completed the requirements by 1998, including the thesis, and soon after that I decided to expand my research and turn the thesis into a book. I felt that more people would benefit from the ideas I proposed, and I was really hoping that eventually humanity could reach the critical number of people supporting the unity paradigm in order to bring separation, hate, and crime to an end (based on the well-known 'hundredth monkey' phenomenon).

The book was finally published in 2007 under the title *"WE ARE ALL ONE: The End of All Worries, Scientific and Spiritual Testimonies to the Unity of All Things"* and it crowned all my research and personal experiences up to that date. In fact, some of its contents are a meaningful extension of this autobiography. The title of the book itself is sufficiently suggestive, and for more details one could visit http://the-end-of-all-worries.com.

As far as my professional development was concerned, in 2009 I completed my second Master degree with a university from Romania, this time in Mathematics Education. This was another rewarding experience since it gave me the chance to study and complete academic requirements again in Romanian for the first time since my university graduation in 1979.

Soon after that I started collecting material for my second book. My intent this time was geared toward writing more for educators, students, and parents, in an attempt to present deeper reasons and unique approaches as far as global education was concerned. My six articles published during the 1990s in an educational journal available nation-wide, came in as the starting point. I completed the book containing 25 chapters on a variety of educational issues and I published it in 2011 under the title *"TEACH FOR LIFE: Essays on Modern Education for Teachers, Students, and Parents."* Details are available at http://teachforlife.positive-imaging.com.

Long before I had decided to write my books, I had been determined to improve myself musically. It seemed that music had always been a major part of my life and I completely agree with an Austin radio disc-jockey who one day said on the air: "Life without music makes no sense!" Consequently, based on my experience as a drummer and vocalist from Romania, I continued my progress once I arrived in Texas. In this respect, ever since I moved in my first apartment, I continued teaching myself the basics of playing guitar, and I started learning to play bass and a little bit of keyboard. The latter brought back vivid memories of many a night when my two musically talented uncles Mircea and Radu (my mother's brothers) would display their expertise as they were playing accordion for fun when I was little. Over time, Mircea developed into an accomplished semi-professional keyboard player, while Radu embraced music as his vocation becoming a professional

organist. So my musical inclination was most likely influenced by them and also by my mother, a good singer in her own right.

However, it soon became obvious to me that playing in bands around Austin could most likely be a dead-end road, so I have decided to continue my practice and my passion for music all by myself. This road took me to a four-track recorder and many hours of self-taught recording in my little improvised home-recording studio. With all the instruments available in my 'music room,' every time I would 'receive' an inspiration I would tape it and eventually develop it into a potential piece of music. Consequently, over the last 30 years, I accumulated a large number of musical ideas and in the end, as a 'one-man-band,' I finalized enough tracks of mostly original music to complete two albums of about an hour each.

More recently I expended my musical universe to include my son Sergio (virtuoso guitar player) and my nephew from Romania, Cristian (singer and guitar player), and I would practice and record with them whenever possible. My 'music room' in Austin hosted a few of my jams with Sergio and they evidence his abundant talent. In addition, over the summers of the last few years (including 2012) I had the chance to play along with Cristian in Romania and we even came up with a name for our 'band,' "Generations." We videotaped some of our improvised 'shows' and they will be our treasures for years to come. So, I am happy to say that musically I was fortunate to reach most of my 'impossible' pre-1981 dreams. Not only was I able to see live in concert many of the bands I idolized over the Free Europe Radio years (from AC/DC and Deep Purple to Jethro Tull, and from Pink Floyd and Yes to Whitesnake), but I also became able to involve my son and my nephew in the creation of long lasting family musical legacy. All of these are now a precious addition to my 700-vinyl-record collection along with about the same number of tapes, compact discs, and DVDs that constitute my 'music library.'

Beside my books and music I was happy to also experience first-hand what it means to play in a film. As soon as I became a full-time mathematics teacher at ACC, this opportunity manifested itself. My newly made friend and colleague Paul was also a very talented actor. From time to time we would have passionate conversations on philosophical themes, which one day took me to an old true story from my last few years spent in Romania. We later called it *FEMEIA CU VACA* (The Woman with the Cow) and Paul and I wrote a screenplay for a full-length movie based on this and other true stories from my life in Romania (one can find the complete story of 'the woman with the cow' in my book *WE ARE ALL ONE*). We sent it to several screenplay contests and we received some positive feedback but no prices or further offers. A few years later though, Paul came up with the idea of a short 20-minute film treating the exact theme of *FEMEIA CU VACA*, this time having all action taking place in Austin, Texas. He financed virtually the entire project and I got to play one of the significant parts. We called it *JUST ANOTHER DAY* and we sent it to several short films festivals. In spite of some positive reviews, the film, like the screenplay, did not reach a higher ground in the fierce nation-wide competition. However, we are proud of both and we hope that their message centered on the 'non-accidental nature of the human existence' can motivate people to think outside the box of consecrated existential philosophy.

In retrospect, it is evident that my long-time search for solutions to some of the most ardent human problems has been a fruitful one, and it materialized so far in my two books, some of my songs, the screenplay, and the short film. It seemed that if I kept my passion alive and I was inspired to select positive choices along the way, I would be able to initiate meaningful cooperation with others who happened to be on a similar path. That is how my friendship with Paul, my colleague at ACC came about, and even more amazingly, that is how I had been instinctively guided to meet Flem and Jo, my new friends from Houston. On Saturday, November 8, 2008 I had decided to attend a workshop offered by physicist Thomas Campbell in Austin (at the Unitarian Church–coincidence?); he was in fact promoting his 800-page trilogy "My Big TOE," as in 'Theory of Everything' - a fascinating presentation on the merging of philosophy, physics, and metaphysics. At one point during the meeting I noticed a gentleman 1-2 yards away from me, who was freezing in the air-conditioned room. I took my light jacket that I had hung on the back of my chair and I handed it to him. He silently accepted it and appreciated my gesture. When the allotted lunch time came about, my accent revealed my foreign nationality as we exchanged a few words while he thanked me for the jacket. That started a short conversation that would be passionately continued over lunch.

In fact the discussion turned more or less into a monolog as I was respectfully asked to describe my defection from Communist Romania. Flem, Jo, and three of their good friends, Cheryl Anne, Amparo, and Nannette, came all the way from Houston to attend the workshop. Flem and Jo had a close affinity to Eastern-Europe since back during the years 1970 forward, they very much enjoyed trips to the old Yugoslavia when, contrary to its portrayal in some media, it was a combination of socialism, capitalism, and communism, as well as trips to Croatia and Slovenia after the breakup of Yugoslavia. Obviously, my escape from Romania via Yugoslavia instantly revived their pleasant memories, and gave them a whole new perspective on that area. Moreover, our common interests in the theme of the workshop were a clear indication that we could find much more to talk about if time permitted. However, the only extra few minutes together were at the end of the day before their return to Houston. I accompanied them to their car which was relatively close to mine, and as we were saying goodbye I remembered that I had a couple of extra copies of my book *WE ARE ALL ONE* in my car. I politely asked them to accept a gift that happened to contain a brief description of my defection from Romania; I signed the books, and after we exchanged phone numbers we shook hands and they took off.

About ten days later I received a telephone message from Flem. It was the greatest compliment and praise I have ever received for my book, the *WE ARE ALL ONE* he had just finished reading. Obviously it made me very happy to find such appreciation for my work and subsequently I found out that Flem and Jo were member/organizers of the Theosophical Society of West Houston. The common ground we had discovered in Austin (along with our common interest in rock-and-roll music) had just been expanded because of all of this and it cemented our friendship forever. Over the following years I was invited to present at several monthly meetings of the society and Flem ordered many copies of both of my books. His noble intent was and is to spread the message of the common interests of all people of the world, of unity and free choice, along with the need for meaningful world-wide education.

20

The Year Is 2012

My Father's Passing

Ever since 1981 I have traveled to many and different places, enhancing my understanding of the world via first-hand experience. However, nothing compared to a sudden trip to Romania on the 14 of April, 2012. It was about 3:15 a.m. that Saturday morning when our Austin telephone rang with a totally disturbing message about my father in Romania: "He fell to the ground, and died!" These were my sister Ligia's words, in tears, as she was conveying the sad news to us in Texas. It was totally unexpected. It is true that in 2000 my father had a quadruple bypass surgery, but he recovered completely and had done relatively well ever since. Especially not presenting obvious symptoms lately, I was shocked and so were Valentina and our son Sergio when we told him later that morning. To me, the explosive way I received the sad news (with absolutely no prior warning or expectation), confirmed a pattern I had identified for a number of years up to that point. Over time, I noticed that whenever I was to receive bad news it came to me with no warning at all; it was like I would not entertain any thoughts about the respective event until it would hit me. It happened exactly that same way, as my sister called in the middle of the night with the news about our father's death.

From that moment on, we did the best we could to secure a flight for me to Romania that same day, which wasn't an easy task. Apparently, airline companies do not provide immediate service for extreme situations such as mine anymore, so we had to keep trying to find an available seat with an airline company all the way to Bucharest. In the end, our nephew, Valentin from Romania, located an advantageous flight for me from Austin to Bucharest, with an 8-hour delay in Paris, France. The longer than normal delay did not matter as long as I would make it to Ucea the next day (having in mind the 8-hour time difference between Texas and Romania).

My father in 2011

The flight departed at about 1:30 p.m. and it was one of the most significant experiences of my life. On one hand I had to concentrate on the connections in order to make it on time, and on the other hand I couldn't escape thinking about the reason I was flying so unexpectedly to Romania. First, I flew from Austin to Atlanta, and after a short connection time, from Atlanta to Paris. Over the 8-hour trans-Atlantic flight I experienced some of the most moving mind-voyages I had ever had. Tired after a virtually sleepless night, I did take a few short naps, but in the meantime I entertained some deep meditative states of mind full of vivid images of my life in Romania and of course, in my father's presence. At one point along the way I was instinctively driven to grab my note book and write down what I thought I would like to be said on my behalf at his funeral procession. It all flew almost subconsciously on three hand-written pages and I saved it to be finished and typed upon my arrival.

The long layover in Paris gave me even more time to contemplate my 'adventure' and I made sure I would not fall asleep, afraid that I would miss my connection to Romania. There were 8 long hours of self-search between grading a few papers I took with me, sitting at different gates where chairs were available, and grabbing a couple of sandwiches and a bottle of water to keep me busy and fed. At last, the flight was announced, although with about 40 minutes of an extra delay, and I was on my way on the last leg of my flight from Paris to Bucharest. Once in my seat, I finally let myself drift to sleep, confident that I would be awakened at my arrival in Romania. Indeed, I slept the entire 2 hours of the flight, and upon my arrival in Bucharest I met my other nephew, Paul and his fiancé Iulia who came to pick me up at the Bucharest airport.

About 3.5 hours later we arrived to Ucea de Jos, my native village, and I couldn't wait to see my mother and my sister. It was by now about 11 p.m. when I stepped onto the familiar homestead where I grew up. Powerful emotions were trying to win me over as I was about to enter the house, but I kept reminding myself that we all had to be strong, to understand the situation as it was, and to encourage each other in order to pass through these tough times without escalating the pain to unbearable levels. I opened the door and, as cheerfully as I could under the circumstances, I embraced my mother who was basically confined to bed due to a two-month recovery from a basin fracture. Naturally she started crying while I did my best to keep my tears to a minimum, and then I embraced my sister; it was hard to let go! The pain I felt from both of them, although contained, surpassed any of my preconceived expectations. It was all overly understandable: my 78-year old mother had just lost the love of her life and her trusted partner of the past 58 years, and my sister had found our 83-year old father the previous morning laying on the ground, dead of a cardiac arrest. In those moments I felt I had to balance somewhat this excruciating pain, so I happily injected into the discussion some description of my long last-minute flight. In spite of the first and very natural reaction to our unfortunate reunion, I was actually content to realize that both my mother and my sister had in fact come to grips commendably with the situation.

That Sunday, the 15th of April, was actually the Christian Greek-Orthodox Easter holiday so throughout the funeral ceremonies it was repeatedly mentioned that my father had chosen to depart during the most sacred time of the year. Not only that, but apparently he had always wished to die suddenly, without inflicting too much burden on the loved ones. Indeed he did. Per tradition, as an ex-priest and theology professor, his body was set in the church for visitations up to the time of the burial, which was scheduled for that coming Tuesday. Therefore, at the end of my 30-minute visit with my mother and my sister at home, I left for the church.

I didn't know what to expect. It was by then almost midnight and a tumult of thoughts swirled through my head as I was climbing the stairs. As soon as I opened the familiar heavy old church door, the candle smell brought me to the reality of the moment. I stepped in quietly and I walked slowly toward the casket in the eyes of the 15-20 people present who were obviously surprised to see me. My father's body looked like he was sleeping; I had a weird strong feeling that at any moment he could open his eyes and turn his head. His face was serene, displaying even a slight smile, as if to say: "I am sorry I had to go, but I did it the way I always wanted to." With my hands on the casket, I silently sent him my best wishes and I reconfirmed my belief in a happy after life with the possibility of many returns, subjects he and I had debated for numerous years.

After I embraced my nephew Cristian who was there at the time, I shook hands with everybody else in the church, thanking everyone for their care and support. About 2 hours later my body gave in to the cold, the tiredness, and the lack of sleep, so I had to retire for the night, with the plan to return the next morning at about 10 a.m. for the Second Easter-day mass.

I entered the church a few minutes after 10 a.m. and I was impressed by the large number of people present. It was a double reason for a full church on the second Easter day: the Easter mass, and the last two days people could see my father's body laying in his well-dressed coffin. Many came to pay their respect and to offer their condolences to us, members of the family, and we were very touched.

After the Easter mass most people left for lunch with the plan to return that evening for the "saracusta," which is a special ceremony offered the night before the burial. Our entire family was present. My mother made it despite her weakness, and of course we were there to help. The proceedings were impressive once again. The bishop along with 13 priests offered the mass and he concluded with a sensitive and moving speech in front of the full church.

View from above

The next day was *the day*. The funeral special mass was scheduled for 1 p.m., when the archbishop could also make it. So after the regular third-Easter-day mass was over, the church was flooded with people one more time and 35 priests joined hands to make the occasion truly memorable. I hired a photographer to take pictures and film some of the ceremony, anticipating its importance to the community and, of course, to our family. The church could not accommodate the 4 or 5 hundred people who decided to be part of this unique event. Consequently, the outdoor speakers did well to carry the indoor sound to the people gathered in front of the main entrance, so everyone had the chance to be reached and touched at least that way. The mass itself embodied a tapestry of sentiments. On one hand it underlined the pain of losing a remarkable person, and on the other hand it presented the entire event as a part of the joyful tradition of the resurrection of Christ that was still celebrated on the third-Easter-day. This fortunate mix helped our family and especially my mother as we were all trying our best to accept my father's sudden departure. The fact that he apparently chose those particular days and the fact that he got his wish to die without suffering or inflicting a heavy burden on the family, contributed immensely to this acceptance. The two impressive eulogies offered by the archbishop and a respected theology professor (an old friend of my father) were basically carved around his life and they also emphasized the significance of the time of his death. In the meantime, since I wasn't able to properly edit my thoughts to be read at that moment, I promised to send them later, for another occasion. In closing, the local priest of Ucea de Jos presented his extensive commemoration of my father's life and it was very warmly received.

What followed was the hardest to take. Several priests picked up the casket; the multitude of people in the church made room for the procession to move outside as they were heading for the cemetery located immediately behind the church building. My sister and I helped our mother follow the convoy and in a few minutes we were all near the family vault previously prepared for my parents' afterlife by themselves. That was the hardest time for my mother: to watch the group of priests lowering her husband of 58 years into the ground, must have been the most difficult sight she had ever witnessed. As my sister and I were consoling our mother, we both dealt with the same pain: this was the end of an era in our lives, an era when my father did, to the best of his knowledge and possibilities, the best he could for our wellbeing. Now he was gone. We, on the other hand, were parents ourselves and in the depth of our beings we knew we had been doing the same for our children and we just had to keep going.

The burial concluded relatively quickly. Since she was exhausted after a remarkably hard day, I drove my mother home and then I joined the priests, the rest of the family, and the people heading to the reception in my father's honor at the newly built auditorium of Ucea de Jos. It was almost full. Our extended family from Victoria, Valentina's mother and nephews, did impressively well to provide a three-course meal and drinks for close to 400 people (Valentina's sister Carmen and her husband Olimpiu were out of the country at that time). It took a few hours of socializing before I was able to go back home and see my mother. She was in the care of a couple of neighbors (lady friends) and they had already received the food we had sent from the reception. I spent some time with her, the family, and some other neighbors and supporting friends who had made it to the house by then, and around midnight I retired to get some rest and to prepare for my morning trip to the Bucharest airport on my way back to Austin, Texas.

At 8 a.m. the next morning we were all gathered at the gate of my parent's house as I was about to embark on my 3.5-hour drive to the airport. Suddenly my leaving became excruciating. I felt that I was leaving my mother, my sister, and her two sons in the hands of pain and there was nothing I could really do to help. For all those years, my father was the brick that united the family especially after my 1981 defection from Romania. He had always made a sustained effort to keep family, relatives, and friends together or at least in communication with each other. Now he was gone. With her older son Irineu and his wife living in France, and with her younger son still a student in Bucharest, my sister (her husband not fully cooperating) was left virtually alone to rebalance the family. I was convinced she could do it, but at the point of my departure tears vehemently engulfed our emotions and the pain-knot in my chest reminded me that it would not be easy. However, I did my best to send my cheerful wishes in a positive and optimistic way as I embraced everyone, with the promise that we will see each other with more time in July when we will come to Romania for our summer vacation.

The drive to the airport brought a refreshing change in my emotional state of mind and the rest of the flight to Austin gave me more time to reflect on the entire trip. My son, Sergio, picked me up from the airport late at night, sharing his sorrow on losing his grandfather. At home, Valentina anxiously awaited our arrival and we briefly shared our thoughts before retiring for the night.

The next morning I went back to school and I was pleasantly surprised to receive a card full of nice and supportive messages from all my colleagues. The semester slowly got back to normal but I kept having a recurring question in my head: how will it feel on our summer vacation in Romania when I will not find my father home in his usual routine? The answer would inevitably be: it is all okay; he is now there, where we will all go when we finish our life's purpose; he is well and he would not want any of us to keep suffering because of his leaving. That was the exact message I repeatedly conveyed to my mother, in a heartfelt effort to help her cope with the hardest loss of her life.

This same message was also the core of my two-page letter sent to be read by the priest of Ucea de Jos at the traditional 6-week commemoration of my father's departure. It seemed well received and that was one way for me to be part of that church procession. It was also a good way to close a 6-week period of family events intertwined with an arsenal of my inner debates over the meaning of life, our own dharma, and our expectations once we pass from this existence.

The Summer of 2012

In light of all these experiences, the transition from spring to summer was a special one. My 5.5-week ACC summer semester ended early July and we had already set up our usual summer trip to Romania scheduled for the 11th. However, this time there was nothing 'usual' about it, at least for me: as soon as we would make it to Ucea, the absence of my father will be notable. With this in mind, obviously, my mother and my sister were anxious to be all together again, and so was I.

However, that summer had developed itself into a much more crowded vacation than usual due to a sequence of other pre-scheduled events. First, only two days after our arrival, I played both volleyball and tennis in the annual sports meeting in Victoria, "Cupa Chimistului" (the "Chemist's Cup"). At the end of a very long and exhausting day, although we had a pretty good volleyball team helped by my long-time friend Vasi, we came short of even the third place, but I managed to get a second place in tennis.

Sand volleyball in Victoria

Then was our nephew Paul's wedding on the 28th of July. It was a true celebration that lasted two days and it was very similar to Valentin's wedding three years earlier. Conforming to the Romanian tradition such occasions are always marked by great cuisine, music, and shows. The preparations had been exhausting and the attention to detail was as sharp as it could be. Although Paul's wedding reminded me much of Valentin's, this time we were joined by three special guests from Texas: Sergio's girlfriend, Kyle (his best friend from Austin), and our great family friend Deborah who made it to the wedding as she was vacationing in Spain (her husband Robert understandably chose not to make the trip to Romania). This tumultuous traveling in and out of Romania gave me the opportunity to become really familiar and comfortable with the 3.5-hour drive to the Bucharest airport which is not a light endeavor considering the roads and traffic in Romania.

On the 4th of August we drove one more time to Bucharest as Sergio's girlfriend and Kyle had their scheduled flights back to the U.S., while Valentina, Sergio, and I were heading to Munich, Germany for her college reunion; since many of her college class mates from Cluj, Romania, were by now living and working in Germany, Munich seemed a good place for the meeting. As destiny has it, Rudi, one of my good high school friends whom I had been keeping in touch with over the years, also lived in Munich, agreed to pick us up at the airport and we spent that evening together with him and his wife Bruni. In 1974 Rudi's family, a member of the Sasi minority of German origin in Romania, had received the emigration visa to then West Germany as part of Ceausescu's international financial deals. Our get together that night was a moving experience. As we were driving from the airport to a restaurant for dinner, he related to us that only two days earlier they had the funeral of his mother. I mentioned, of course, my April visit to Romania for the funeral of my father and we shared our thoughts about such sensitive and significant events in our lives. After dinner we said goodbye to Rudi and Bruni as they dropped us off at the hotel where we met Valentina's college classmates' families ready to get the reunion started. We spent the entire next day, Saturday, enjoying the festivities with food, drinks, and music, and we were looking forward to the second leg of our trip outside Romania we had scheduled for the summer.

Months earlier, we made plans to couple Valentina's reunion trip to Germany with four days in Verona, Italy, a famous touristic place also known for its summer season of outdoor opera plays in the ancient Verona Arena. Consequently, on that Sunday we took a train from Munich to Verona, a trip that would carve special memories. As we were enjoying the train ride, an announcement came through loud speakers: due to a rainstorm in the Alps a mudslide had made the railroad tracks useless at just about the point of entry to Italy. To solve the problem, the plan put in place was to move the entire train load of people into buses that would drop us all off at the first functioning Italian train station so that we could continue our trip by train. It all went well, but that had set us a couple of hours behind our scheduled arrival at the small Verona hotel.

The first two days in Verona were great. We visited several recommended sites and tasted the well-known Italian cuisine including delicate wines. After two days of exhausting sightseeing on foot, we were finally ready for our first time outdoor 4-hour opera. Under the clear night sky of Verona, several thousand people stepped into the ancient arena taking their seats on the cool rock stands that had witnessed centuries of shows since the Roman time; a thought went through my head: if they could only speak! As I was marveling at the thousands of candles lit by the audience just a few minutes before the show, I was wondering how many more thousands had sat around this arena over the years and what kind of memories had they taken with them at the end of those shows. We were set to see the famous opera *Carmen* by George Bizet. I was certain I would treasure every minute of my time there, especially enjoying the spectacle side by side with Valentina and our son Sergio. Since our seats were near the side of the gigantic stage, we were privileged to witness every bit of the preparation between the four acts of the play, which enhanced considerably our understanding of what it took to stage such a grandiose presentation. The play was a reproduction of what the great director and producer Franco Zeffirelli envisioned *Carmen* to be. Of course we immediately recognized the musical theme, but to blend it in with such a theatrical and well-orchestrated drama was out of this world. The hundreds of professional actors, singers, and assistant personnel made it all flow very naturally despite the length of the show. Although we were physically spent at the end of our second day of sightseeing, emotionally, that evening truly put the icing on the cake of our vacation away from Romania, carving the four-hour extravaganza into an unforgettable experience.

The Verona Arena

The next day, our last day in Italy, was dedicated to a bus trip to a near-by lake, Lake Garda. Valentina and I went on this trip by ourselves since Sergio chose to spend the day in Verona. The bus took us through beautiful Italian countryside full of grape vine plantations and small farm communities, until we reached the shore. It was picture-perfect scenery. The large lake was surrounded by small towns like the one we were in, which based their living on tourism, and were separated by low mountainous relief. The lake's clear water offered an ideal refreshing medium for several people to escape the heat of the Italian summer, and a near-perfect floating surface for a few small boats. While marveling at all of this, we took long water-front walks but we also ventured on the beautiful narrow streets jammed with souvenir shops and restaurants. An impressive ancient castle was guarding the tourist area from one side as we were searching for a nice place to have a late lunch. The small restaurant did not disappoint. We took our time savoring some of their specialties and cooled off with a couple of cold beers before heading back to Verona. The early evening bus dropped us off close to the Arena and the heavy shopping district, which allowed us to select a few souvenirs to commemorate our stay in Italy.

Our next morning's early flight connection took us back to Bucharest via Munich and that evening we made it home to Victoria ready to make the best we could of the 10 days we had left in Romania, and we did. Soon after our return from Italy, I took my mother and my uncle Mircea for a short car trip to the near-by Sambata Monastery beautifully located at the foot of the Carpathian Mountains, part of the chain of Fagaras Mountains. We visited around for a while but the main purpose of the trip was for me to meet an old and special friend: Olga, the Youth Communist Party secretary at the Victoria Chemical Plant of 1981. The circle was about to close. We had not seen each other in the 31 years since our vacation trip to Yugoslavia and we had made arrangements by phone to meet that day. She was at the end of a three-day back-pack hike in the mountains, accompanied by her sister and a small group of close relatives. She was now living in Canada and she was happy to relive one of her greatest adventures, a hike in the Fagaras Mountains which I had already accomplished before our trip to Munich and Italy.

The moment we met was special. She dropped her back-pack, we hugged, and immediately took a few pictures to immortalize the reunion. We only had a couple of hours together that day, but over lunch, together with my mother and my uncle, we had enough time to roll back some of the memories of the last 31 years. While I summarized my 1981 escape beyond the time in Sarajevo where we saw each other last, I expected Olga to comment on what had happened immediately after my disappearance. She briefly did. Apparently, the group leaders (the Securitate officer, the translator, and the guide) did not make my absence into a disastrous event, and this with the clever intent not to alarm the group. She went on to relate how in 1988 she had also defected from Romania via Yugoslavia, spent several months in a refugee camp, and in 1989 had emigrated to Canada. She eventually had built a career, got married, and more recently she realized one of her long-time dreams since living in Canada: to hike again in the Fagaras Mountains; she had accomplished this for the last two summers. We briefly talked about our old hobbies and our lives of the last few decades and it came time for her to depart since, while in Romania, she stayed with her sister who lived close to Brasov. We said goodbye and promised to do the best we could to see each other again, hopefully with future summer occasions like the one we enjoyed that time.

In the meantime our vacation was drawing to an end. Our flight back to Texas was scheduled for the 19th of August and we wanted to squeeze in as much as possible over the last few days. The highlight of that week was a family reunion at home when we celebrated a double anniversary: Valentin's and Mihaela's wedding of three years earlier and our religious wedding of 1989. We all had a great time as we savored the exquisite menu prepared at the family restaurant, but most importantly we tremendously enjoyed each other's company before our imminent departure.

In retrospect, the summer of 2012 had a very busy vacation in store for us which ended with my first day of school on the 20th of August and Valentina's a few days later. Our son Sergio had stayed a few more days in Romania and then flew to Berlin, Germany for his university semester abroad. In his effort to learn German and his love for philosophy and literature, Berlin seemed to be the best place for the first semester of his junior year in college. Over all, we had a great time everywhere we went and we came back to Austin refreshed, energized, and ready to start a new school year with the Fall semester of 2012.

However, most of my memories from the summer had been ever so softly shadowed by a thought related to a large volume of information regarding 2012 as the year of world-wide changes on our planet. From ancient predictions that included the Mayan calendar with its famous date of the 21st of December, to the astronomical reality of a rare alignment of the Sun, Earth, the large planets in our solar system and the center of our galaxy, all 'evidence' pointed to the possible reality of such changes. In fact, from a social and economical perspective, big changes had already manifested in massive public unrest and heavy financial decline in many European and Middle East countries. Moreover, it has been claimed recently that a sophisticated, yet secretive computer program meant to study world-wide information patterns on the internet, is predicting a 'black-hole' in communication over several months beginning late December 2012.

As I'm contemplating this information, I don't know how much trust we can really put in all or any of it, but my hope is that our planet and the human race are more resilient than some believe. I think we should all keep our optimism high and do what we can to help the state of the world around us in a positive way. In fact that is all we can do anyway; worrying about doom-and-gloom has never helped to prevent it. Who knows, maybe this is the precise time in history when human beings may reach the critical number of positive thinkers that will tilt the future of our species away from destruction, into the light of a bright, happy, peaceful, and safe new millennium, which is in the common interest of all.

I wish you well!

Epilogue

I would like to conclude this volume with another anonymous wisdom story of the ages I find very suggestive. Here is my rendition of it.

"With the little money she had, a woman bought a small piece of totally inhospitable land; it was all full of weeds and unwelcome bushes, and rocks reigned all over the unfertile soil. However, at the end of two years of hard work, dedication, persistence, patience, and positive attitude, the woman transformed her piece of land into a beautiful, picture-perfect garden: a large variety of vegetables were thriving on well-kept rows sheltered by a multitude of colorful flowers joyfully decorating the place. At about that time, an old friend of our woman paid her a visit. They had not seen each other in years, and of course they stopped by the garden. As soon as they arrived, the visitor was completely taken by the fascinating beauty in front of them, and exclaimed: 'Wow! My dear! What a beautiful garden God blessed you with!' To this, our woman gently responded: 'Yes, you're right. But you should have seen this place when God had it all by himself!'"

Closely resembling the meaning of this story, a Romanian saying summarizes it beautifully: "The person sanctifies the place!" Let us be those persons, or, as Gandhi expressed it so eloquently, let us *become* the changes we want to see in the world!

I wish you all well, in peace, love, and cooperation for a better future.